Rethinking
Christ and Culture

A Post-Christendom Perspective

Craig A. Carter

BrazosPress

Grand Rapids, Michigan

Published by Brazos Press
a division of Baker Publishing Group
P.O. Box 6287, Grand Rapids, MI 49516-6287
www.brazospress.com

Printed in the United States of America

Scripture quotations are taken from the HOLY BIBLE, NEW INTERNATIONAL VERSION®. Copyright ©1973, 1978, 1984 by International Bible Society. Used by permission of Zondervan. All rights reserved.

Library of Congress Cataloging-in-Publication Data is on file at the Library of Congress, Washington, DC.

For Rebecca

Contents

Preface

I hope that this book will be useful for professors who wish to help their students grapple with the challenges of the postmodern, post-Christian society in which we live. I also hope it will be of some help to ordinary Christians whose classroom is the culture and whose daily lives consist of trying to make sense of it. Most of all, however, I hope it will spark the imaginations of those creative, risk-taking church leaders who are on the cutting edge of ministry today. We live in a time when old paradigms are falling apart and new ones are emerging only gradually, and our greatest need is for a more fertile and more thoroughly sanctified imagination.

I am aware that the thesis of this book—that we must move from a Christendom to a post-Christendom way of thinking about the Christ and culture problem—will be judged by many individuals to be far too radical for their tastes. That is perfectly understandable so far as I am concerned. I know that not everyone feels the pressure of the post-Christendom trend equally at the same time. Western Christendom was not built in a single day, and it will take a long time for it to die out everywhere. So I hope it does not sound arrogant when I say that I have not written this book for yesterday, but for tomorrow and, perhaps, for today.

Although I have not written this book for yesterday, I have no doubt that ancient wisdom is the key to future faithfulness. Despite all our technological gadgets and our late-modern pretensions, there is truly nothing new under the sun. The church of Jesus Christ has been in situations like our present one before, and all the temptations we face are recycled ones. The devil has hardly any imagination and no real creativity (which must gall him to no end!). Only God can really make all things new. So we need to detach ourselves from our immediate context long enough to look at other times when the church has faced the kinds of problems we face now, and we need to learn both how to do it and how *not* to do it.

I am convinced that the future for the church lies in taking a radical approach and refusing to be either liberal or conservative. The church in North America

7

has been divided into two wings, liberal and conservative, for over a century now, and I regard both liberalism and conservatism as dead ends. Scratch a liberal and you find a fundamentalist in reaction against his or her upbringing. Both are severely compromised by the Enlightenment project of autonomous human reason as the highest authority, of science and technology as the way of salvation, and of progress as the inevitable destiny of the human race. This kind of faith is a secularized form of a heretical deviation from Christianity, and it is dying.

I grew up in fundamentalism and have watched many of my peers journey toward a more liberal expression of the Christian faith. But for some reason, even as I became discontented with the anti-intellectualism, the lack of social concern, the separatism, the individualism, the shallowness, and the legalism of my fundamentalist background, I was never tempted by liberalism. I seemed instinctively to know that it was too much like what I was troubled by in my own background, even though it tried its best to appear different. Indeed, it tries too hard and protests, I think, far too much. I have come to see that both conservative and liberal Christians have made peace with modernity their own way and have, for the most part, accepted dutifully the place that modern Christendom designates for religion—as a prop for the morale of the nation-state in public and as a consolation to individuals in private.

One often hears an author say that writing a book is a lonely process, but that has not been my experience. The stimulating conversations, loving support, and challenging interactions with students, colleagues, and friends that I have experienced while writing this book have made it extremely enjoyable. I have learned much from them, and I am grateful for their input.

But I also have found fellowship with the dead in Christ by reading the writings of the saints who have gone before, and quite often I have felt more in tune with some of them than with my contemporaries. Many times during the writing of this book I have felt inspired, challenged, and humbled by the stories of the martyrs, saints, and pilgrims who have gone before and who have borne a faithful testimony to our Lord Jesus Christ. What a diverse group they are: desert fathers, bishops, monks, nobles, tradesmen, housewives, scholars, missionaries, pietists, Anabaptists, nuns, pastors, social activists, poets, politicians, martyrs, evangelists, and educators. There have been so many incredibly diverse ways of witnessing to Christ in church history that one cannot help but be hopeful, if only we can allow our imaginations to be stimulated by their examples.

The wonderful thing about the Christian faith is that this is not an alienating experience—to find fellowship with the dead, that is—because of the hope of resurrection. I am not merely an isolated individual living in a certain place and time cut off from them forever; I am part of the worldwide church of Christ of all ages. My destiny in Christ is to be part of this body of believers of all nationalities, languages, times, and places for eternity, and so a feeling of solidarity in the faith with those of past ages is more than a dream; it is a reality. The Scripture says of Abel: "And by faith he still speaks, even though he is dead" (Hebrews 11:4).

But the living speak too, and several living individuals deserve particular mention here. First, I want to thank Jeff Greenman, now of Wheaton College, but formerly my administrative colleague at Tyndale University College and Seminary. He and I sketched out the basic plan for this book on a piece of scrap paper in O'Hare Airport while we were on our way home from a Society of Christian Ethics meeting many years ago. Jeff has also been a constant source of encouragement as this project crawled along. He read the next-to-final version of the manuscript and made some excellent suggestions. I listened to everything he said and tried to incorporate his suggestions, except for a very few points where I was stubborn. No one should blame him for whatever is lacking in this book; he did everything a friend could do to make it as good as it could be.

The same goes for others who have been helpful along the way. The original inspiration for this book came from a panel discussion about the fiftieth anniversary edition of H. Richard Niebuhr's *Christ and Culture* at the Society of Christian Ethics annual meeting and particularly from some comments by Duane Friesen on that occasion. His later article in the *Society of Christian Ethics Annual* is mentioned at the appropriate place in this book as having been very important for my thinking.

I thank many people who took time out of their busy schedules to read the manuscript and to talk to me about it. Dan Goodwin, Ted Newell, Bob Williams, Greg Maillet, Seth Crowell, Steve Carter, and Stephen Dempster, who are all faculty members at Atlantic Baptist University, spent an evening discussing it with me. Myron B. Penner also read it, and our conversation at the annual meeting of the American Academy of Religion in November of 2005 was extremely important to me in terms of seeing connections between postmodernism and a post-Christendom perspective. Jonathan Wilson also took time to read most of the manuscript, and I thank him for our good conversation at AAR that year as well.

I also thank the students in my spring-summer class on Christ and culture at McMaster Divinity College in June 2005 and in my fall intensive course on Christ and culture at Atlantic Baptist University in November 2005 for discussing the ideas in this book and for giving me valuable feedback. Sincere thanks also go to President Brian Stiller, Provost Earl Davey, and the Cabinet of Tyndale University College & Seminary for a sabbatical year in 2004–5, during which this book was written. Rodney Clapp and the team at Brazos were supportive and helpful, and I appreciate so much the great work they are doing for the Lord. Rodney's insightful comments on the next-to-last draft saved me from some blunders that I definitely would have regretted later, and I really appreciate his help.

I would like to thank Bradley Longard for his help with the creation of the index. I also want to thank my son, Stephen, for giving me a student's reaction to part of the manuscript. My oldest daughter, Rebecca Carter-Chand, read the entire manuscript and made some helpful suggestions. It has been my privilege to discuss many of the ideas in this book with her over the past decade as she has grown up and progressed through high school, university, and graduate school. Our relationship as parent and child now has matured into a wonderful friendship, and I am delighted to dedicate this book to her with my love. To my wife, Bonnie, I once again acknowledge my gratitude and freely confess that I could never accomplish projects like this without her constant support, encouragement, and love.

Introduction

Do not love the world or anything in the world. If anyone loves the world, the love of the Father is not in him.

1 John 2:15

Christendom is . . . the betrayal of Christianity; a "Christian world" is . . . apostasy from Christianity.

Søren Kierkegaard, *Attack Upon Christendom*

Throughout the world, the Church is concerned today with the problem of the secularization of the modern man. It would perhaps be more profitable if the Church were at least to begin to become concerned with the problem of its own secularization.

Karl Barth, *God in Action*

You are the salt of the earth. But if the salt loses its saltiness, how can it be made salty again? It is no longer good for anything, except to be thrown out and trampled by men.

Matthew 5:13

Thus a world, which has become evil, succeeds in making the Christians become evil too.

Dietrich Bonhoeffer, *Ethics*

1

Reading Niebuhr
in a Post-Christendom Situation

H. Richard Niebuhr's classic book *Christ and Culture* has helped to shape the outlook of several generations of students, pastors, professors, and laypeople since its publication in 1951.[1] Having remained in print continuously for a half a century, it recently came out in a fiftieth anniversary edition. Much of its influence derives from its use as a textbook in numerous college, university, and seminary courses in social ethics, church history, and related disciplines. What is amazing is its appeal to people at all points along the liberal-conservative continuum. Both liberals and evangelicals view it as expressing the range of possible ways of engaging culture. Very few books have achieved this kind of acceptance across the theological spectrum. Even people who have never read the book can name Niebuhr's five types and tell you clearly which one they favor. Occasionally one comes across authors who mention "Christ transforming culture" and expect the reader to catch the reference to *Christ and Culture*. The concepts set forth in Niebuhr's book have become part of the way that many people think about the relationship of Christ and culture today.

The most influential ideas and theories in culture are so ingrained in our thinking that they seem to be neutral descriptions of reality itself. These are ideas and

1. Quotations of H. Richard Niebuhr's *Christ and Culture* are taken from the fiftieth anniversary edition, with a new foreword by Martin E. Marty, a new preface by James M. Gustafson, and an introductory essay by the author (New York: Harper, 2001). All future references to this work in this chapter will be in the form of page numbers given in parenthesis within the text.

theories we seldom question or doubt. In the natural sciences, for example, the theory of evolution functions as a background belief most of the time. It leads scientists to develop a myriad of research programs focused on how a particular organism managed to survive or how it might have evolved. Rather than setting out to validate the theory of evolution, scientists just use it, meaning that they presuppose it rather than debate it. They use it as an overarching framework or paradigm within which many specific theories may be developed, tested, and either validated or discarded. One reason most scientists do not find the theory of evolution too restrictive is that the theory itself is so general that it allows room for many different explanations of particular phenomena. Scientists are so busy working on vast numbers of specific problems within the overall framework of evolution that the theory of evolution itself seems like a neutral, objective framework that they never need question. Only at times of major upheaval, which Thomas Kuhn famously calls "paradigm changes,"[2] are such large, overarching frameworks as the theory of evolution actually challenged. During what Kuhn calls times of "normal science"[3] (which is by far most of the time), scientific activity happily plods along with a focus on the details, not the big picture.

Christ and Culture is based on a very large, general background assumption: the theory of Christendom, which is taken for granted by both author and readers. Each of Niebuhr's five types presupposes the existence of Christendom, and the debate between them is carried out within a Christendom paradigm. The book could just as well have been entitled *Christ and Culture in the Context of Christendom*.

The Christendom Assumptions behind *Christ and Culture*

In 1951, when *Christ and Culture* was first published, Christendom was taken for granted within North American Protestantism. So it was quite natural that, rather than challenging it in his book, Niebuhr presupposed it. But what is Christendom? Christendom is the concept of Western civilization as having a religious arm (the church) and a secular arm (civil government), both of which are united in their adherence to Christian faith, which is seen as the so-called soul of Europe or the West. The essence of the idea is the assertion that Western civilization is Christian. Within this Christian civilization, the state and the church have different roles to play, but, since membership in both is coterminous, both can be seen as aspects of one unified reality—Christendom.

Of course, during the past sixteen hundred years, Christendom has assumed many different specific forms, but this basic definition captures the essence of the

2. Thomas Kuhn, *The Structure of Scientific Revolutions* (2nd ed.; Chicago: University of Chicago Press, 1970).
3. Ibid., 10.

idea in all its many and varied forms. A closely related term is Constantinianism,[4] which is often used to describe the union of church and state in which the civil power incorporates the church into the state. I prefer the term *Christendom* simply because it is a better-known term and less likely to be misunderstood.

Within the framework of Christendom, Niebuhr provided a range of options on how Christ and culture might be related, which seemed helpful and persuasive to a great many scholars, pastors, and other thoughtful Christians. He identified two extremes: Christ against culture (which sees Christ in conflict with culture) and Christ of culture (which blends Christ into culture as the symbol of what is highest and best in that culture). The first is the view of Tertullian, the Mennonites, and Leo Tolstoy; and the second is the view of nineteenth-century, liberal culture-Protestantism. Niebuhr also identifies three mediating positions: Christ above culture (the position of Thomism), Christ and culture in paradox (Lutheranism), and Christ transforming culture (Calvinism). All three attempt to bring together a Christ who is a prophet of the transcendence of God with the realities and compromises required by the culture of fallen and finite human beings. It is taken for granted by Niebuhr that, since Western culture is Christian, Christians therefore have a responsibility for culture and must be realistic in relating faith in a Christ who really does not fit within any human culture to Western Christendom. Christendom is presupposed, and the problem is how to relate Christ to it.

The greatest single attack on Christendom during the past two centuries came from the prophet of Copenhagen: Søren Kierkegaard. In the book *Attack Upon Christendom*, Kierkegaard pilloried the state-church system that rested on the fiction that every Dane was a Christian and that the state-supported clergy were "witnesses to the truth."[5] He called the state church "an apostasy from the Christianity of the New Testament,"[6] and he regarded Christendom as "the betrayal of Christianity."[7] For Kierkegaard, true Christianity is a prophetic rebuke to the world as it is and cannot help but come into conflict with the world, which in-

---

4. The term *Constantinianism* refers to Roman emperor Constantine the Great, who tolerated and then encouraged Christianity beginning in 312. He ended the great persecution of 303–12 and called the Council of Nicea in 325 in order to unify the church in the face of the Arian threat. Although he was not baptized until his deathbed, he came to symbolize the Christianization of the Roman Empire in the fourth century. Although the majority of Christians view this as a triumph for the church, a minority regards it as a tragic compromise of the gospel for the sake of social acceptance and power. John Howard Yoder, for example, uses the term *Constantinianism* to refer to an eschatological heresy in which the promises of the coming kingdom of God are seen as being fulfilled in history and in the Christendom that results from the Constantinian shift. For an extended discussion of Constantinianism as an eschatological heresy, see my *The Politics of the Cross: The Theology and Social Ethics of John Howard Yoder* (Grand Rapids: Brazos Press, 2001), ch. 6.

5. Søren Kierkegaard, *Attack Upon Christendom* (trans. Walter Lowrie; Princeton: Princeton University Press, 1968), 10.

6. Ibid., 19.

7. Ibid., 33.

evitably means suffering for all those who dare to bear witness to the truth. The easy compatibility of the state church of Christendom with the world is proof of its apostasy—its abandonment of the gospel.[8] For the church to align itself with the culture so as to become a part of that culture—the religious dimension of a pagan culture—is for the church to lose its true identity as the witness to the new culture, the new world being brought into existence by the redemptive act of God in Jesus Christ. Christendom has assumed many different forms and has managed to persist, in the form of a civil religion supported by the churches, even in countries in which there is no state church, such as the United States.[9]

Attacks on Christendom by isolated prophets like Kierkegaard, however, did not prevent Niebuhr from presupposing Christendom as he approached the Christ and culture problem. Christendom functions in Niebuhr's thought as the great unexamined presupposition. Within the framework of Christendom, Niebuhr provided a range of options on how Christ and culture might be related, which seemed helpful and persuasive to a great many scholars, pastors, and thoughtful Christians. By defining five types of relationship between Christ and culture and claiming to see some good in all of them, the book provides a way of conceptualizing the problem that appears to be objective and neutral, even while pushing people away from sectarianism and isolationism and toward responsible involvement in transformation.

Most of the attention of socially engaged people is so focused at the level of practical action—electing a certain candidate, running a soup kitchen, demonstrating against polluters, and so on—that the big-picture questions are not revisited very often. They are like scientists practicing normal science. Whenever the big picture is discussed, it becomes convenient to frame the question of how Christ and culture should relate in Niebuhr's terms. Even then, however, we seldom notice that the overall background belief, which lies just out of sight in the background of Niebuhr's book, is the theory of Christendom. Like the theory of evolution in biology, the theory of Christendom frequently functions as the overall framework for Christian social ethics, while not often being referred to or thought about explicitly. Yet the existence of this theory, rather than some other, gives direction to the research program by making some ideas comprehensible within the overall framework and others not. Christendom just is; no thought is given to the possibility that it should not exist or might one day cease to exist. No argument for it is given, no reference to it is made, and thus no questioning of it is possible.

Rather than engaging in debate on the level of specific social-ethical issues (like war or abortion, for example) or even debating on the second level (i.e., discussing which of Niebuhr's five types is the best), my intention is to move

8. Ibid., 271.
9. John Howard Yoder explores this process in *The Priestly Kingdom: Social Ethics as Gospel* (Notre Dame: University of Notre Dame Press, 1984), 135–47.

to the third level—the level of questioning the Christendom assumptions that linger just out of sight behind *Christ and Culture*. I contend that we are on the verge of a paradigm shift. My thesis is that the theory of Christendom must not only be questioned, but must be rejected today as the general paradigm in the context of which approaches to social ethics are developed. This is so for two very good reasons: first, because Christendom is dead in some places and dying in others[10]; and, second, because it would be detrimental to true Christian faith to try to resurrect it, even if turned out to be possible to do so. An important implication of this thesis is that once one rejects the Christendom assumptions behind Niebuhr's book, the whole typology becomes suspect. I will argue that the types make sense only on the basis of the two assumptions that Christendom does exist and should exist.

The reason why Christendom must be rejected is rooted in the nature of Christian discipleship. Building and sustaining Christendom requires activity incompatible with being a follower of Jesus Christ, such as using violent coercion to maintain the position of Christianity within society. Within Christendom, the New Testament message of radical discipleship ("take up your cross and follow me") is transformed into a message of social conservatism (or, in certain circumstances, of social revolution) in such a way that being a disciple becomes a matter of conforming to the world in one's outward behavior, while believing something unique about Jesus and God in one's private, inner being. But is that the New Testament concept of what it means to follow Jesus? John Howard Yoder, in his classic work *The Politics of Jesus*, argues that it clearly is not.[11] Yoder argues that the New Testament teaching on discipleship is that Jesus calls us to follow him in the path of suffering by renouncing violence, confronting the powers of this world with the message of Christ's lordship, and being willing to suffer at the hands of those who resist the message of the gospel. For Yoder, believing inwardly and conforming outwardly is the way of Christendom, but it is not the way of Jesus.

Dietrich Bonhoeffer never read *The Politics of Jesus*, but he was a careful and honest reader of the Bible, and he exemplifies what it means to resist the powers and bear witness to Jesus Christ even to the point of suffering for the faith. At the beginning of his great book *The Cost of Discipleship*, he says: "Cheap grace is the deadly enemy of our Church. We are fighting to-day for costly grace."[12] What is costly grace? Bonhoeffer writes: "Such grace is *costly* because it calls us to follow, and it is *grace* because it calls us to follow Jesus Christ."[13] Bonhoeffer's

10. See, for example, *The Decline of Christendom in Western Europe 1750–2000*, ed. Hugh MacLeod and Werner Ustorf (Cambridge: Cambridge University Press, 2003).

11. John Howard Yoder, *The Politics of Jesus: Vicit Agnus Noster* (2nd ed.; Grand Rapids: Eerdmans, 1994).

12. Dietrich Bonhoeffer, *The Cost of Discipleship* (trans. R. H. Fuller; rev. Imgard Booth; New York: Simon & Schuster, 1995), 43.

13. Ibid., 45 (emphasis original).

description of the problem in Western Christianity sounds a great deal like that of Kierkegaard:

> As Christianity spread, and the Church became more secularized, this realization of the costliness of grace gradually faded. The world was christianized, and grace became its common property. It was to be had at low cost. Yet the Church of Rome did not altogether lose the earlier vision. It is highly significant that the Church was astute enough to find room for the monastic movement, and to prevent it from lapsing into schism.[14]

Christendom meant cheap grace; yet the vision of costly grace was kept alive for a time in the monastic movement, where following Jesus still involved sacrifice and commitment. However, what began as "a living protest against the secularization of Christianity and the cheapening of grace" ended up being relativized by the worldly, mainstream church as something heroic, "which the mass of the laity could not be expected to emulate."[15] By its very separation from society, monasticism (and its call to discipleship) was marginalized. According to Yoder, the Anabaptist movement of the sixteenth century was a challenge to Christendom to make the kind of discipleship that characterized the best of monasticism the content of the preaching of the church. In other words, instead of preaching cheap grace in order to make possible the building and sustaining of Christendom, the Anabaptist challenge was to make following Jesus the norm for all disciples and the content of the message of the church to the world.[16] For Yoder, the basis for this was, as it was for Bonhoeffer, the plain teaching of the New Testament.

The End of Western Christendom

In chapters 2 and 3 I argue that Niebuhr's recommendation in *Christ and Culture* was for the churches to see their mission as being to transform society (Christ transforming culture), rather than withdrawing from culture and losing influence in the culture (Christ against culture). His view was that this is the responsible and realistic thing to do, even if it means some compromises along the way. The separated church, he repeatedly stresses, has no positive effect on the wider society and is therefore selfish in its quest for purity. This has always been the basic calculus of Christendom thinking: a few compromises for the sake of great influence on the wider society.

In the temptation narratives (Matthew 4:1–11 and parallels), the devil promised Jesus so much power to do good and so much influence over the whole world if only he would compromise on that one little point of worshiping the devil instead

14. Ibid., 46.
15. Ibid., 46–47.
16. See Yoder, *Priestly Kingdom*, 105–22.

of God. Would a technicality like bowing the knee to the devil really be so important, compared to the tremendous good that Emperor Jesus could do as the ruler
of the whole world? Did not God want the messiah to rule the world? Was Jesus
not called to be the messiah? Was this not the providentially provided means to
the already agreed upon end? Could it even be a helpful shortcut? Would it be
responsible to refuse this offer? Is the way of preaching, healing, and suffering a
realistic path to the throne? Is the cross really necessary?

Jesus said no to the devil's offer, but the bishops of the Christian church in
the fourth century said yes, and Christendom was born. Western Christendom
has had a long run, and as the devil promised, it has not all been bad. There have
been until recently laws against abortion and euthanasia and laws mandating a
weekly day of rest for exploited workers. There has been freedom to preach the
gospel, and the Scriptures have been preserved and distributed. The church has
been allowed to exercise great influence within society. In some ways, the devil
has kept his side of the bargain: the church gained influence. But now the times
are changing.

We live now in the long, sad denouement of Western Christendom. A resurgent
paganism that never really died, but merely went underground, is now reasserting
itself. The secularization of Western society has been going on for a long time.
We can point to the 1960s as a time of revolution against the Judeo-Christian
establishment. The nineteenth century was a time of growing secularization influenced by anti-Christian thinkers such as Darwin, Marx, and Freud. Some would
go back to the seventeenth-century and eighteenth-century Enlightenment and
the French Revolution as the beginning of a process of revolutionary secularism.
Others would locate the origins of secularism as an ideology in the Renaissance
or even in certain late medieval movements of thought. All would acknowledge
the great influence of ancient Greco-Roman pagan culture on thinkers of the
Renaissance, the Enlightenment, and modern secularism.[17] But no matter how
we write the history, we must face that we live in a society whose intellectual elites
are united in little except a common conviction that Christianity is intolerant
and backward and, therefore, represents a barrier to social progress. Privatized
Christianity can be tolerated, but Christianity must be banished from the public
square, except when it is trotted out as part of a civil religion designed to rally
the citizens in time of war.

The Christianity against which they have reacted, of course, is the Christianity of Christendom: the Christianity of ruling elites and state churches, the
Christianity of violent coercion and intolerance, the Christianity of power and
privilege, the Christianity of racism, patriarchy, and colonialism, the Christianity of the Inquisition and the Holocaust. Christendom Christianity is weighed
down with so much cultural baggage that it could not, under present condi-

17. Peter Gay speaks of the Enlightenment as "the rise of modern paganism" in *The Enlightenment*,
vol. 1: *The Rise of Modern Paganism* (New York: Norton, 1995).

tions, become dominant in Western culture again without being perceived to be a tool of totalitarianism.[18]

But the gospel of Jesus Christ is not Christendom Christianity. The gospel is good news for the poor. The gospel is countercultural, nonviolent, and subversive of empire. The gospel empowers women, teaches the equality of all races, and identifies with Jews as brothers and sisters. The gospel works by persuasion, tolerates rejection, and respects even those who do not listen. The gospel creates genuine community out of those who, humanly speaking, have little in common. The gospel is of no use to most political rulers because it outlaws violence and renounces greed. The gospel identifies with no culture exclusively but is embraced by individuals and minority groups in every culture all over the world. The gospel has never disappeared throughout the long centuries of Christendom, in spite of everything.

The only feasible strategy for Christian faithfulness in a post-Christendom world is to let go of the Christianity of Christendom while clinging tenaciously to the gospel. Unfortunately, however, not all Christians have come to this conclusion yet. In fact, both the conservative and liberal wings of the church continue to operate as if Christendom were going to go on forever. For the past fifty years, both liberal Protestants and evangelicals have been animated by a consensus that Niebuhr's Christ transforming culture type is the best one for our situation. Niebuhr placed this type last in his book and offered no criticisms of it, thus making it appear as his favored position. Christ transforming culture involves the church seeing its responsibility as trying to guide Western culture in a less violent, more just, and more peaceful direction gradually and realistically. For both liberals and evangelicals, Christendom is not dead, but it is seriously ill and needs to be revived. We hear this in the conservative rhetoric of how our society has lost its Judeo-Christian heritage and how Christians must rally to restore Judeo-Christian values to public life. We hear it in the liberal rhetoric that warns that the church must not, at all costs, become irrelevant, but must adopt the agenda of the world so as to nudge society closer to the kingdom of God.

Liberal Protestantism has accommodated itself to culture at the point of the sexual revolution. The fruits of the sexual revolution are easy divorce, shallow interpersonal relationships and promiscuity, sexually transmitted disease and sterility, homosexual activity, routine abortion, contraceptives and antibiotics as substitutes for sexual responsibility, increased poverty among women and children, and children growing up without secure relationships with both parents. All this is tragic—yet liberal Protestantism does little to stand against it.

On the other hand, conservative Protestantism has accommodated itself to culture by blessing the commercialization of all of life and the exploitation of the poor through global capitalism. The fruits of the worship of the market are the

18. For a good example of a public intellectual making this point, see Margaret Atwood, *The Handmaid's Tale: A Novel* (Toronto: Seal, 1998), a major novel that now has been made into a film.

commercialization of nearly all public space, the constant preaching of materialism through advertising, the destruction of the environment, the mad scramble for money, and the trampling of the poor by faceless corporations that view people as nothing but units of labor and consumers. All this is tragic too—yet conservative Protestantism does little to stand against it.

Ironically, having set out to transform culture, both liberal and conservative forms of Christianity in North America today find themselves greatly transformed by late-capitalist, liberal-individualist culture during the last century. It is little more than empty rhetoric, then, for liberals and conservatives to claim to be transforming culture and to accuse those who reject the Christ transforming culture model as irresponsible and irrelevant. What could be more irrelevant than Christian leaders who beg the government to pass laws to coerce their own church members into caring for the poor or refusing the abortion temptation, when those Christian leaders cannot convince their own flocks to do these things on the basis of the Bible? There is a glaring parallel between liberal Christians lobbying the government to tax the capitalists in their own flocks and redistribute the money to the poor, on the one hand, and conservative Christians lobbying the government to outlaw abortion, so members of their own flock will not have it as an option. No wonder politicians often have so little respect for religious lobbyists.

Too many Christians regret the demise of Christendom; they need not. We need to face reality; Christendom did not work. There is no way it ever could have worked. No one can coerce another person into believing the gospel and experiencing the life-giving power of salvation. The church cannot evangelize the world when the world is already officially Christian. The killing, the struggle for power, the greedy fight over wealth that goes on all the time within and between nation-states should not have had to reflect poorly on the Christian church because the church should never have accepted the job of helping to rule the world. When the Roman emperors offered the church the job of being the religion of the empire, the bishops of the church should have done what Jesus did in the wilderness when the devil made him the same offer. The Crusades, the Inquisition, the judicial murder of heretics, the blessing of wars of conquest in the Americas, the justification of slavery, anti-Semitism, and finally, as the climax of all the evils of Western civilization, World War II with the Holocaust and the use of atomic weapons as tools of terror against civilians—all this history should never have been part of church history. But it is part of our history—because of Christendom.

To be sure, these evils are not the whole story of Christendom. Heroic, self-sacrificing monks, nuns, pastors, missionaries, and social activists have been at work sharing the gospel all through the period of Christendom. The gospel has never completely been eclipsed, the church has never disappeared, and there have always been true witnesses in every century. I am not forgetting all the good that has been part of Christian witness in Western culture for the past fifteen hundred years. But to have all the humble Jesus-like witness of all the faithful ones, many of whose names will never be known, obscured by imperial greed, violence, and lust for power is what I deeply lament and mourn. I mourn that, even though humble servants of God like David Brainerd (1718–47) gave their lives to take the gospel to the native people, other Christians launched wars of genocide against the First Nations of North America and thus overshadowed Brainerd's holy witness.

But as a way of relating Christ and culture, Christendom was not biblically justified, it was not theologically sound, it was not pastorally responsible, and it was not evangelistically effective. It was not a series of excusable mistakes made by people who could not have been expected to know better because they were children of their times. It was a reversion to the worst excesses of the kingdom of David and Solomon, excesses that had been expressly condemned by the eighth-century prophets, decisively judged by God in the exile, and consciously rejected by Jesus, who chose the way of the cross over the way of the zealot's sword. David and Solomon at least had the excuse of living in an age prior to the climactic self-revelation of God in Jesus Christ; but the founders and developers of Christendom did not. In other words, the worst thing about the whole sorry Christendom episode was that its founders and apologists were people who knew about Jesus, who had the Gospels to read, and who had been part of the early church. They had no excuse; they should have known better. Although this may seem like a harsh judgment, consider the alternative. If Christendom was not a perversion of the gospel, then the gospel, the Bible, Christianity as a whole, and Jesus himself are all called into question by the evils of Christendom. Since I believe the gospel, I find it necessary to believe that Christendom was a perversion of the gospel, a parody of the church, and a betrayal of the teachings of Jesus.

But one might be tempted to say that the end of Christendom solves the problem. We will not have to worry about the church being identified with the power structures of society once Christianity has been privatized and paganism has taken over. But it is not that simple. We actually have a very large problem in that Christians have gotten so used to being in charge that it is not easy to let go of power and prestige. Many Christians are tempted to do whatever it takes to retain their places as religious chaplains to the culture, as court prophets to the king, as religious professionals delivering the necessary rite-of-passage services to an increasingly pagan culture. Once the choice of serving culture instead of serving Jesus has been made, it is not inconceivable that the religious establishment will simply go with the flow and adopt the new religion of the ruling powers. And what if that new religion is some form of paganism? Well, pagan priests will likely be paid just as well in the future as Christian priests were in the past, and the same amount of cultural prestige will still be available. Did not more than a few pagan priests join the Christian church as Europe was being converted to Christianity a millennium ago? Would it really be shocking to see the reverse happening now that the shoe is on the other foot?

Secularism is not a permanent basis for a society. Like atheism, it is fundamentally nothing more substantial than the denial of Christianity. It has no positive program, no coherent philosophy, and no answers to the basic questions of law, ethics, and meaning. But it is not possible for a society to go from one religion to another overnight unless it is done at sword point. The West is not being converted by force from Christianity to Islam. It is moving from an official status of being Christian to one of pagan pluralism—hence the necessity of secularism as a kind of sop to the Christians while the strength of paganism gradually builds itself up and consolidates its grip on the institutions of society. And the historical paganism of Western Europe is reasserting itself, make no mistake about it. Christendom was more about covering up paganism than about actually converting it, and now that the veneer has worn thin, a pagan polytheism that never really died is stirring again. In the future, the question will be under what conditions Christianity can be tolerated.

In this situation, asking the question of how the church can have influence on the culture is the wrong question to ask if one's goal is to be faithful to the gospel of Jesus Christ. The real question demanding a response is whether the church will abandon the gospel in order to function as the religious chaplaincy of the post-Christian Western world, or whether it will cling to the gospel and accept exile from the halls of power. As every soldier knows, there are times when the choices are not victory or defeat, but rather, defeat with honor or defeat without honor. (And if anyone thinks that defeat for Christendom means defeat for God and his kingdom, that just shows once again how invidious was the linking of the gospel and Western culture in the first place!)

The United Church of Canada has clearly chosen the post-Christian West over Jesus.[19] For all its talk of being radical and its self-image of being in opposition to the culture, the reality is that the United Church has given up on the Christian sexual ethic of chastity and embraced the promiscuity ethic that says that personal sexual fulfillment trumps social and family duties. It has embraced Western liberal individualism and rejected biblical discipleship. It has removed God's self-revelation in Jesus Christ from the center of church proclamation and inserted a vague spirituality and natural theology in its place. Instead of calling people to repentance and faith, the United Church calls them to therapy and self-actualization. Instead of preaching salvation from sin through repentance and faith, it preaches acceptance for every lifestyle. Wherever the secular Canadian culture goes, the United Church will be not far behind; in fact, it will try to be there a bit ahead of the majority culture if at all possible (thus enhancing its progressive self-image). Getting there ten years before the rest of the culture (as on the homosexuality issue) is what passes for being prophetic and progressive in the United Church of Canada today. A constant scramble to find the head of the parade is what mission means in liberal Protestantism today.

The contemporary Roman Catholic Church, by contrast, appears to be heading in the exact opposite direction. Under Pope John Paul II, and now under

19. Of course, I am generalizing here. I have friends within the United Church of Canada who seek to be biblical and faithful Christians, but they are a powerless minority within the structures of the church. The point is not that their witness is insignificant; it is rather that no one should be deceived about where the political power lies in that institution.

Benedict XVI, the Roman Catholic Church appears to be prepared to challenge Western culture, particularly its promiscuity, materialism, and moral relativism. Pope Benedict XVI appears (like the first Benedict) to favor a smaller church with a more distinctive witness, rather than a culturally accommodated one. By opposing abortion, unjust war, capital punishment, and euthanasia, the Roman Catholic Church witnesses to a consistent respect for human-life ethic. By rejecting sexual promiscuity, same-sex marriage, and permissiveness, it witnesses to a Christian ethic of chastity. By opposing materialism, unrestrained capitalism, and consumerism, it witnesses to the spiritual nature of humanity and the responsibility of society to care for the poor and the needy. The Roman Catholic Church is also displaying a strong tendency to uphold historic Christian orthodoxy on the doctrines of the Trinity and the incarnation in the face of pressures to water down the uniqueness of Jesus Christ. These tendencies bring the Roman Catholic Church into direct opposition to Western culture at many points.

While the United Church of Canada may continue to play a public role, that role will consist of being a court prophet by saying whatever the leaders of culture want to hear and by blessing policies based on non-Christian ideologies, once it is clear that these policies are favored by the majority in the culture. The role played by the Roman Catholic Church will be public in a different way in that it will bring the church into conflict with Western culture at many points. If these two religious bodies continue in these two opposite directions, which one will end up having the most influence and being perceived by future historians to be most relevant? In my opinion, the one that scorns relevance and gives up hope of influence will, ironically, be most likely to be judged centuries from now to have been most relevant and influential. If history has not taught us this lesson, it is because we have misread it on account of the blinders of a Christendom mentality.

The possibility of simultaneously being faithful disciples of Jesus and chaplains to the powers that be is over, if it ever really existed except as an illusion. But instead of despair, our response to the post-Christendom world should be faith in the sovereignty of God, the lordship of Jesus, and the power of the Holy Spirit. God can rule without Washington's permission and will continue to do so long after the American empire has joined the Babylonian, Assyrian, Persian, Greek, Roman, British, and Soviet ones on the scrap heap of history.

Moving toward a Paradigm Shift

I have been reading Niebuhr for over twenty years now. I first encountered the book in seminary, and I had an unusual reaction to it. I found it deeply troubling, whereas most people see it as benign if not commonsensical. For years I could not put my finger on the problem with the book, but I knew somehow that the Christ transforming culture type, which is obviously Niebuhr's preferred position, often seems (paradoxically) to lead to the accommodation of Christianity to the culture. Like many young people from pietistic and/or fundamentalist backgrounds, reading Niebuhr made me feel ashamed of the separatism of my heritage.[20] Yet, I also sensed that Niebuhr was much too unsympathetic to the Christ against culture type and that faithful Christian discipleship would need to draw deeply from the confrontation with culture produced by the Christ against culture type if there was to be any hope of real transformation. For a while I said I was in favor of "Christ against culture for the sake of culture," which was a way of saying that attempting to transform culture without also being against vast tracts of it was a recipe for gradual accommodation. Now I want to say that faithfulness to Jesus Christ necessarily involves elements both of radical discipleship and of the "seeking the peace of the city" message of Jeremiah to the exiles in Babylon. The challenge is to find ways to serve the people around us in ways that mirror Jesus's love and compassion for the lost. Sometimes, despite our best intentions, our trying to follow Jesus will be interpreted by many people as being against culture.

As I struggled with the task of trying to express what is wrong with *Christ and Culture*, I happened to read Yoder's *Politics of Jesus* in 1982.[21] Like many others, I found reading this book to be a transformative experience. The difference between the Christ of *Christ and Culture* and the Jesus of *The Politics of Jesus* was absolutely fundamental to everything else these two authors were trying to say. For Yoder, Christendom was not the presupposition or background theory. For Yoder, Christendom was a failed project, one for which Christians should repent.[22] Yoder's Jesus was the founder of a new society, not merely a prophet who pointed away from all culture as hopelessly enmeshed in compromise and sin as was Niebuhr's Christ.

As I continued to read Yoder, I discovered that following Jesus means being part of a countercultural community that affirms his lordship over against the totalizing claims of principalities and powers such as the nation-state, modernity, autonomous reason, and the market. This kind of community is necessarily *against* culture in many ways, but the kind of all-or-nothing choice demanded by Niebuhr in *Christ and Culture* is a false dichotomy. One can stand against killing, the exploitation of poor workers, consumerism, and the sexual revolution without being against classical music, the family farm, and the practice of medicine. What one cannot do is to stand against things like consumerism, promiscuity, and killing without experiencing some degree of what the New

20. James W. McClendon Jr. writes of this phenomenon in his foreword to Charles Scriven's *The Transformation of Culture: Christian Social Ethics after H. Richard Niebuhr* (Scottdale, PA: Herald, 1988), 9.

21. I eventually wrote a doctoral thesis on Yoder, published as *The Politics of the Cross: The Theology and Social Ethics of John Howard Yoder* (Grand Rapids: Brazos, 2001).

22. Yoder argues for this explicitly in "The Disavowal of Constantine: An Alternate Perspective on Interfaith Dialogue" in *The Royal Priesthood: Essays Ecclesiological and Ecumenical* (ed. Michael G. Cartwright; Grand Rapids: Eerdmans, 1994), 242–61.

Testament calls persecution. For Niebuhr, Christ is an otherworldly symbol of ultimate perfection that finally does not fit within this world. For Yoder, Jesus is God incarnate and calls us to follow him here in this world. For Niebuhr, Christ is so at odds with the values of this world that he remains detached from it. His followers have to compromise with reality in order to function within the world. For Yoder, the teachings of Jesus, which he calls his followers to live out, are so at odds with the world that they got him crucified. Nevertheless, Jesus calls us to follow him by taking up our crosses too because, while it is hard to follow Jesus, it is not impossible.

Yoder's account of Jesus as Lord represents a new beginning in social ethics because it is a post-Christendom account of who Jesus is and what kind of disciples we are called to be. This Jesus is also the Christ, the messiah, and the God-man of the creeds, but he is so in the midst of history. In other words, the incarnation really happened. And so, discipleship takes place within history as well. This kind of discipleship involves confronting the principalities and powers with the proclamation of the lordship of Jesus Christ. It involves a nose-to-nose confrontation with the powers that be. But it does not involve compromise or accommodation. Instead of a grab for power and the resort to violent coercion that always accompanies the grab for power, this kind of discipleship rejects violence and accepts the cross. Its goal is not to transform society, but to witness to the truth that, in the resurrection and ascension of Jesus Christ, the world has *already* been transformed. The purpose of the church is to proclaim this truth and to embody it in its own communal life. This can be done without Christendom and, in fact, cannot be done through a Christendom strategy. This kind of discipleship views both the political left and the political right as insufficiently radical because they both cling to nostalgia for Christendom.

During the last quarter of the twentieth century, more and more voices from various traditions joined in questioning the Christendom mindset. *The Politics of Jesus* finally found some traction outside Anabaptist circles as a call to an ethic of discipleship based on the example and teachings of Jesus largely as a result of the work of Stanley Hauerwas and his students.[23] Lesslie Newbigin came home to England from India to find the repaganizing of the West in full force, and his reflections on the West as a mission field inspired the missional church movement.[24] Postmodernism was causing some to rethink our apologetic strategy and turn away from evidentialist apologetics, with its Enlightenment presup-

23. See Stanley Hauerwas and William H. Willimon, *Resident Aliens: A Provocative Christian Assessment of Culture and Ministry for People Who Know That Something Is Wrong* (Nashville: Abingdon, 1989); and Stanley Hauerwas, *The Peaceable Kingdom: A Primer in Christian Ethics* (Notre Dame: University of Notre Dame Press, 1983).

24. See Lesslie Newbigin, *Foolishness to the Greeks: The Gospel and Western Culture* (Grand Rapids: Eerdmans, 1986); and idem, *The Gospel in a Pluralist Society* (Grand Rapids: Eerdmans, 1989). For a book that reflects the growing influence of Newbigin, see Darrell L. Guder, ed., *Missional Church: A Vision for the Sending of the Church in North America* (Grand Rapids: Eerdmans, 1998).

positions, to a more holistic apologetic focused on community.[25] Postliberalism arose within liberal Protestantism as a protest against the Enlightenment captivity of the church, with Hans Frei leading the way by recalling our attention to the way that Scripture functions as the master narrative that makes sense of our lives and the whole cosmos.[26] Growing interest in the theology of Karl Barth in North America during the past twenty years has brought many North American theologians and ethicists into contact with a seminal thinker whose theology is in significant ways a post-Christendom theology. His highly significant and important rejection of natural theology is one crucial element in the development of a theology that resists being coopted by the political powers that be.[27] The emergent church movement sprang up, led by twenty-somethings who had grown up in a postmodern culture and who had never really thought in terms of a single unified culture at all. Instinctively they thought in terms of cultures, with the church being one among many. Robert Webber's *The Younger Evangelicals* catalogs the profound differences in the way these younger leaders think from the ways in which the current evangelical establishment thinks.[28] A new generation of postmodern missional leaders is recovering the biblical and apostolic mission of the church as a community of disciples clearly distinguished from the world and thus able to call people out of the world and into the church. Christendom is dying, but Jesus and his church are thriving!

Mission after Christendom

Increasingly, the Western church is a minority church within a pluralistic pagan society. The world around us is not uniformly hostile to Jesus or to the gospel, but it contains a mixture of different attitudes. In some quarters, there is hostility to everything that smacks of the colonialist, patriarchal, imperialist past of Western civilization. On the other hand, a growing number of people are amazingly ignorant about what Christianity is all about. Some are eager to absorb Jesus into a Hindu-like pantheon of heroes, avatars, angels, and saints. Others, still rebelling against their own Christian upbringing, feel the sting of their own consciences and react sharply against any hint of Christian morality. Everywhere one goes, one

25. See, for example, Brad J. Kallenberg, *Live to Tell: Evangelism for a Postmodern Age* (Grand Rapids: Brazos, 2002). The late Stanley J. Grenz was a mentor to many younger evangelicals who are moving in this direction.

26. Hans W. Frei, *Eclipse of Biblical Narrative: A Study in Eighteenth and Nineteenth Century Hermeneutics* (New Haven: Yale University Press, 1974).

27. See Karl Barth, *Church Dogmatics* II/1 (trans. Geoffrey W. Bromiley et al.; ed. Geoffrey W. Bromiley and Thomas F. Torrance; Edinburgh, Scotland: T & T Clark, 1957–77), 3–254. For an evangelical development of aspects of Barth's approach to theology, see John R. Franke, *The Character of Theology: A Post-conservative, Evangelical Approach* (Grand Rapids: Baker, 2005).

28. Robert Webber, *The Younger Evangelicals: Facing the Challenge of a New World* (Grand Rapids: Baker, 2002).

encounters the view that if Christianity has any place in the postmodern world at all, it is in the private sphere of home, family, and individual belief. Many people are empty and disillusioned with materialism, hedonism, and individualism, and many of them are longing for community and longing for permanent relationships, yet come across as suspicious, having been abandoned by parents, and as cynical, having been hurt too often. Others are eager to enlist Christianity (or a particular brand of Christianity) in their power base as they lunge for power in the political arena. "Give me your vote and I'll make people obey your moral principles," they say. We need spiritual discernment in the face of too many choices and too much novelty. In this type of situation the old labels of left and right and liberal and conservative seem curiously quaint.

But, of course, the situation is not really new. The twenty-first century is more like the first three centuries after Christ than any century between the fourth and twentieth. The church has been here before. Before Christendom there was a church, and even during Christendom the worst excesses of state-church violence and decadence never obscured the existence of faithful Christian communities of discipleship. That is why looking at history can be helpful as we seek to be faithful to Jesus Christ in our time. But continuing to look at history through the Christendom paradigm will not help. It will lead only to disaster because it will either cause us to repeat the same old mistakes or get us stuck in quandaries in which all the alternatives involve compromising our commitment to Jesus as Lord. Niebuhr's *Christ and Culture* has been an important book to many people because it deals with a very real and very practical issue. But it belongs to the old paradigm. We should not stop thinking about the issue, but we need to start thinking about it from within a new paradigm. And we find that new paradigm in the life, death, resurrection, and teaching of Jesus. Despite having been obscured by centuries of misinterpretation caused by the Christendom mentality of Christian leaders, the gospel of Jesus Christ preached in the power of the Holy Spirit still has the power to reach us and change us. It has displayed that power over and over again in the history of Christendom, and there is no reason to think it cannot happen again after Christendom.

The demise of Christendom opens the door to genuine Christian missions and evangelism in Western culture. In order to take advantage of the opportunities that lay before us, however, it is necessary that we repent of Christendom publicly and state in no uncertain terms that we want nothing to do with ruling over non-Christians, coercing people into faith, or gaining political and economic power for ourselves. The church must accept its new situation as a minority subculture within a pluralistic world with grace and quiet confidence. If God is real, if Jesus is God, and if the Holy Spirit is the driving force behind the church, we do not need guns, laws, and the favor of non-Christian rulers in order to succeed in our mission. We have the opportunity to live by faith in God, rather than by faith in the state. After Christendom is an exciting time to be in ministry. Instead of lamenting the passing of Christendom, let us humbly say amen to postmodernist and postcolonialist attacks on the evils of Christendom. Then, let us get on with the task of sharing the good news that there is another way to live—a way that sometimes requires dying but never killing, a way that involves following Jesus as his disciples rather than trusting in religious rituals to make up for our refusal to follow him, a way that involves serving others rather than dominating, controlling, and exploiting them.

I am convinced that faithful pastors and church members who work together to gather, nurture, and sustain worshiping communities of faith in which the Bible is preached, God is worshiped, friendships are nourished, and the poor are welcomed do more to change the world than all the liberal lobby groups and conservative political action groups put together. Why? Because these communities function as outposts of the kingdom of God, and they nourish a living faith in Jesus Christ, the Lord of heaven and earth. But how does that change the world, you ask? Well, to be precise, it actually proclaims that the world has already been changed and that the Lord Jesus Christ now reigns. The real problem with the world is not that we have yet to hit upon the right socio-economic-political system—although that is what liberals believe. And the real problem is not that we do not have God-fearing, Bible-preaching people running the government—although that is what conservatives believe. The real problem is sin; that is, fallen human nature and the openness created by that sad reality for what the New Testament calls the "principalities and powers" to take over human society and promote what John Paul II labeled "the culture of death." And the answer is not a better distribution of wealth (the liberal solution) or more restrictive laws (the conservative solution), but rather the acknowledgement of Jesus Christ as Lord. Followers of Jesus may well press for a better redistribution of wealth and may well work for a consistent ethic of life, but they recognize that they are thereby tackling the symptoms, not the roots, of the real problem. The root problem is addressed by faith in Jesus Christ and by liberation from earthly powers through baptism. Of course, it does not instantly solve everything. But it goes to the heart of the issue for individuals, for groups, and for the world as a whole.

The Argument of This Book

In part 1 I examine *Christ and Culture* in detail. In chapter 2 I summarize the argument of Niebuhr's book at length and look carefully at its structure. Internal tensions within the book will be uncovered, and questions will be raised about its assumed stance of objective neutrality and pluralistic approach. In chapter 3 I critique the book, both from a rhetorical perspective and also from a theological perspective. Chapter 4 examines the theory of Christendom in more depth and seeks to isolate exactly what in this paradigm is inconsistent with the gospel. This analysis requires a careful look at the events of the fourth century and argues for the thesis that the acceptance by Christian bishops of violent coercion as part of the work of evangelism is the key element of the Christendom theory that makes it incompatible with the gospel. Chapter 5 clarifies what I see as the alternative to Christendom.

In part 2 I offer an imaginative alternative to Niebuhr's typology. If coercive violence in the service of the gospel is the key element in a theory of Christendom that obscures the gospel and ruins Christian witness, then how could Niebuhr's typology be reconstructed so as to distinguish between Christian movements that did witness faithfully to the gospel and those that did not? It is not my view that all of Western church history from the fourth to the twentieth centuries is a write-off. I would not say that no faithful witness has been rendered. That would be an irresponsible overreaction to the obvious failures of Christendom. To the best of my understanding, even those groups that spoke of the fall of the church in the sixteenth century (which included most Protestant movements, not just the so-called radical ones) did not claim that the gospel had not been preached, believed by people, and lived out by many different Christians in many different ways during the previous thousand years. I certainly do not want to say that. But I do want to say that Christendom thinking was of no help to those who believed, preached, and suffered for the gospel. The church witnessed to the gospel despite, not because of, Christendom. And the message of the gospel was brutally deformed, obscured, and hidden all too often by war, violence, greed, power politics, and the alignment of church leaders with rulers bent on self-promotion and lust for power—exactly the dangers that Jesus warned his disciples about in no uncertain terms in Matthew 20:20–27.

So a useful typology of ways of relating Christ and culture needs to take account of the key issue of coercive violence and also needs to distinguish a range of ways in which both groups that rejected coercion and groups that accepted coercion interacted with culture. By forcing all those who rejected violent coercion into the Christ against culture type, Niebuhr failed to take sufficient account of the many Christian leaders, movements, and institutions that both rejected violent coercion *and* had a transformative or leavening effect on culture. His advocacy of the Christ transforming culture type ignored that many Christian leaders, movements, and institutions that claimed to be transforming culture by means of violent coercion actually ended up conforming to culture at precisely the points where the gospel requires a contrast. Thus, the whole Niebuhrian Christ transforming culture project is revealed to be deficient in two key ways: first, it seeks transformation in such a way that it loses touch with the gospel and thus negates its right to be viewed as authentically Christian witness; and, second, precisely because its main thrust is away from the unique message of the gospel, it tends merely to confirm the world in its rebellion, rather than actually transforming that rebellion into repentance and conversion. The alternative typology presented here allows for some key distinctions that Niebuhr's typology does not; for example, between those who use violent coercion to transform culture (such as Oliver Cromwell) and those who transform culture without resorting to violence (such as Martin

Luther King Jr.). This new typology thus allows us to reimagine the relationship between Christ and culture without playing off responsibility against faithfulness and without getting trapped into a tragic choice of either compromised involvement or irresponsible withdrawal.

This book attempts to describe both the intellectual act of acknowledging the lordship of Jesus Christ and the ethical act of following him not as two separate things, one of which logically follows from the other, but rather as one integrated movement of a life toward God. This entails asking hard questions about the relationship between orthodoxy and discipleship on the one hand and about the nature of the witness of the church on the other. I argue that to claim to believe in Nicene orthodoxy without living a life of discipleship in which nonviolence and orthodoxy merge together in one living faith is, in the end, incoherent. If Jesus really is God in the flesh, then his teachings must be believed and his commands must be obeyed. His last command to the disciples was to make disciples of all nations, "teaching them to obey everything I have commanded you" (Matthew 28:20).

I also intend to argue that the mission of the church is to witness to the gospel of Jesus Christ, which means that the transformation of the wider culture in which the church lives will always be a secondary by-product of the church's main mission rather than its primary goal in this age. In many ways these arguments are subversive and counterintuitive for most Western Christians, who have been conditioned by centuries of Christendom thinking. But in the post-Christendom situation we have no choice but to learn to think differently about issues of Christ and culture. My final chapter attempts to clarify the choice the church needs to make at this point in history in order to be faithful to Jesus.

This book is an exercise in envisioning the future by fashioning new categories with which to reinterpret the past. One of our perpetual problems is our inability to see ourselves, our world, and our history more clearly and more truly than we do. The story of the church's relationship to Western culture is full of instruction for those who can read the lessons rightly. But not everyone can read the lessons, for not all have eyes to see. I hope to begin anew from the same data that Niebuhr looked at in writing his book. My question is this: What if one reexamines Niebuhr's data from the perspective, not of Christendom, but of the conviction that following Jesus is both possible and essential to true Christian discipleship? I hope you find that question to be as stimulating as I have found it to be. The first step, then, is to return to Niebuhr's great work and examine it carefully.

Part 1

Rethinking Christ and Culture
after Christendom

Commonly, only those who are squarely within the dominant culture believe that there is some neutral place to stand outside all culture.

Darrell Guder, Missional Church

The historical fact that movements which at the outset use anti-cultural rhetoric turn out to be very culturally creative must for Niebuhr be a vice of the movements described, rather than indicating a possible flaw in his categories, or in his assumptions about sociology.

John Howard Yoder, Authentic Transformation

Therefore, I urge you, brothers, in view of God's mercy, to offer your bodies as living sacrifices, holy and pleasing to God—this is your spiritual act of worship.

Romans 12:1–2

Only *false* gods can accept *forced* homage.

Gustavo Gutiérrez, Las Casas (quoting Tertullian and Lactantius)

[The Romans] rob, butcher, plunder, and call it empire; and where they make a desolation, they call it "peace."

Agricola, a chief speaking to his fellow Britons, as recorded by Tacitus

2

The Argument
of Niebuhr's *Christ and Culture*

We need to begin by looking at the argument of Niebuhr's book. In the next chapter, I will offer a critique of the book. But in fairness to Niebuhr, we need to examine carefully what he had to say before attempting criticism. If you have already read Niebuhr for yourself, this chapter will provide a quick review. If you have not read Niebuhr, I highly recommend that you do so. If you do not have time to do that, at least read this chapter carefully. It is crucial to a critique of any writer that we first of all state his or her position in a way that he or she would be able to *recognize* as his or her own position. In other words, the test of the success of this chapter is whether Niebuhr, if he were he alive and aware of it, would say: Yes, that accurately represents what I tried to say in my book. Of course there would always be quibbles. But have we gotten the main points right? If we fail this test, our critique can never be convincing because it can always be dismissed as resting on a caricature.

The shape of Niebuhr's book is quite straightforward. In the first chapter, Niebuhr sets out what he calls "The Enduring Problem." For Niebuhr, the problem is that the Christ of the New Testament is so fixated on the absolute sovereignty of God that his teaching is so radical that it cannot be lived out in this world. Living within human culture requires compromise because human culture is fallen and sinful. But Jesus's teaching is full of absolutes that cannot be simply applied to our human, fallen situation. Therefore, the Christian is forced to figure out how best to relate two fundamentally incompatible things, Christ and culture, in his or her own life. In the next five chapters, Niebuhr describes five typical ways that this has been done in Christian history. Some Christians follow Jesus so strictly that they find it necessary to separate from culture altogether. Others identify Christ with culture so completely that the tension between the two disappears. Niebuhr views these two approaches—the Christ against culture and the Christ of culture approaches—as the extremes and then discusses three mediating positions that try to balance the necessity of living in human culture with being a disciple of Jesus Christ. He looks at the biblical basis of all five types and gives examples of each one (see table 1). In his final chapter, "A Concluding Unscientific Postscript," Niebuhr asserts that all five types have some degree of validity and deals with the question of how one makes choices in the task of relating Christ and culture. His answer is a social existentialism in which we choose which approach is best for our situation based on many factors, including historical trends and communal consciousness of the Spirit's leading. Since the definition of terms is crucial in determining the outcome of any debate, it is crucial that we understand clearly what Niebuhr means by the key terms *Christ* and *culture*.

Table 1. Niebuhr's Typology of Christ and Culture

	The Two Extremes		The Church of the Center		
	Christ against culture	Christ of culture	Christ above culture	Christ and culture in paradox	Christ transforming culture
Niebuhr calls examples	radicals	liberals	synthesists	dualists	conversionists
Biblical support	• 1 John • Revelation	• apocryphal Gospels (gnostics) and lives of Jesus (liberals)	• NT sayings like: "Render to Caesar the things that are Caesar's, and to God the things that are God's"	• Paul's Letters	• Fourth Gospel
Examples	• Tertullian • monasticism • Mennonites • Tolstoy	• Gnosticism • Abelard • Kant • Schleiermacher • Ritschl	• Justin Martyr • Clement of Alexandria • Thomas Aquinas • Joseph Butler	• Marcion • Luther • Kierkegaard • Roger Williams	• Augustine • Calvin • F. D. Maurice

Niebuhr's Definition of the Problem

In his first chapter, Niebuhr begins by giving some examples of what he means by the problem of Christ and culture. He claims first, quoting Rabbi Joseph Klausner, that Jesus came into conflict with Jewish culture because, while Judaism "is not only religion and it is not only ethics: it is the sum total of all the needs of the nation, placed on a religious basis," Jesus set aside "all the requirements of a national life" and "set up nothing but an ethico-religious system bound up with his conception of the Godhead." Niebuhr views Jesus as a kind of anarchist who is unconcerned about the maintenance of Jewish culture and social order: "For civil justice he substituted the command to nonresistance, which must result in the loss of all social order."[1]

Niebuhr's second example of the Christ and culture problem is the conflict between the gospel and Greco-Roman civilization. Niebuhr quotes Edward Gibbon's statement of the Roman viewpoint that Christians are "animated by a contempt for present existence and by confidence in immortality" (5). According to Niebuhr, history shows that not only the Romans found themselves in conflict with Christianity at this point, but also various nationalistic and communistic societies in modern times that "have discerned in Christ a foe of cultural interests." It is not just a matter of political persecution, for the problem raised by Christ is "broadly cultural" (4).

A third example of the Christ and culture problem is the closely related charge that Christ and his church are intolerant. Again, Niebuhr quotes Gibbon, who argues that the Romans were "bound to reject Christianity just because Rome was tolerant" (7). Rome tolerated many different religions, looked benignly on hundreds of local cults, and allowed various deities to be worshiped within the empire so long as none of these religions claimed to be the one and only true religion. The situation in the ancient Roman Empire was very similar to the situation in modern democracies in that, as long as it did not call into question one's loyalty to the empire (or the modern nation-state), religion was/is considered harmless. Eventually, however, as a way of maintaining imperial unity, emperor worship came to be expected of all the subjects of the empire. Although an exception was made for the Jews, who constituted a separate nation with an ancient tradition of monotheism and who just wanted to be left alone, no such exception was made for the Christian movement because Christianity was quite different. For one thing, it was spreading throughout the empire geographically. For another, it was having an influence on all social classes and races. Christianity represented a threat to kings because, as Niebuhr puts it, "monotheism deprives them of their sacred aura." The same dynamic became apparent in the modern era in "the anti-Christian and especially anti-Jewish attacks of German national socialism" (8). Niebuhr is aware that the modern demand that religion be kept out of business or politics or that Christianity learn to get along with other religions is a covert way of organizing society on the basis of a different religion: "What is often

---

1. H. Richard Niebuhr, *Christ and Culture,* with a foreword by Martin E. Marty, a new preface by James M. Gustafson, and an introductory essay by the author (San Francisco: HarperSanFrancisco, 2001), 3. All future references to this work in this chapter will be in the form of page numbers in parentheses within the text.

meant is that not only the claims of religious groups but all consideration of the
claims of Christ and God should be banished from the spheres where other gods,
called values, reign. . . . The charge lies not only against Christian organizations
which use coercive means against what they define as false religions, but against
the faith itself" (9). Niebuhr recognizes that the Christian belief in the lordship
of Christ makes it impossible for Christians to be confronted with the claims to
lordship of other powers and authorities without bearing a witness to Christ that
may, and often does, cause offense.

However, the debate about Christ and culture is not always carried on between
Christians and non-Christians. Often, the debate occurs between Christians and
within individual Christian consciences. We see it happening throughout church
history—in the efforts of Paul to translate the gospel into Greek forms of thought,
in the Constantinian settlement, in the monastic movement, in Thomism, in the
Reformation, and in the social gospel. For this reason, Niebuhr argues: "It is not
essentially the problem of Christianity and civilization; for Christianity, whether
defined as church, creed, ethics, or movement of thought, itself moves between
the poles of Christ and culture" (11). The problem of Christ and culture is thus
defined in terms of the dilemma faced by Christians in the world who wish both
to serve Jesus Christ as Lord and also to live in this world in some fashion.

At this point, Niebuhr turns to a definition of the term *Christ*. After defining
a Christian as one who believes in or is a follower of Christ (11), Niebuhr then
points out that there are many differing interpretations of who Christ is (12). Is
he a teacher and lawgiver or a revealer of truths and laws in himself; that is, the
living revelation of God? For some Christians, Christianity is neither new teaching
nor new life but rather a new community: the church. Yet, the New Testament
portrait of Christ remains the authoritative one by which all later ones need to be
corrected (13). Liberal Protestantism interprets Christ as love and in so doing has
not distorted the reality of who Christ is. But Jesus does not teach love for the sake
of love, he teaches a particular kind of love: "The virtue of love in Jesus' character
and demand is the virtue of the *love of God and of the neighbor in God*, not the
virtue of the love of love" (16, emphasis original). Niebuhr interprets Jesus's love
of God as the key to his whole life and ministry. Rather than attributing infinite
value to the human soul, Jesus attributes infinite value to one thing and only one
thing—God. This emphasis is not the same as liberalism's emphasis on Jesus as
the example of the "man for others," the ultimate exemplar of neighborly love.

Liberalism's emphasis on love has been followed by eschatological interpretations that view Jesus as the man of hope and existentialist interpretations that view
him as radically obedient. Liberalism was preceded by an orthodox Protestantism
for whom Jesus was "the exemplar and the bestower of the virtue of faith, and by
a monasticism which was astonished and charmed by his great humility" (19).
Although the Christ of the New Testament has all of these virtues, all of them are
subordinated to and expressive of his relationship to God. Jesus was extreme in
his single-minded devotion to God: "In his moral sonship to God Jesus Christ is

not a median figure, half God, half man; his is a single person wholly directed as man toward God and wholly directed in his unity with the Father toward men" (29). So Niebuhr can say: "Thus any one of the virtues of Jesus may be taken as the key to the understanding of his character and teaching; but each is intelligible in its apparent radicalism only as a relation to God" (27). For Niebuhr, then, Jesus is a radical monotheist[2] who basically rejects culture: "In his single-minded direction toward God, Christ leads men away from the temporality and pluralism of culture" (39). Yet Jesus is also the moral Son of God, who functions as "the moral mediator of the Father's will toward men" (28). Rejecting culture, Jesus focuses completely on the will of the Father; embodying God's will, Jesus thus mediates God's will to humanity.

Next, Niebuhr turns to a definition of the term *culture*. For some Christians, culture is godless in the neutral sense of being secular, while for others "it is Godless in the negative sense, as being anti-God or idolatrous" (30). Niebuhr refuses to adopt either of these two definitions. He also rejects any definition of culture as a particular culture, such as Greco-Roman or Western culture (30–31). Niebuhr also resists narrowing down the definition of culture to a particular aspect of human social organization, such as science or political structures. Niebuhr presses for the widest possible definition of culture, concluding that "what we have in view when we deal with Christ and culture is that total process of human activity and that total result of such activity to which now the name *culture*, now the name *civilization*, is applied in common speech" (32).

While professing to be unable to define the essence of this culture, he nevertheless enumerates some of its characteristics. First, culture is always social; one person does not create a culture alone (32). Second, culture is human achievement; it is what humans impose upon nature (33). Third, it is therefore designed by humans for certain ends and thus represents "a world of values" (34). Fourth, these values are concerned predominantly with "the good for man," which means that cultural values must serve the human good because humanity "is the measure of all things" (35). It is not made clear why culture must be defined in an anthropocentric manner: Niebuhr does not appear to consider the possibility of a Christian culture directed toward the service of God in all things. He appears simply to be describing non-Christian cultures as we find them, especially when he notes that even when cultures serve the gods they do so for humanistic ends. As a description of particular, historical, non-Christian cultures, this seems unobjectionable. Yet the reader is left wondering how Niebuhr cannot so much as even acknowledge the attempt in Western Christendom to develop a culture centered on God. (We will reflect further on this question in the next chapter.) Fifth, Niebuhr says that culture "is concerned with the temporal and material

---

2. The title of one of Niebuhr's later books is *Radical Monotheism and Western Culture* (Louisville: Westminster/John Knox, 1970). If one had to pick one label to describe Niebuhr, "radical monotheist" might well be the best.

realization of values" (36). Even when the goods that humans seek to realize in culture are not material, culture is nevertheless the material realization or expression of such goals. Sixth, since culture deals with material and therefore transient materials, "the conservation of values" is as important as their initial realization (37). Niebuhr's seventh and final characteristic of culture is the pluralism of all culture: "The values a culture seeks to realize in any time or place are many in number" (38). For Niebuhr, this is necessarily the case because the good for human beings is different for "male and female, child and adult, ruler and ruled," for members of "special vocations and groups," and for individuals with "their special claims and interests."

Thus, for Niebuhr, cultures are faced continuously with the task of balancing freedom and welfare, justice and order. A very large claim has been made here under the cover of giving a definition. Niebuhr asks the reader to accept without discussion that there is no one, unified good for human beings. In other words, the search for the unified good for humanity that animated ancient Greek philosophy is dismissed as a chimera, and the pluralism of modern liberal individualism is taken for granted as the truth. Implicit in this claim is the further premise that cultures both are and should be polytheistic, because monotheism imposes a uniform conception of the common good on all people. But modern liberal individualism can never be more than a provisional arrangement, suitable for a fallen world, because if there is one God, who is the highest good in the universe, and if this one God is also at the same time the only one in whom individuals and cultures alike find their ultimate fulfillment and most complete meaning and purpose, then clearly culture must be unified in the worship of the one, true God. This will happen when the kingdom of God has fully come, but to force it on society now would necessitate a degree of coercion that would negate the message of the gospel as good news of liberation.

For Niebuhr, then, the problem of Christ and culture is that culture is human centered and pluralistic and therefore constantly needs to balance irreconcilable values in order to maintain social peace, while Christ exhibits a single-minded devotion to God, which places him in irreconcilable tension with culture as so defined. That the tension is irreconcilable is the crucial point for Niebuhr, and it is the reason why it becomes our task to somehow bring about a suitable relationship (which must always fall short of reconciliation) between the two. The problem of Christ and culture, therefore, becomes ours to manage.

Christ against Culture

In chapter 2 Niebuhr turns to a discussion of the Christ against culture position. In the first section, entitled "The New People and 'the World,'" Niebuhr begins by acknowledging that this position seems to be the most consistent one because "it appears to follow directly from the common Christian principle of the Lordship of Jesus Christ" and because "it is widely held to be the typical attitude of the first Christians" (45). According to Niebuhr, both claims are "subject to question," and in a sense the thrust of Niebuhr's whole book is directed to disproving the claim of the Christ against culture type to be the correct one for Christians, although Niebuhr nowhere states this as his intention in so many words.

Niebuhr looks at the First Epistle of John as the most important biblical example of this type. He views First John as being focused on the lordship of Christ as much as on the idea of love. Obedience to the command of the visible and tangible Jesus Christ of history, who is "inseparably united with the unseen Father in love and righteousness," is of paramount importance, and this obedience requires "the rejection of cultural society" (47). For the author of First John, the world is "a realm under the power of evil" (48). Niebuhr interprets the author as working with an interim ethic that did not expect the world to last very long (49). Many second-century writings, such as *The Teaching of the Twelve* and *The Shepherd of Hermas*, also exhibit the Christ against culture approach, but the most outstanding example is Tertullian.

Tertullian combines a strong emphasis on the lordship of Christ with "a rigorous morality of obedience to his commandments" (52). According to Niebuhr, although Tertullian comes close to identifying sin with human culture, his main concern is "pagan religion, with its polytheism and idolatry, its beliefs and rites, its sensuality and its commercialization" (53). For Tertullian, the problem of living as a Christian in a society permeated by paganism in all these forms is acute. Yet it is by no means evident that this highly educated, articulate lawyer and theologian would have taken the same attitude toward a society largely purged of paganism. So the question is this: is it more correct to say that Tertullian was opposed to *culture* as such or only to the particular, historical, pagan culture he faced in his day?

In the second section of this chapter, Niebuhr gives ten pages to "Tolstoy's Rejection of Culture." He mentions only in passing other examples of the Christ against culture type: the monastic movement, Protestant sectarianism, Mennonites, and Quakers. Tolstoy was a tortured and tragic figure who took a unique and individualistic stance, which has produced many admirers and few imitators. The fairness of using him as one of two major examples of this type, which is supposed to include many movements, denominations, and organized societies, is somewhat questionable. He is a bit of an easy target for Niebuhr, who points out the many inconsistencies in a man who believed that "property claims were based on robbery and maintained by violence" (62) and yet who continued to live on his vast estates. Niebuhr points to the curious fact that Tolstoy differs from most radical Christians throughout the centuries in that there is lacking in him "a personal devotion to a personal Lord" (64). For Tolstoy, the law of Christ appears more important than Christ himself, and Christ appears to be detached almost completely from historic Christianity. As Niebuhr himself points out, that Tolstoy is such an exception among radical Christians should alert us to the danger of overemphasizing him as an example of the radical type.

In the third section of chapter 2, entitled "A Necessary and Inadequate Position," Niebuhr presents his evaluation of the Christ against culture position. Niebuhr praises the exemplars of this type as having a very great appeal, rooted in their sincerity and their "reduplication" of Christ, and he admits: "In history these Christian withdrawals from and rejections of the institutions of society have been of very great importance to both church and culture" (66). Nevertheless, he argues that anticultural Christians have never influenced culture without the mediation of Christians who embody the other types. Niebuhr argues that both withdrawal/renunciation and responsible engagement are equally necessary. According to Niebuhr, it is impossible to rely solely on Jesus Christ to the exclusion of culture. One should note, however, that the dichotomy between Christ and culture is not something advocated by exemplars of the Christ against culture type; it is Niebuhr's own view embodied within his definition of Christ as described above. He defines Christ as pointing away from culture toward God, as though one had to choose either God or culture. He allows no choice between a godly culture and an ungodly one, no possible contrast between a Christian community (e.g., a monastic one) and a pagan society (e.g., the Roman Empire). Why not? His definitions simply exclude such possibilities. For him, to move closer to Christ (and God) is by definition to move away from culture. But this conclusion is not deduced from historical data; it is contained in the definitions, which function as a premise. This definition of culture certainly does not prepare us for Niebuhr's advocating, by the end of his book, the Christ transforming culture type.

In the final section of this chapter, Niebuhr says that there are four "theological problems" with the Christ against culture type. First is what he calls the "denigration of reason and the exaltation of revelation" (76). By this phrase Niebuhr means that those in the Christ against culture type believe that human reason is "not only inadequate because it does not lead to knowledge of God . . . ; but it is also erroneous and deceptive" (77). But of course, as Niebuhr himself admits, Christians from a wide variety of backgrounds, and not just the radicals, believe this to be true. Second, Niebuhr says that the radicals have an inadequate appreciation of the effects of sin on Christians. While they make a valid contribution in explaining the inheritance of sin in social terms, they cannot get away from sin by withdrawing from the world—the implication being that they try to do so. Since Niebuhr himself acknowledges that the radicals understand quite well that the main difference between the Christian and the non-Christian is that the former owns up to his or her sinfulness (78), the nature of the objection is unclear. Third, Niebuhr accuses exponents of the Christ against culture type of legalism (79–80). Although the charge seems to be appropriate with regard to Tolstoy, it definitely is not appropriate with regard to First John and is doubtfully appropriate with regard to Tertullian. Fourth, Niebuhr suggests that the emphasis placed on Jesus Christ by the radicals leads to the danger of ignoring the creator of nature (the Father) and the Spirit immanent in creation and the Christian community (80–81). For Niebuhr, the doctrine of the Trinity means that the radical thrust of the Son's teaching must be tempered by the more conservative thrust of the Father and the work of the Spirit as evidenced in tradition. He says that those who advocate the Christ against culture type risk "converting their ethical dualism into an ontological bifurcation" (81).

Full evaluation of these crucial theological issues must wait until the next chapter, but for now we must at least raise the question of whether the tendency toward an ontological dualism is to be discerned in radical Christian communities of discipleship throughout history or in Niebuhr's own definitions of Christ and culture. It is hard to know how to reconcile Niebuhr's assertion that the radicals tend to lose "contact with the historical Jesus Christ of history, for whom a spiritual principle is substituted" (81–82), with his earlier assertion that "it is exceedingly important for the First Letter of John that Christians be loyal to no merely spiritual Christ but to a visible and tangible Jesus Christ of history, who is, however, not only the Jesus of history but the Son of God, inseparably united with the unseen Father in love and righteousness" (47). Perhaps on page 81 he is thinking of Tolstoy, while on page 47 he obviously has First John in mind. But if so, how can Tolstoy and First John both be examples of the same type? Indeed, how could they be more different from each other?

Christ of Culture

In chapter 3 Niebuhr takes up the Christ of culture type, the accommodationist approach. In the first section, he looks at Gnosticism and Abelard as examples of this type in the ancient and medieval periods. What all examples of this type have in common is that "they feel no great tension between church and world" (83). They are the "healthy-minded" and the "once-born," in the terminology made famous by William James (84). This is the approach that sees Christ as being compatible with the best and highest of human wisdom.

The gnostics were condemned as heretics, but they thought of themselves as loyal Christians. According to Niebuhr, they sought to reconcile the science and philosophy of their day with the gospel (86). If their ideas look bizarre to us, he says, we must remember that they were working with cultural ideas that were in their day the equivalent of psychotherapy and quantum mechanics in our day insofar as they represented the "latest thought." Gnosticism was a refined philosophy and very much an individualistic matter: "As a religion dealing with the soul it laid no imperious claim on man's total life," and that meant that "a Gnostic had no reason for refusing to pay homage to Caesar or to participate in war" (87). Niebuhr's treatment of Gnosticism is much more benign than that of the church fathers, such as Irenaeus and Tertullian, who battled it as dangerous heresy. The word *Gnosticism* is derived from a Greek word meaning "knowledge," and it refers to a second-century movement that may have been a deviation from Christian teaching or a previously existing pagan movement that assimilated segments of Christian teachings. Gnosticism was based on a matter-spirit dualism in which salvation consisted of escape from the material world. Since the true God could have no contact with matter, the Old Testament creator God was seen as a demiurge distinct from the unknowable divine being. As a divine being, Jesus Christ was not really and truly human, but only temporarily inhabited a human being or apparently took human form. Gnosticism thus involves a denial of creation, incarnation, and redemption.[3]

According to Niebuhr, in Abelard we see a medieval approach to the Christ and culture problem that is "akin" in spirit to the gnostics (89). But Abelard was not a gnostic, and all that Niebuhr appears to mean by his comparison is that, like the gnostics, Abelard reduces Christian faith to "what conforms with the best in culture." Niebuhr points out that "the moral theory of atonement is offered as an alternative not only to a doctrine that is difficult for Christians as Christians, but to the whole conception of a once-and-for-all act of redemption" (90). For Abelard, Jesus is the great moral teacher who did something similar to that done by Socrates and Plato before him, only in a higher degree.

In section two, Niebuhr discusses "culture-Protestantism" and Albrecht Ritschl as the prime modern examples of the Christ of culture type. Since the eighteenth century, figures such as John Locke, Immanuel Kant, and Thomas Jefferson have shaped liberal Protestantism with their emphasis on reason, ethics, and culture. The Schleiermacher of the *Speeches on Religion*, though not so clearly the later Schleiermacher of *The Christian Faith*, was part of this movement (93). Other important figures include Hegel and Emerson, but Niebuhr chooses to focus primarily on Ritschl. Ritschl's starting point, like all those in liberalism, was the struggle of humans to gain mastery over nature, beginning with human nature. As a Kantian, Ritschl was concerned with "the effort of the ethical reason to impress on human nature itself the internal law of the conscience." Ritschl called his goal "the kingdom of God," but by that he meant "the ideal goal of virtuous existence in society of free yet interdependent virtuous persons" (96). For Ritschl, the kingdom of God was the full implementation of nineteenth-century cultural ideals, and Jesus Christ was the embodiment of those ideals (98). Later nineteenth-century figures mentioned by Niebuhr who embody culture-Protestantism are Adolf von Harnack in Germany, Leonhard Ragaz in Switzerland, and Walter Rauschenbusch, Shailer Mathews, and D. C. Mcintosh in the United States. All of these figures have in common the idea that "the human situation is fundamentally characterized by man's conflict with nature" and that Jesus Christ is "a great leader of the spiritual, cultural cause, of man's struggle to subdue nature, and of his aspirations to transcend it" (101).

3. For more information, see F. L. Cross and E. A. Livingston, eds., *The Oxford Dictionary of the Christian Church* (3rd ed.; Oxford: Oxford University Press, 1997), 683–85 s.v. "Gnosticism" (with bibliography).

In the third section of this chapter, Niebuhr writes "in defense of [this] cultural faith." He does not dismiss it out of hand, but sees in it one answer to the Christ and culture problem, which taken by itself is inadequate, but which acting in tension with the others has a contribution to make. He astutely points out that very often the critics of this approach merely wish to defend ideas drawn from older cultures, and so their criticism is not of the Christ of culture type itself, but only of the particular cultural values the liberals of the day wish to lift up as the meaning of Christianity (102). To be conservative is not necessarily to be biblical. Niebuhr commends advocates of the Christ of culture type for often speaking powerfully to the leading groups in society because "the Christ-of-culture position appears in these and other similar ways to make effective the universal meaning of the gospel, and the truth that Jesus is the savior, not of a selected little band of saints, but of the world" (105). According to Niebuhr, the gnostics helped to keep "the church from becoming a withdrawn sect," and "the Culture-Protestants are preachers of repentance to an industrial culture endangered by its peculiar corruptions" (107). But, he asks, is this not to turn Christ into a chameleon to which each culture in turn attaches its highest ideals? Niebuhr replies in the negative, suggesting that to find "kinship between Christ and the prophets of the Hebrews, the moral philosophers of Greece, the Roman Stoics, Spinoza and Kant, humanitarian reformers and Eastern mystics, may be less indicative of Christian instability than of a certain stability in human wisdom" (107). This attempt to bring all religions and philosophies into harmony with Christ as the symbol of that harmony is characteristic of liberal Protestantism, and we note that Niebuhr presents it here without critique.

In the fourth section of this chapter, Niebuhr turns to some "theological objections" to the Christ of culture type. The basis of most objections to the Christ of culture position is "the charge that loyalty to contemporary culture has so far qualified the loyalty to Christ that he has been abandoned in favor of an idol called by his name" (110). Niebuhr states that "the major part of the Christian movement" has rejected the Christ of culture position, though he does not give any evidence for this assertion. From our post-Christendom vantage point, it looks like the Christ of culture position dominated nineteenth-century German culture-Protestantism and so-called mainline Protestantism during at least the first half of the twentieth century.

Niebuhr portrays the Christ of culture and the Christ against culture positions as being alike in their suspicion of theology: "Extremes seem to meet also in the radical and the cultural Christian views of sin, of grace and law, and of the Trinity" (112). How so? As for sin, the radicals locate it in social institutions and the liberals locate it in the animal passions. As we saw above, however, this is not true of most of Niebuhr's examples of the Christ against culture type. According to Niebuhr, both the liberals and the radicals "incline to the side of law in dealing with the polarity of law and grace" (113). How this tendency toward emphasizing the law is different from simply taking ethics and sanctification seriously is not made clear. As for the Trinity, Niebuhr says that both the radicals and the liberals have problems with this doctrine. While this is true for the Christ of culture position, it is less clear that it can be said of such exemplars of the Christ against culture type as monasticism, Tertullian, or First John.

Christ above Culture

Chapter 4 of *Christ and Culture* deals with the Christ above culture position. In the first section of this chapter, Niebuhr makes some comments on the three mediating types, which he designates collectively as "the church of the center," before taking up the Christ above culture position as such. He notes that the church of the center constitutes "the great majority movement in Christianity" (117). Here we see an attempt to hold together belief in both Christ and the world as expressed in the phrase *Jesus Christ as the Son of God, the Father Almighty who created heaven and earth*. There is agreement that humans are to be obedient to God in Christ in "the concrete, actual life of natural, cultural man," and this is seen by Niebuhr as holding to the essential truth of the doctrine of the Trinity, rather than overemphasizing the lordship of Christ at the expense of the revelation of the Father in creation and the Spirit in history (118). According to Niebuhr, while the radicals "are tempted to exclude [sin from] their holy commonwealths" and cultural Christians "tend to deny that it reaches into the depths of human personality," the church of the center affirms both the universality and radical nature of sin (118). This is a debatable assertion, since one of the most common criticisms of the synthesist position is that it does not take sin seriously enough, a point that Niebuhr himself later notes (148). Niebuhr also views the church of the center as rejecting the legalism to which both the radicals and cultural Christians are tempted (119). Niebuhr is unclear, however, about whether he means that radicals have been tempted in this way or that, according to his ideal type, they should be tempted in this way, or both.

In the second section of this chapter, Niebuhr summarizes the Christ above culture type or synthesist approach. He distinguishes the synthesist approach from the accommodationist and radical approaches by pointing out that "there is in the synthesist's view a gap between Christ and culture that accommodation Christianity never takes seriously enough, and that radicalism does not try to overcome" (121). Niebuhr finds no New Testament book to point to as a basis of this type, but he does claim that certain quotations from the Gospels can be viewed as supporting it, such as: "Render to Caesar the things that are Caesar's," "Think not that I have come to abolish the law and the prophets," and "Let every person be subject to the governing authorities" (123). Ancient church examples are Justin Martyr and Clement of Alexandria, but the greatest historical exemplar of this type is Thomas Aquinas. As a monk, Thomas represents a protest movement against a worldly church, but a protest movement that has been "incorporated into the church without losing its radical character" (129).

Thomas begins with the question "what is my purpose, my end?" and uses Aristotle's philosophy to give an answer. Aristotle taught that nothing but the universal good could totally satisfy the human being, and Thomas identifies this good with God (131). Thomas views the contemplative life as the highest form of human life, and he views all other ways of life as ministerial to this highest good. Thus, for Thomas, there are many subordinate goods corresponding to various stations in life and ways of life, all of which lead progressively onward to the highest good, the beatific vision, which lies beyond this life. For Thomas, this life is governed by law, which is discoverable by human reason apart from revelation (135). The divine law corresponds in some ways to the civil law, but it also transcends it. So there is overlap and synthesis, but not identification of the two. Niebuhr distinguishes Thomas as an example of synthesis from Pope Leo XIII, whom he views as an example of cultural Christianity because the goal of this nineteenth-century pope was to recreate the union of the church with medieval culture rather than to synthesize the church of his day with nineteenth-century culture (139).

Niebuhr titles the third section of this chapter "Synthesis in Question." But instead of criticizing this type, he spends most of his time defending the contribution made by the Christ above culture position from the attacks of the radicals. For example, he insists that the synthesists offer to Christians "an intelligible basis for the work they must do in co-operation with nonbelievers" and specifically draws a contrast with Tertullian on this point (143). The "radical critics too often forget how exalted a view of the law and the goal of love is presented by Clement and Thomas" (144). The only real criticism of the synthesist position he discusses in this section is that all attempts at synthesis can be only provisional because they all tend toward the absolutization of that which is relative (145). While it is true that "the effort to synthesize leads to the institutionalization of Christ and the gospel" (146), Niebuhr argues that the answer is to attempt the synthesis with humility, recognizing that it is God's work and therefore never within our power to accomplish fully (147). The major objection to the synthesist position, however, is mentioned only at the end of the chapter: the synthesist position does not face up to the radical evil present in all human work (148), a charge that comes primarily from the dualists, the subject of Niebuhr's next chapter.

Christ and Culture in Paradox

Chapter 5 of *Christ and Culture* deals with the second mediating position: the Christ and culture in paradox or dualist position. In section one, "The Theology of the Dualists," Niebuhr explains that this type arises historically out of an attack on the synthesist position (149). The term *dualist*, as Niebuhr uses it, does not mean a Manichean dualism in which the world is divided into the realms of darkness and of light, the kingdoms of Satan and of God. Although the dualists dissent from the way in which synthesists go about holding together Christ and culture, they, unlike the radical Christians, also want to do so as well, just in a different way. Niebuhr explains: "For them the fundamental issue in life is not the one which radical Christians face as they draw the line between Christian community and pagan world. Neither is it the issue which cultural Christianity discerns as it sees man everywhere in conflict with nature and locates Christ on the side of the spiritual forces of culture" (150). Where then do the dualists draw the line, if not between church and culture or between nature and culture? They draw the line within the human heart, and the division is between our righteousness and God's righteousness. The conflict is between God and us. Sin for the dualist is the "will to live as gods, hence without God" (155), and this sin makes everything cultural feel sordid and abhorrent (154). Niebuhr says: "Thus in the dualist's view the whole edifice of culture is cracked and madly askew" (155). The dualist has to resort to the language of paradox in order to express both the reality of sin and the reality of grace as grace, which comes to us in the midst of sin. The dualist, says Niebuhr, does not meet God as a simple unity because God is revealed in nature as wrath, whereas God is revealed in Christ as mercy (158). The temptation is always to "separate the two principles; and to posit two gods, or a division in the Godhead," but the dualist resists the temptation and lives in the tension (159).

In the second section of this chapter, "The Dualistic Motif in Paul and Marcion," Niebuhr puts forward Paul as the biblical example and Marcion as the ancient example of this type. Here Niebuhr introduces the term *motif*, which he has not used up to this point but which he will favor for the rest of the book. A motif, he says, is somewhat more vague than a type in that one finds it hard to come up with clear-cut consistent examples of it: "In the case of dualism even more than in that of the previous answers to the Christ and culture question we ought to speak of a *motif* in Christian thinking rather than of a school of thought" (159, emphasis original). Niebuhr claims that the dualistic motif is more pronounced in Paul's thought than in the synthetic or radical ones. For Paul, Christ solves the problem of the contrast between the righteousness of God and the unrighteousness of humanity by means of his revelation, reconciliation, and inspiration (160). All cultural institutions and all human works were relativized for Paul by his encounter with God in Christ. They were all included under sin, and religion was not excepted. Yet all these cultural institutions—including religion—are redeemed by Christ in the sense that the believer lives in them with perfect freedom, no longer under their control (162). Then Niebuhr makes an astonishing statement: "It would be false to interpret all this in eschatological terms" (162). By this statement Niebuhr appears to mean that Paul's eschatology should be interpreted as a realized eschatology with no future component. But he does not even bother to argue for this controversial conclusion; he merely asserts it as if it were obvious to everyone. A page later we see why it is crucial for Niebuhr to insist on a realized eschatology: "With this understanding of the work of Christ and the works of man, Paul could not take the way of the radical Christian with his new Christian law by attempting to remove himself and other disciples out of the cultural world into an isolated community of the saved" (163). A realized eschatology is completely internal to the individual and thus cannot be expressed in community, and Niebuhr is concerned here to interpret Paul as a foe of the Christ against culture type. For Niebuhr's very Lutheran Paul, the Christian life is an inward experience. Insofar as Paul has a social ethic, it is basically negative: marriage prevents sexual promiscuity, the state prevents anarchy, and so on (165).

Niebuhr says that Marcion could be viewed as a radical because he founded a sect (167, 169), he but chooses to view him as a follower of Paul who takes Paul's ideas to an extreme (168). Marcion's dualism was much sharper: this world is evil and the Old Testament God is an inferior deity. Marcion tried to "draw Christians out of the physical as well as the cultural world as much as possible" (169). While a dualist lives in the tension, Marcion breaks the poles apart.

In the third section of this chapter, "Dualism in Luther and Modern Times," Niebuhr names Martin Luther as the foremost example of this type. Luther argued that there are two kingdoms—the kingdom of God and the kingdom of the world—and that only fanatics confuse the two (171). Although Luther rejected the synthesist approach, he firmly maintained the unity of Christ and culture (172). Luther accepted the absolute lordship of God but avoided the radical approach by understanding the gospel as focusing not on "the overt actions of man," but on "the springs of conduct" (173). Faith is a matter of trusting God, and this trust sets us free to serve God in the world as good citizens: "Christ deals with the fundamental problems of the moral life; he cleanses the springs of action. . . . But by the same token he does not directly govern the external actions or construct the immediate community in which man carries on his work" (174). For Luther, this means that Christians can simply follow the rules of culture as they find them, and thus he could affirm culture to a very great extent. To be a good Christian one merely has to be a good judge, farmer, soldier, mother, or whatsoever role one has been assigned. The Christian prince will not be any different from a non-Christian prince: "There is no way of deriving knowledge from the gospel about what to do as physician, builder, carpenter, or statesman" (176). Only a few vocations were ruled out by Luther; most were affirmed as they are (175).

In the fourth section of this chapter, Niebuhr discusses "The Virtues and Vices of Dualism." The strength of this type is that it mirrors the experience of Christians who live "between the times" (185). The two main criticisms of it are the charges of cultural conservatism and antinomianism (187). It can be seen as antinomian in that it relativizes all the laws of society, of reason, and of all other human works, which often leads Christians of this type to overstress (like Luther) the duty to be obedient to the powers that be as a way of warding off anarchy. The charge of cultural conservatism thus seems "to be directly connected with the dualist position" (188). The history of Lutheranism in Germany from the

Reformation to World War II illustrates the danger of a national church allying itself with a conservative state.

Christ Transforming Culture

In chapter 6 Niebuhr deals with the Christ transforming culture type. The first section deals with "theological convictions." Niebuhr says that the conversionist type is "most closely akin to dualism" (190), but the difference is that the conversionist motif is "more positive and hopeful" in its attitude to culture (191). This optimism, says Niebuhr, stems from three doctrinal convictions. First, the conversionist has a higher view of creation than the dualist and so emphasizes the incarnation of the Son in creation as part of the work of redemption (192). Second, the conversionist stresses the created goodness of humankind and sees the fall more as the perversion of the good than as identical with physical existence (193–94). Third, the conversionist views history as "the story of God's mighty deeds and of man's responses to them." So rather than living in expectation of a final ending of the world, the conversionist lives "in awareness of the power of the Lord to transform all things by lifting them up to himself" (195). In other words, there is great optimism that human culture can be transformed for the glory of God (196).

In the second section, "The Conversion Motif in the Fourth Gospel," Niebuhr attempts to root the Christ transforming culture type in John's Gospel, but he admits that although all the ideas of conversionism are found within it "the work itself is a partial demonstration of cultural conversion" (196). This would seem to be something of an understatement, given that an argument could be made that, of all the New Testament documents, this one most clearly leans in the direction of the Christ against culture type. Nevertheless, Niebuhr argues that the great note of incarnation struck at the beginning of the Fourth Gospel affirms the goodness of creation and corrects the Hellenistic notion that "the physical or material as such is subject to a special wrath of God" (197). Niebuhr recognizes that it is paradoxical that John uses the word *world* not only for the good created order, but also for "mankind in so far as it rejects Christ, lives in darkness, does evil works, is ignorant of the Father, rejoices over the death of the Son" (198). Niebuhr correctly notes that John is not referring to two different realms but to one, originally good but now fallen, world. For John "sin is the denial of the principle of life itself; it is the lie that cannot exist except on the basis of an accepted truth" (199). Niebuhr continues to read the New Testament in terms of a wholly realized eschatology and understands John's message as one of the eternal being applied to history: "John's interest is directed toward the spiritual transformation of man's life in the world" (204). Niebuhr notes the "particularist tendency" of John but simply falls back on his standard explanation that no exemplar of any type is totally consistent.

In the third section, "Augustine and the Conversion of Culture," Niebuhr focuses on Augustine as the great exemplar of the Christ transforming culture type. He interprets Augustine as "one of the leaders of that great historical moment whereby the society of the Roman empire is converted from a Caesar-centered community into medieval Christendom" (209). He is in himself an example of what conversion means: the Roman rhetorician becomes a Christian preacher, the Neoplatonist philosopher learns of the incarnation, and the Ciceronian moralist experiences grace (208).

For Augustine, the doctrine of creation means that nothing is fundamentally evil; all evil is the perversion of something fundamentally good (211). This idea is the basis of his optimism that the world can be regenerated by being reoriented to Jesus Christ (213). But even the great Augustine did not work out his own ideas in a fully consistent manner. His individualistic and futuristic eschatology is criticized by Niebuhr as a betrayal of the fundamental movement of his thought. Niebuhr's frustration is evident: "Why the theologian whose fundamental convictions laid the groundwork for a thoroughly conversionist view of humanity's nature and culture did not draw the consequences of these convictions is a difficult question" (216). Niebuhr chalks it up to Augustine's "defensiveness" and gently shakes his head. Calvin gets much briefer treatment (one page) than those who identify the Christ transforming culture position with Calvinism might imagine, and the pithy sentence "Calvin is very much like Augustine" sums up Niebuhr's evaluation of him (217).

The fourth section of this chapter is not, as in the previous chapters, a critique of the weaknesses of this type. Instead, it deals with the thought of English socialist F. D. Maurice, who is held up as the exemplar of the Christ transforming culture type. Maurice's brand of Christian socialism is viewed as a positive approach to the transformation of society, and the key issue is selfishness: "The conversion of mankind from self-centeredness to Christ-centeredness was for Maurice the universal and present divine possibility" (225). Salvation is understood in social terms by Maurice: "The full realization of the kingdom of Christ did not, then, mean the substitution of a new universal society for all the separate organizations of men, but rather the participation of all these in the one universal kingdom of which Christ is the head" (226). We are unsurprised to learn that Maurice had a realized eschatology: "With universality Maurice mated the idea of eschatological immediacy" (227). Niebuhr brings this chapter (and the original lectureship) to a close with a paragraph that begins with these words:

> In Maurice the conversionist idea is more clearly expressed than in any other modern Christian thinker and leader. His attitude toward culture is affirmative throughout, because he takes most seriously the conviction that nothing exists without the Word. It is thoroughly conversionist and never accommodating, because he is most sensitive to the perversion of human culture, as well in its religious as in its political and economic aspects. It is never dualistic; because he has cast off all ideas about the corruption of spirit through body, and about the separation of mankind into redeemed and condemned. (229)

Astonishingly, although Paul, John, Tertullian, Clement of Alexandria, Augustine, Thomas Aquinas, Luther, and Calvin have all come in for significant critique at Niebuhr's hands, Maurice appears to have gotten it pretty much right! That this type comes last and that Niebuhr surprisingly offers no criticisms of it whatsoever leads one to suspect strongly that this is the approach with which Niebuhr personally identifies.

Niebuhr's "Concluding Unscientific Postscript"

In the final chapter of his book, Niebuhr states: "Our examination of the typical answers Christians have given to their enduring problem is unconcluded and inconclusive" (230). He contends that theology cannot give us "*the* Christian answer" (232, emphasis original) and that each believer must make a decision in faith. The second section of this chapter, called "The Relativism of Faith," argues for viewing our decisions made in faith as being relative. We are dependent on partial, fragmentary knowledge; we have differing amounts of faith; we begin from a particular historical situation; and we are concerned with relative values (234). So we can become nihilists and skeptics, flee to authority, or accept our relativities with faith in the infinite absolute (238). Niebuhr obviously recommends the third of these three responses, and he argues in the third section of this chapter for a "social existentialism" in which the "responsible self" makes decisions in the context of its social context. Niebuhr takes pains to point out that, unlike Kierkegaardian existentialism, his social existentialism does not result in individualistic decisions made on the basis of what is "true for me" (245). Rather, they are made in the presence of Christ and a great cloud of witnesses. And so, "in our historical present we make our individual decisions with freedom and in faith; but we do not make them in independence and without reason" (249). The final section of this chapter deals with what "freedom in dependence" means. It means that we choose and reason in faith and that "faith exists only in a community of selves in the presence of a transcendent cause" (253). For Niebuhr, "without the historical incarnation of that faith in Jesus Christ, we should be lost in unfaithfulness" (255). Jesus is presented here as the exemplar of faith; we need faith like his (rather than faith in him).

Niebuhr's book thus ends with an unresolved tension between the final two chapters. In chapter 7 he says that there is no one Christian answer to the problem of Christ and culture, yet in chapter 6 he gave strong signals that he favored the Christ transforming culture position. Certainly most readers tend to view the transformationalist type as the most adequate. How do we reconcile this tension? There probably is no need to resolve it. Niebuhr appears to hold that, while the transformationalist approach is his preferred approach, he still is open to learning from the others.

3

A Critique
of Niebuhr's *Christ and Culture*

In the last chapter, we spent considerable time observing Niebuhr's argument in an attempt to understand his classic work. I have already begun to raise questions about the cogency of his arguments, however, and in this chapter I move directly to critique. First, I will consider the rhetorical power of this book and offer some comments on why it had such a wide influence. Then, I will offer a theological critique of the book and attempt to show why the theological assumptions behind it are seriously inadequate. Finally, I will ask if Niebuhr's analysis can be saved; that is, whether it would be beneficial to continue to use this typology in the future.

The fundamental problem behind the specific problems to which I will call attention in this chapter is that Christendom functions as the unarticulated presupposition of Niebuhr's work. The arguments of the book work rhetorically because (or to the extent that) the writer and reader share Christendom assumptions. The theological weaknesses are mostly related to the distorting effects on the gospel caused by the theory and practice of Christendom. The issue of whether Niebuhr's typology can be saved depends on whether it can be revised so as to become compelling in a post-Christendom context. As it stands, however, Niebuhr's typology belongs to the passé era of Christendom.

The Rhetorical Power of *Christ and Culture*

Why has *Christ and Culture* remained in print for half a century and been so widely influential? Part of the answer to that question has to do with the rhetorical power of Niebuhr's presentation. I speak of "rhetorical power" instead of "clarity of analysis" or "theological sophistication" or some other such phrase because I am convinced that part of the reason for the book's influence is that Niebuhr told a very good story. I am confident that Niebuhr himself, with his appreciation for the power of narrative, would not be offended by such a characterization of his work. Niebuhr was a "strong poet" who imposed his understanding of reality upon us by the compelling way in which he spun a narrative that made sense of our lives.[1] In order to understand why his story made sense to so many people in the post–World War II period of North American history, we need to recall something of what was going on in church and society at the time, what was going on in the theological situation at midcentury.

Historical Context

Modernity and Christendom were not dead, by any means, in 1950s North American Protestantism. Interesting developments were taking place in both the liberal (mainline) wing and conservative (fundamentalist) wing in the decade after World War II. On the one hand, liberal or mainline Protestantism was at the height of its power, having lost most of its radical social-gospel edge but not yet having entered into its period of steep decline, which began in the 1960s and has not yet been arrested. The optimistic, humanistic liberalism of the nineteenth century had been savaged by the tragic events of the first half of the twentieth century: two world wars, the Depression, the Holocaust, the development and use of the atomic bomb, racism, eugenics, increased barbarism in war, the rise of Communist totalitarianism in the Soviet Union. These horrific events had shaken the twin doctrines of the Enlightenment: the doctrine of progress through science, technology, education, and democracy and the doctrine of the perfectibility of humanity.

These chastening events were the background for the rise of neoorthodoxy in America, in which Niebuhr and his brother Reinhold were key players. At the time, it seemed to offer a genuine alternative to the discredited liberalism of the past. From a vantage point of a half a century down the road, however, it is now clear that it was really only the last gasp of Protestant liberalism. The genuinely postliberal Barthian revolution had not really come to America, and the neo-orthodoxy of the 1950s is better understood as neoliberalism.[2] In Europe, Barth

---

1. That is, he was able to tell such a compelling story that others felt unable to deny the reality it depicted.

2. For a good discussion, see Gary Dorrien, *The Making of American Liberal Theology: Idealism, Realism, and Modernity* (Louisville: Westminster/John Knox, 2003), chap. 7, especially pp. 465–69 and 477–83.

had launched a genuinely postliberal movement in theology, a christocentric trinitarianism that recovered premodern classical orthodoxy and brought it into conversation with modern and emerging postmodern thought. The result was a theology that is not simply premodern, definitely not modernist, and yet not postmodern in the commonly understood (though inadequate) sense of relativistic and nihilistic. Barth's theology could be described as a new way of doing theology in which the trinitarian theology of the ancient Greek fathers (especially the Cappadocians) and of the Reformers (especially Luther and Calvin) was brought into conversation with the modern situation dominated by liberal Protestantism and pre–Vatican II Roman Catholicism. Barth's determination to move decisively beyond culture-Protestantism cost him alliances and friendships with people like Bultmann, Tillich, and Brunner in the 1930s, but North American textbooks would tend to lump Barth with these figures throughout most of the twentieth century. It would not be until the last quarter of the twentieth century that the implications of his truly postliberal theology would begin to be grasped in North America. In fact, it is questionable if the full implications of Barth's theological moves are yet understood in much of North American Protestantism, although that is rapidly changing, thanks to the work of writers such as George Hunsinger, Bruce McCormack, John Webster, and others.

In the 1950s neoorthodoxy (sometimes confusingly called Barthianism) was not clearly differentiated from the neoliberalism of Reinhold Niebuhr and Paul Tillich. As a result, Barth's christocentric trinitarianism was rejected without being fully understood by many theologians, although it was understood by others and still rejected. Richard Niebuhr appears to fit into the latter category. While he seems to have understood Barth, he simply chose not to follow him at the key points of Christology and revelation. Although Richard tended to be somewhat more appreciative of Barth's position than did Reinhold or Tillich, conventional accounts of this period tend to lump them together as neoorthodox. Actually, the neoliberalism of Reinhold and Tillich was extremely different from Barth's orthodoxy, and the term *neoorthodox* is insufficiently nuanced to contain all their theologies. As Gary Dorrien shows, the label *neoorthodox* is nearly useless because it lumps together a group of theologians who were quite different from each other.[3] The only thing they had in common was that they did not want to be known as either fundamentalists or liberals in the tradition of Ritschl and Harnack. Reinhold, Tillich, and their followers and associates are better described as chastened liberals or revisionists. The term *revisionist* is often used to describe the descendents of liberals who have been chastened by the horrific events of the twentieth century and wish to carry on the liberal project of revising Christian faith so as to identify it with the highest and best in Western culture—only they

3. See ibid. These theologians include Barth, Bultmann, Tillich, Brunner, and the Niebuhr brothers. See also Hans W. Frei, *Types of Modern Theology* (New Haven: Yale University Press, 1992), in which he uses Bultmann, Tillich, and Barth to exemplify three of the five main types of contemporary theology. This is the opposite extreme of understanding them as three representatives of a single school.

wish to carry this project on in a more humble and subdued manner. Richard occupies a position somewhere between that of Barth and that of Reinhold and Tillich. What further confuses the interpretation of Richard's book is that he wrote it before the division between neoliberals (or revisionists) and Barthians appeared in North America.

Christ and Culture was written when liberal Protestantism dominated public life in North America. The effects of the secular ideology of liberal individualism that would later fragment liberal theology had not yet become dominant in North America. The social-oriented liberalism of the first half of the twentieth century was about to explode into what Lonnie Kliever aptly calls "the shattered spectrum":[4] that is, black theology, feminist theology, Latin American liberation theology, gay liberation theology, process theology, and so on. This would take place in the 1960s, but it had not yet happened in 1951. Also, other Christian perspectives were still not mounting a significant public challenge to neoliberal Protestant dominance. Fundamentalism had gone underground and could easily be ignored. The Roman Catholic Church was in a defensive, isolationist mode, with Vatican II still a decade away. The boomer generation was coming of age, the economy was growing, Protestant churches were full, and liberal Protestants had concluded that even though the kingdom of God had been delayed, the New Deal was not a bad substitute, all things considered. Mainline, neoliberal Protestantism thought of itself as mainstream Christianity. *Christ and Culture* clearly bears the marks of its origin in the mind of one of the leaders of mainline Protestantism and therefore of North American culture in general.

It is very important to understand this book as a product of, and apology for, Christendom. This is one of the advantages that half a century of historical perspective gives us as interpreters, especially since that half century has witnessed the unraveling of Christendom. By calling *Christ and Culture* a product of and apology for Christendom, I mean that it takes Christendom for granted as its starting point and assumes that Christendom is real, permanent, and on the whole a good thing. Although there is no state church in the United States, there is a strong sense of America being a Christian nation and of the church having a key role to play in maintaining public morality, inspiring patriotism in the citizenry, and giving religious legitimacy to the government. In many ways, the role of mainline Protestantism in the United States during the 1950s was that of a very active and very influential, though unofficial, state church. While the state churches of Europe were collapsing, American Christendom was in full flower; evangelicals and Roman Catholics basically were still regarded as sectarians; and the splintering of liberal theology and the decline of mainline denominations still lay in the future. Christendom was alive and well in the United States of the 1950s, and theologians like Niebuhr felt a responsibility to write and act in the

---

4. Lonnie D. Kliever, *The Shattered Spectrum: A Survey of Contemporary Theology* (Atlanta: John Knox, 1981).

public interest. That what was good for America might not be good for the church was unthinkable; the debate would be over whether it was good for America. The strong call to cultural responsibility and the transformationist or conversionist vision played well in this context. For example, Paul Ramsey describes the effect that *Christ and Culture* had after its publication in 1951:

> When Richard Niebuhr's book first appeared almost everyone in America rushed to locate himself among the "transformationalists": naturalists, process theologians, personalists, idealists, Lutherans and Anglicans who were sometimes Thomists, as well as those you would have expected. It was as if the "typology" or clustering of Christian approaches to man's work in culture and history had suddenly collapsed in 1951, so universal was the conviction that, of course, the Christian always joins in the transformation of the world whenever this is proposed.[5]

Liberal Protestantism, at the height of its cultural influence in North America, viewed *Christ and Culture* as a justification of its cultural leadership, as well as a call for it to continue.

Meanwhile, in the conservative branch of Protestantism, strange rumblings were being heard about the possibility of fundamentalists emerging from cultural isolation to challenge liberal Protestantism for cultural leadership. Leaders like Carl F. H. Henry, Harold Ockenga, Billy Graham, E. J. Carnell, and Harold Lindsell were in favor of fundamentalists ending their isolation and reengaging culture in hopes of overturning the liberal dominance of the public square. In his manifesto *The Uneasy Conscience of Modern Fundamentalism*, Carl F. H. Henry declares:

> Whereas in previous eras of Occidental history no spiritual force so challenged the human scene as did Christianity ... the challenge of modern Fundamentalism to the present world mind is almost nonexistent on the great social issues. Through the Christian centuries, assuredly, the evangelical challenge came always in a specifically redemptive framework. But in modern times the challenge is hardly felt at all. For Fundamentalism in the main fails to make relevant to the great moral problems in twentieth-century global living the implications of its redemptive message.[6]

Henry called fundamentalists to abandon their ghetto and have an impact on the mainstream of national life and the great moral issues of the day. At the time it seemed like an impossible dream, which just goes to show how bad most of us are at prophecy. The founding of the National Association of Evangelicals, *Christianity Today* magazine, and Fuller Seminary were key events in the coalescing of a new movement called neoevangelicalism (later shortened to evangelicalism). At first leaders of this movement were dismissed as "fundamentalists with PhDs,"

5. Paul Ramsey, *War and the Christian Conscience: How Shall Modern War Be Conducted Justly?* (Durham: Duke University Press, 1961), 112–13.

6. Carl F. H. Henry, *The Uneasy Conscience of Modern Fundamentalism* (Grand Rapids: Eerdmans, 1947), 37–38.

but their growth and success was phenomenal. The mostly Calvinist leadership of Baptists and Presbyterians showed real political talent in maintaining control of the movement, while managing to form alliances with Pentecostals, conservative Christian Reformed intellectuals, conservative Lutherans and Anglicans, and various representatives of the Wesleyan-Holiness tradition, as evangelicalism moved to challenge mainline Protestantism.

The year 1976 was declared by *Time* magazine to be the "Year of the Evangelical," and every president from Jimmy Carter to George W. Bush has claimed to be born again. Whether a non-born-again presidential candidate would now be electable is questionable. Whereas prior to 1950, fundamentalism distrusted higher education so much that they shunned seminaries and used Bible colleges to train their pastors, enrollment at evangelical seminaries has exploded in the United States. Galvanized by the legalization of abortion, evangelicals have moved into electoral politics with a passion. The rise of the religious right in politics has caused a fundamental realignment of politics in the United States, although the Democratic Party (with the notable exception of Bill Clinton) has been slow to adjust. Evangelicalism has arrived in a big way in America.

The situation is somewhat different in Canada. Evangelicalism in Canada is not tied as closely to conservative politics, and neoconservative policies have found little traction with the Canadian voters in a major way. Perhaps part of the explanation is that the percentage of the Canadian population professing to be evangelical is smaller than in the United States, as is the percentage of the population that attends church. But with regard to seminaries, the story is the same as the United States. The last third of the twentieth century witnessed an explosion of growth in evangelical seminaries across Canada. Evangelicalism in the United States has a major effect on Canadian evangelicalism, and most U.S. parachurch ministries have Canadian parallels. Canadian evangelicalism is more irenic than its U.S. counterpart but is becoming a larger percentage of Protestantism as liberal Protestantism continues to decline. It has even taken some important steps toward engaging the wider society through the Evangelical Fellowship of Canada, though this organization usually works on Christendom assumptions, insofar as that is possible in the extremely secular Canadian political context.

When Niebuhr's book appeared in the 1950s, its call for responsible involvement in society, combined with its sharp attack on the Christ against culture position, meant that its message was attractive, especially to younger evangelical leaders as they strove to overcome the separatism, isolation, and suspicion of political involvement inherent in their fundamentalist past. It could be argued that Roman Catholics went through a similar process as they entered the mainstream of political and cultural involvement in North America after Vatican II. They, too, often found the message of *Christ and Culture* compelling. What this meant was that hardly anybody was against the basic premise of the book. No wonder it has been in print for so long and has been assigned as required reading in so many college and seminary courses! Niebuhr's book appealed to a wide spectrum of Christians who either already were doing what the book advocated (mainline Protestants) or who wanted desperately to get into the game (evangelicals and Roman Catholics). It was truly a tract for the times.

The Story Niebuhr Told

Niebuhr did not simply write a sociological study of the various ways in which Christians, at various times and places, have sought to relate Christ and culture; he told a story that made sense as a connected narrative and in which many diverse readers could see themselves. The story began in the first century with a few small bands of zealous, deeply committed, but somewhat naïve believers huddled together in their little enclaves waiting for Jesus to return at any moment. Of course they did not try to transform culture; they could not conceive of such a thing. In their zeal for holiness, readiness for martyrdom, and heroic anticultural stance, we see sincerity, faithfulness, and a reduplication of Jesus's own lifestyle. But we do not see an adequate model for discipleship today. Our Lord did not return in the second or third century, and Christian history did not come to an end. Instead, a Roman emperor embraced the faith, and Christianity became the official religion of the most powerful empire on earth. As that empire crumbled over the next few centuries, the church inherited great civil and social responsibility for society in the face of potential chaos and violence. Did not Christians have a duty to their fellow human beings to step into the gap and even get their hands dirty stemming the tide of lawlessness and barbarism?

Niebuhr does not want to slam the fundamentalists, the monks, and the apolitical and uninvolved little bands of Christians today. They are sincere folk with a genuine commitment to Christ. Surely those who continue the socially responsible work of attempting to mitigate the worst of the violence and evil in the world by responsible involvement in governing society should not be denounced as compromising and worldly. Surely we can see that there is a perfectly reasonable division of labor between those who pray full-time for society and those who rule society, and each group benefits the other. Monasticism has functioned as a part of Christendom for fifteen hundred years, and pacifist sects, fundamentalist separatists, and pietistic holiness groups can be understood as Protestant equivalents.

Those who claim that all Christians should separate from social responsibility (the Christ against culture type) are as extreme as those who hold that Christianity and culture can meld into one entity. Since Jesus was so oblivious to culture and since culture includes all of human life as created by God, reasonable Christians with a genuine commitment to Christ and a strong social conscience must search for the right way to relate Christ and culture. But this task is so complex and so treacherous that those engaged in it can learn something even from the Christ against culture people and the Christ of culture people. It is always good to be reminded that the Christ of the New Testament will never fit completely into any human culture. And it is good to be reminded that the Christ of culture people are bearing witness to the truth that all culture does, in some mysterious way, belong to Christ and cannot be separated from his lordship. So all five types have validity and there is room for all Christians in Christendom—even monks, Mennonites, and dispensationalists—if only they will agree that those who labor in governing our culture also do the Lord's work.

This is a compelling and persuasive story. Notice how reasonable and nice it is. No one is demonized; no one is completely wrong. There is a place for many different kinds of social involvement and many different ways to relate Christ and culture. In his final chapter, Niebuhr argues that we cannot give "*the* Christian answer" in the sense of an answer for all Christians at all times and in all places. Yet, he admits, we must give some answer. Niebuhr recommends "social existentialism," which he contrasts to individualistic existentialism. In his social existentialism, the "responsible self," who is embedded in a particular Christian community at a particular time in a particular place, makes a decision drawing on its context for help. So the individual Christian, who finally is responsible for deciding, is also responsible for deciding within the context of the Christian story and the Christian community. This means that there are no absolute principles and no divine commands to limit our decisions. The history of the development of the church is the work of the Spirit and thus revelatory. Notice how the autonomous choices of Christians end up being elevated to the status of revelation of the Holy Spirit! This methodology for Christian social ethics cannot be described as anything but liberal.

Niebuhr's methodology is not all that different from the relativistic methodology of those leaders of culture-Protestantism who backed the war policy of the kaiser in 1914 and who filled the ranks of the German Christians in the 1930s, to the shock and dismay of people like Barth and Bonhoeffer. Of course, Niebuhr did not support German nationalism or militarism. That is not in question. But what is in question is whether his social existentialism provides the theological resources to say a firm no to such movements. Can we picture Niebuhr's social existentialism inspiring a Barmen Declaration? That requires more imagination than I can muster, and that is why, in the end, we must see *Christ and Culture* as a Christendom work, just as nineteenth-century culture-Protestantism was a Christendom project.

If nothing else, Niebuhr's stance of neutral objectivity gives the game away and makes it clear that this is a modernist book. The authors of *Missional Church* perceptively note: "It is usually only those who are squarely within the dominant culture who believe that there is some neutral place to stand outside all cultures."[7] Niebuhr's stance in this book is to hover above the fray, looking down on all the other actors, each of whom is revealed to have his or her own agenda. But Niebuhr's own agenda is unstated and officially neutral because it is rooted in his relativistic epistemology. In a postmodern world, we see clearly that nobody, including Niebuhr, comes from nowhere. Everyone has an agenda and everyone

---

7. Darrell L. Guder, ed., *Missional Church: A Vision for the Sending of the Church in North America* (Grand Rapids: Eerdmans, 1998), 113–14.

evaluates others in the light of his or her own presuppositions. To claim that one is neutral because one is relativistic just does not wash. No one really is neutral. Of course, that does not prove Niebuhr wrong about anything. But it does demonstrate that his stance in this book is consistent with a Christendom mentality in which liberal Protestantism is the unofficial state church of Western culture, which is the dominant culture of the modern world.

However, we saw in the previous chapter that the shape of the book clearly indicates that Niebuhr favors the Christ transforming culture type. Each of the types tends to incorporate compensations for the shortcomings of the previous ones, and the final type, unlike all the others, contains no section dealing with shortcomings and criticisms. So does this represent a contradiction in the book? No, not at all. Niebuhr is not claiming that his is the only correct view—he leaves his readers to draw that conclusion if they want to do so (and, of course, many do). In fact, many teachers of this book testify that most students read it and think that the Christ transforming culture type is the best.[8] But Niebuhr's own view is more modest. While he thinks his conversionist approach is best, he would not dream of saying that all other Christians necessarily should agree with him. He is allowed to have his favored view, as are all others, and together we will constitute a complete approach to the problem as the total Christian church. Ironically, Niebuhr's assumed stance of modesty only tends to make his favored view seem even more objectively superior than it would otherwise. Most readers think they have figured out that the transformationist view is best, even though, in reality, they have been led to this conclusion, gently yet firmly, by a master rhetorician.

Niebuhr's intention in this book, however, is not just to argue for the superiority of the transformationalist approach under the guise of a benign relativism. He also has an even more important agenda; namely, to argue against the first type, the Christ against culture position. In many ways, this is the main point of the book because only the radical type challenges the book's unstated Christendom presuppositions. John Howard Yoder points out that Niebuhr seems to want it both ways in that he wants his types to be understood as ideal constructs with a heuristic purpose, which means that we do not expect historical figures to conform exactly to the types and we do not blame them for not doing so. But, on the other hand, Niebuhr also wants to argue against the radical (or Christ against culture) position on the basis that the radicals are inconsistent in that they fail to consistently adhere to the Christ against culture type as defined by Niebuhr.[9] In fact, much of the rhetorical power of Niebuhr's book comes from

8. See the Ramsey quotation above. John Howard Yoder also makes the same point in "How H. Richard Niebuhr Reasoned: A Critique of *Christ and Culture*," in *Authentic Transformation: A New Vision of Christ and Culture*, by Glen H. Stassen, D. M. Yeager, and John Howard Yoder (Nashville: Abingdon, 1996), 41–43.

9. Ibid., 45. My critique of Niebuhr's book is highly influenced by Yoder's excellent critique. His work is an original, powerful, and comprehensive treatment of this problem, and in this chapter I can only hope to represent it faithfully and perhaps extend it a bit further in certain areas.

the radicals' failure to be consistent in adhering to the Christ against culture position. For example, after listing the many ways in which Tertullian rejected aspects of culture in the name of the lordship of Jesus Christ, Niebuhr concludes: "The great North African theologian seems, then, to present the epitome of the 'Christ-against-culture' position. Yet he sounds both more radical and more consistent than he really was. As we shall have occasion to note, he could not in fact emancipate himself and the church from reliance on and participation in culture, pagan though it was" (55).

For Niebuhr, it is a weakness and a sign of inconsistency that Tertullian could not extract himself completely from the world. But why does Niebuhr assume that acknowledging the lordship of Christ must mean extracting oneself from all "reliance on and participation in culture"? Does Tertullian interpret the lordship of Christ in that way? No. Niebuhr assumes this because he has already defined Christ as detached from culture and he has defined culture as everything that people do on earth. But what if Tertullian believed that the lordship of Christ requires us to reject only those aspects of culture that are evil, such as militarism, idolatry, brutality of gladiatorial games, and greed for money? What if Tertullian believed that there is nothing inconsistent with the lordship of Christ about being well educated, articulate, creative, industrious, and committed to public service? Niebuhr's categories simply have no room for someone with the views of the historical Tertullian. Niebuhr insists, on the basis of nothing more substantial than his own definitions of Christ and culture, that Tertullian could not reject killing in war and still embrace culture transformatively.

Both Niebuhr brothers made their own personal journeys away from liberal pacifism and toward a more realist stance during their professional lifetimes. They lived through a time when pacifism was a front-burner issue and war was a brutal reality. In this respect they were hardly unique. Mainline Protestantism as a whole tended strongly toward pacifism prior to World War I, then heeded Woodrow Wilson's call to join in a crusade, "the war to end all wars." They then turned back to pacifism in disillusionment after the horror and futility of that pointless disaster became clear. But then they had to confront the rise of Nazi evil in the 1930s and finally backed the U.S. decision to enter World War II in order to stop Hitler. This is not just an issue of Niebuhr's personal biography; it is the historical situation in which *Christ and Culture* was both written and read. Liberal Protestantism had tried to follow Jesus and be pacifist but found that it was, in the end, impossible for a state church (even an unofficial one) to be pacifist. The choice of the Niebuhr brothers and liberal Protestantism in general was to view following Jesus as impossible as long as one was committed to making Christendom work, and that was their commitment. And so, the story that Niebuhr told in his book was a Christendom story about how the radical following Jesus approach is inadequate.

Before concluding this section, there is one important methodological issue to address. James Gustafson, a pupil of Niebuhr, in his preface to the fiftieth anniversary edition of *Christ and Culture*, presents a rebuttal of the kind of critique I have mounted here and that has been made by several others and originally by Yoder.[10] Gustafson says that *Christ and Culture* is not a taxonomy of the writings of the authors used in the book and it is not a history of ethics. To read it in these ways is to misread Niebuhr's intentions, which were to employ the ideal-typical method of Troeltsch in the study of Christian ethics: "The typology is an ideal construct of ideas, not generalizations about literature. . . . Ideal types are ideal constructs of ideals along a clearly stated axis by which particular aspects of issues of literature are illumined. The purpose of taxonomy is to develop headings about generalizations from a variety of literature which shares similarities" (xxx). According to Gustafson, what this means is that the

> interpretive, illuminating power of the fivefold typology and of each type is the principal criterion by which to evaluate the expositions and analyses in each of the chapters and in the book as a whole. As Max Weber explained, typologies are heuristic devices; they should help the reader to understand the particular texts, events, or social structures on which they are brought to bear. (xxxi)

Gustafson apparently thinks that Marsden, Yoder, and company are unfair to Niebuhr because they see discrepancies between the historical Tertullian (and other figures in the book) and the ideal type constructed by Niebuhr. Of course no single figure fits the type perfectly, but does the type help to illumine the choices they and we face in Christian ethics? That is the question Gustafson wants us to use in judging the adequacy of Niebuhr's book. It seems clear to me that that is precisely the question Yoder asks. The problem is not that Yoder fails to ask the question Gustafson wants asked; the problem is that Yoder (and those who follow him on this point) does not give the answer Gustafson wants him to give to that question. The disagreement is over the heuristic value of Niebuhr's typology. More is obscured than is illuminated, particularly by the Christ against culture type.

As a liberal Protestant, Gustafson is heavily invested in the Christendom project. He therefore believes that Niebuhr's typology is characterized by objectivity and trains students how to think and not what to think (xxxii). Only someone who stands within the dominant culture can see things this way. Gustafson is a perfect example, therefore, of the kind of reader who is convinced by Niebuhr's typology. He rejects the Christ against culture position, embraces the amorphous Christ transforming culture position, and thereby justifies the Christendom project of

---

10. Gustafson mentions the work of Stanley Hauerwas and William Willimon in *Resident Aliens* (Nashville: Abingdon, 1989) and that of George Marsden (in a lecture attended by Gustafson). For a Lutheran perspective on Niebuhr, see Angus Menuge, "Niebuhr's *Christ and Culture* Reexamined," in *Christ and Culture in Dialogue* (ed. Angus J. L. Menuge; Saint Louis: Concordia, 1999), 31–55. All of these scholars follow (to Gustafson's chagrin) in the wake created by Yoder's powerful critique of Niebuhr's classic.

Christians compromising the teachings of Jesus Christ in an effort to be realistic and responsible by managing society and making it a bit less violent and cruel than it otherwise might be. Niebuhr's book resonates greatly with those who share this set of priorities.

Theological Weaknesses in *Christ and Culture*

The unwary reader who encounters Niebuhr's book can be led into accepting some very bad theology without noticing what is going on. This is partly because of the impression cultivated by Niebuhr that he is speaking for mainstream Christianity. Those who read the book from within liberal Protestantism have no problem with Niebuhr's liberal theology, but even those who read it from the evangelical and Roman Catholic perspectives tend not to notice the theological problems because of the way Niebuhr appeals to the doctrine of the Trinity and appears to speak out of the great tradition. There are many theological problems in this book, but his definitions of Christ and church are basic to the others.

Christology

Does Niebuhr really believe in the historic doctrine of the incarnation? Does he really believe that, in Jesus of Nazareth, God appeared on earth in flesh and blood? The Jesus of *Christ and Culture* is very different from the very human, flesh-and-blood prophet of the Synoptic Gospels. Yoder notes: "He has excised from his picture of Jesus precisely those dimensions, clearly present in the biblical witness and in classical theology, which would make impossible the interpretation of Jesus as 'pointing away' from the realm of culture."[11] Niebuhr's Jesus is an otherworldly, almost mystical figure who preached an uncompromising message of the sovereignty of God the Father and who had no interest in the mundane things of human life such as politics, family, and social structure. One could say that the feet of Niebuhr's Jesus barely touch the earth. That Jesus is a man who lives in perfect communion with the Father in this world of sin is not that important; his message of radical monotheism is everything. But orthodox Christology views Jesus's divinity as being united with his humanity in such a way that Jesus becomes the perfect human—the Second Adam—who fulfills in his life the intention God had for humanity when God created the human race. Just because he is God, he is the perfect human. And that Jesus could live in the world and obey the Father's will perfectly means that it is possible to follow him in the way of discipleship in such a way as to please God.

Niebuhr sets up a dualism between Jesus and the created order. Of course, not all dualisms are bad. There is an ethical dualism between Jesus and the world, which

11. Yoder, "How H. Richard Niebuhr Reasoned," 60.

in the New Testament means the fallen created order organized in its rebellion against the creator. Jesus and the community he calls out from the world are in conflict with the world over the issue of ultimate allegiance. Jesus and the church live in the kingdom of God because they acknowledge the lordship of God, while Satan and the world oppose this kingdom because they refuse to acknowledge the lordship of God. When Christians bow to the lordship of Jesus Christ, they acknowledge the dividedness of creation, the brokenness of a world created to glorify God, but that is made up of some who bow the knee to Jesus Christ and some who do not. There is thus what we might call an ethical dualism in creation—a religious divide along the fault line of recognition or rejection of the lordship of Jesus Christ. It is temporary and does not arise out of creation, but out of the fall. One day it will be eliminated by the redemption of all creation.

Niebuhr's dualism, however, seems to be more ontological than ethical (though he is inconsistent on this issue). It is not just that Jesus's so-called strenuous commands in the Sermon on the Mount and the rest of this teaching are hard to obey because of the prevalence of sin in the world; Niebuhr seems to believe that these commands are unrealistic given the *reality* of the world. Yet, Jesus's ministry is all about redefining what is real. The idea that the Sermon on the Mount could be lived on this earth by a segment of fallen humanity is rejected as impossible by Niebuhr. He argues that when radical Christians separate from non-Christian culture, they inevitably set up a miniversion of the outside world in the government of the separated community (71). Up to a point this is true, but pushed too far it becomes absurd. For example, if Niebuhr's insight is taken to mean that the leadership structure of a Mennonite church or the government of a Benedictine monastery is essentially no different from the Roman Empire or the elite of the Communist Party of the Soviet Union under Stalin, then we must wonder if the insight has not exceeded the limits of its usefulness. Of course, in a limited sense his point is well taken. Any Christian community is made up of forgiven sinners, not perfected saints. So there will be sin in the church too.[12] We ought not to look for perfection or utopia in separated Christian communities. But in another sense, his argument goes too far in that it erases the great ethical gulf that stands between small, peaceable, minority Christian communities, on the one hand, and nation-states and empires, on the other. It seems to go so far as to assume that the rule of God upon this earth is utterly impossible. Yet Jesus came preaching the kingdom of God (Mark 1:15), and the community he founded is made up precisely of those who acknowledge him as Lord and enter this kingdom.

The liberal Protestantism of the late nineteenth and early twentieth centuries assumed that America could be brought into the kingdom, but the horrific events

---

12. A keen sense of the human capacity for selfishness, self-deception, and rationalization is one of the strongest arguments for the wisdom of an absolute rule against killing. This is precisely why it is disconcerting to see the rule against euthanasia relaxed, even in extreme cases. The radical Christian absolute prohibition of all killing can be regarded as a rule borne out of deep insight into fallen human nature, rather than as an idealization of it.

of World Wars I and II made it clear that their liberal humanistic optimism was naïve. In reaction against this error, Niebuhr lost hope of the kingdom coming on earth, and much of the passion he spent on refuting the Christ against culture position appears to have arisen from his arguing against a position he had formerly held and to which many of his fellow liberal Protestants were still attracted. In fact, in 1935 Niebuhr and two friends had written a book with the title *The Church Against the World*. In the introduction, Niebuhr wrote:

> In the faith of the church, the problem is not one of adjustment to the changing, relative and temporal elements but rather one of constant adjustment, amid these changing things, to the eternal. The crisis of the church from this point of view is not the crisis of the church in the world but of the world in the church. . . . The church has adjusted itself too much rather than too little to the world in which it lies. It has identified itself too intimately with capitalism, with the philosophy of individualism and with the imperialism of the West.[13]

These are good sentiments, but not ones that can be found anywhere in *Christ and Culture*. Between 1935 and 1951 a lot of water flowed under the bridge for Niebuhr. By 1951 he was far less alienated from Western culture and felt much less need to be critical of it or to distance himself from it.

Church

The problem with liberal Protestantism was not that it took seriously the call of Jesus to enter the kingdom of God; the problem was that it thought that entering the kingdom could be detached from personally acknowledging the lordship of Jesus Christ. A nation containing more non-Christians than Christians cannot be brought into the kingdom en masse. That is a typical Christendom error. But instead of recovering a doctrine of the church as the community that acknowledges the lordship of Jesus Christ and thus lives in the kingdom, Niebuhr gave up on the establishing of the kingdom on earth altogether. Thus, his Jesus had to be otherworldly and detached from culture.

Niebuhr still upheld the sovereignty of God and portrayed Jesus as a prophet calling us to acknowledge the lordship of the Father. But Niebuhr criticized the radicals for believing that communities of disciples could acknowledge God's lordship and live under it here on earth. Niebuhr could not acknowledge a link between the incarnation of our Lord and the historical reality of the church as witness to the kingdom. One does not need to go so far as to view the church as an extension of the incarnation in order to affirm the possibility of the life of discipleship. One error is to deify the church, and the opposite error is to deny the reality of the incarnation. Jesus lived a life of total obedience to the Father, and we often think of this in pietistic and moral terms (he never swore, got drunk, etc.). But we need

13. H. Richard Niebuhr, Wilhelm Pauck, and Francis P. Miller, *The Church Against the World* (Chicago: Willett, Clark, 1935).

to think of it in terms of acknowledging the lordship of the Father in all things, not just personal moral issues. Jesus was the incarnation of the kingdom in that he embodied obedience and submission to the Father's will. The question is this: Can the Christian community follow Jesus in submitting to the Father's will and acknowledging the Father's lordship? The answer to this question is complex.

Of course, we cannot be morally perfect. This is how we differ from Jesus. God knows that we are fallen and weak. That is why the Old Testament sacrificial system was given to his people—to allow them a means by which they could confess their sins and be forgiven and restored to fellowship and service. And the church rightly follows the writer of the Epistle to the Hebrews in understanding the death of Jesus as the ultimate fulfillment of the sacrificial system. God knows that we will fail morally, and he has made provision for confession, forgiveness, and restoration to fellowship and service (1 John 1:9). Still, the point is that the Christian community can confess the lordship of Jesus Christ and thus live in the kingdom of God and bear witness to the lordship of God *without being morally perfect*. In fact, it is precisely in the act of confessing our sins and being forgiven both by God and by one another that we most powerfully bear witness to the gospel. We can confess the lordship of Christ in this world as a community of forgiven sinners. Confession, forgiveness, and reconciliation are historical acts that take place here in this world, for Christians are to confess to each other, forgive each other, and be reconciled to each other just as they confess to God, are forgiven by God, and are reconciled to God. The visibility of the community of discipleship consists not in moral perfection, but in its sin and in its confession, forgiveness, and reconciliation.

If God cannot and does not make us into this kind of community, then the reality of the incarnation is in question. The human life lived by Jesus is proof that human life in this world can be lived to the glory of God in the acts of confession, forgiveness, and reconciliation. Of course, it does not demonstrate that that this kind of life can be lived by those who do not confess Jesus as Lord and are not filled with the Holy Spirit. And it does not demonstrate that the life of true discipleship can be lived without the disciple coming into conflict with the world. We can, as a Christian community, follow Jesus in the way of discipleship, but only if we are prepared to meet the same fate he met at the hands of the powers that be. This means that Christian discipleship is hard. But to say it is hard is not to say that it is impossible. To say it is hard is to acknowledge the reality and power of sin. To say it is impossible is to exalt sin to the status of a metaphysical reality that is stronger than the Holy Spirit. To say that Christian discipleship makes sense only in the light of faith in the resurrection of Jesus is to be realistic. What is realistic must be redefined in the light of the resurrection.

Niebuhr's doctrine of the church is weak in that he does not view the church as being able to bear a collective witness to the lordship of Jesus Christ. So he has very little confidence that the church can be a contrast community to the world. That is behind much of his criticism of the Christ against culture position. The authors of *Missional Church* put it this way: "Niebuhr ignores the possibility that the most transforming activity of the church in relationship to the culture might not be to try to wield power in the dominant culture, but instead to demonstrate by the church's own life together the renewing and healing power of God's new community."[14] The church is called to be "a holy nation among the nations," not a vendor of religious goods and services or the religious chaplaincy to secular society. The church is an alternative society to the world. Unfortunately, at the time he wrote *Christ and Culture*, Niebuhr did not have a vision of this kind of church.

Creation

Another major theological difficulty in *Christ and Culture* is the meaning of culture and its relation to creation. When Niebuhr speaks of culture, he is speaking primarily of what humans create. But we must bear in mind that culture in this sense is still a part of creation, for humans themselves are part of the created order. When the New Testament speaks of the world, what is usually in view is not the unfallen creation as it existed before the fall, but rather the presently fallen and rebellious network of human and demonic powers that rule the earth. Niebuhr does not clearly enough differentiate between fallen creation and culture.[15] This leads him to some loose argumentation. For example, in chapter 1 Niebuhr says that in defining the values of culture "man begins with himself as the chief value and the source of all other values" (35). Culture here is defined in a humanistic way so that the dualism between Christ and culture can be highlighted: Christ must point away from culture defined this way. But in chapter 6 Niebuhr argues that culture can be transformed. What does the word *transformed* mean in this context? We are given no specifics. But we must wonder how something that is *by definition* human centered can be transformed by Christ without becoming something else in the process.

The problem is that Niebuhr cannot really conceive of culture as redeemed because he cannot conceive of it as unfallen, and this is why things get so vague when he talks about Christ transforming culture. Would not Christ transforming culture mean the people in the culture bowing to the lordship of Christ? Would that not be exactly what Niebuhr assumed at the beginning of the book to be impossible by definition? If we take Niebuhr seriously in chapter 6, do we not have to go back to chapter 1 and change the definition of culture found there? Would there not be room, then, within the definition of culture to distinguish between the organized opposition to God that presumes to claim sovereignty over this world, on the one hand, and the community of those who acknowledge the lordship of Christ, on the other? Niebuhr uses the definition given in chapter 1 to criticize the Christ against culture position in chapter 2. The radicals are called naïve because they imagine that they can escape the sin that engulfs all forms of

14. Guder, *Missional Church*, 116.

15. Menuge, "Niebuhr's *Christ and Culture* Reexamined," 45, criticizes Niebuhr's lack of consistency on this point. He also endorses the main outlines of Yoder's critique.

human community. But if culture can be transformed by Christ, why should it be impossible for that transformation to begin in the church?

This is the puzzling thing about the whole liberal Protestant tradition from the nineteenth century to the present: its apparent willingness to believe that human society as a whole can be transformed by Christ in ways that the visible community of Christians cannot. In chapter 6 Niebuhr presents as his uncriticized exemplar of transformation Christian socialist F. D. Maurice. Having chided the radicals for naïve optimism and a low view of sin because they attempt to create a counterculture that witnesses to the lordship of Christ, he then turns around and recommends socialism as the meaning of Christ transforming culture! Socialist institutions are supposed to be capable of avoiding sin, even though churches are not! How can such a high view of socialism coexist with such a low view of the church? The point is not that socialism is evil. Even if one votes socialist (as the best choice currently available), one does not necessarily have to elevate socialism to the status of the kingdom of God. As skeptical as he is about the conversion of individuals and the possibility of authentic Christian community, Niebuhr still believes in the conversion of the economic systems of nation-states.

Trinity and Revelation

In criticizing the radical Christ against culture position, Niebuhr brings out the heavy artillery of the orthodox doctrine of the Trinity. But his interpretation of this doctrine is contrary to the meaning that it has had in the great tradition of the church. His doctrine of the Trinity is a liberal, pluralistic, and relativistic doctrine that functions in his theology in the precise opposite way that it functions for the church fathers and the Eastern Orthodox, Roman Catholic, and Reformation traditions. His deployment of this doctrine displays strong overtones of "creeping Unitarianism," which later writings such as *The Responsible Self* and *Racial Monotheism and Western Culture* do little to dispel.[16]

In *Christ and Culture* Niebuhr claims that the problem with the radicals is that they "regard the doctrine of the Trinity as having no ethical meaning" because they concentrate so much on the lordship of Christ that they neglect "nature and nature's God" and the "Spirit immanent in him [Christ] and the believer" (81). This argument is stated in greater detail in Niebuhr's 1946 article "The Doctrine of the Trinity and the Unity of the Church," in which he claims that everyone in the history of the church is a Unitarian of one sort or another.[17] There are Unitarians of the Son, Unitarians of the Father, and Unitarians of the Spirit: "Christianity as a whole is more likely to be an association, loosely held together, of three Unitarian

16. H. Richard Niebuhr, *The Responsible Self: An Essay in Christian Moral Philosophy* (New York: Harper & Row, 1963); idem, *Radical Monotheism and Western Culture* (New York: Harper, 1960).

17. H. Richard Niebuhr, "The Doctrine of the Trinity and the Unity of the Church," *Theology Today* 3 (1946): 371–84.

religions."[18] Unitarians of the Son can be either ethical or mystical in their focus, and they include Marcion, pietists, mystics, and Ritschlians. Unitarians of the creator are interested in natural theology and include Arianism and Monarchianism in the early church and Socinianism, Deism, and Unitarianism in modern times. Unitarians of the Spirit include all Christian spiritualism and are exemplified by mysticism, Spiritual Franciscans, and Society of Friends. Although all these unitarianisms are inadequate, we are not to worry because the mysterious mathematics of the doctrine of the Trinity mean that three heresies add up to orthodoxy![19] In other words, Niebuhr defines the doctrine of the Trinity as the union within one church of three different families of belief, each of which is heretical by itself.

The upshot is that the more radical ethics of Jesus have to be balanced by the more conservative ethics of the Father and the ongoing revelation found in the Spirit immanent in history and tradition. Niebuhr thus attempts to locate his reluctance to make the lordship of the biblical Jesus decisive for Christian ethics in a doctrine of the Trinity that posits multiple ways to divine truth. These ways to divine truth do not simply reinforce one another; they are different and even correct one another. For example: "The Unitarianism of the Creator is always a protest against exclusive reliance on Scriptures for knowledge of God and against exclusive worship of the Christ of Scriptures as the object of trust and the bringer of salvation."[20] Yoder correctly discerns that Niebuhr's doctrine of the Trinity is a way of justifying ethical thought that does not spring from Christ by presenting the authority of God the Father as the basis for natural theology.[21]

This understanding of the Father, Son, and Holy Spirit is incompatible with the New Testament portrayal of their interrelationships. In the New Testament the Son is viewed as the agent of creation (Colossians 1:16; Hebrews 1:10; John 1:3), and he is also identified as the Lord of history (1 Corinthians 15:24).[22] The whole point of the Gospel of John's portrayal of the relationship between Jesus and the Father is that "anyone who has seen me has seen the Father" (John 14:9) and "I and the Father are one" (10:30). The New Testament offers no support for the idea that we might need different revelation, deriving from the Father but discoverable by human reason, to supplement and complement the revelation of God in Jesus Christ. In fact, the whole point seems to be exactly the opposite.

Niebuhr's understanding of the Father, Son, and Holy Spirit is also incompatible with the classical orthodoxy of the Nicene Creed. Thomas F. Torrance, one of the greatest patristic scholars and theologians of the twentieth century, expounds the

18. Ibid., 372.

19. One can only wonder what sort of Unitarians Athanasius and the Cappadocians were. What about Augustine? How about Calvin? This seems to be a rather wildly overstated claim that cannot be taken seriously.

20. Ibid., 379.

21. John Howard Yoder, *The Politics of Jesus: Vicit Agnus Noster* (2nd ed.; Grand Rapids: Eerdmans, 1994), 144.

22. See Yoder, "How H. Richard Niebuhr Reasoned," 62.

faith expressed in the Nicene Creed in his masterful book *The Trinitarian Faith*. On the knowledge of God he says: "Knowledge of the Father, knowledge of the Son and knowledge of the Holy Spirit cannot be separated from one another for God is known only through the one movement of self-revelation of the Father, through the Son and in the Holy Spirit."[23] Torrance reiterates the point first made by Irenaeus that "strictly speaking . . . only God can know himself so that it is that only through God that God can be known."[24] The implication of this is that natural theology is impossible and that the incarnation is the sole source of our knowledge of God:

> It is only in and through the Son, the one and only Son, that the *eidos* of the Godhead is made known, for it is specifically in Jesus Christ the incarnate Son that God has communicated himself to us creaturely human beings within the conditions and structures of our earthly existence and knowledge. Thus it is only in him who is *homoousios* with the Father and *homoousios* with us, that we may really know God as he is in himself and in accordance with his own nature.[25]

Niebuhr's doctrine of the Trinity is not the Nicene doctrine, and his intention of balancing the ethics of Jesus with the ethics of the Father is not the Nicene intention.

On the surface, what we are faced with in *Christ and Culture* is an attempt to refute the Christ against culture position by utilizing the orthodox doctrine of the Trinity. But what we actually have is clear evidence that the doctrine of the Trinity is on the side of those radicals who seek to live out the implications of Jesus's authoritative humanity, which has been affirmed by its union with deity. To be Nicene is to believe in the reality of the incarnation; that is, to believe that God actually walked this earth and called us to follow him. Only a faith that accepts the reality of the incarnation has the theological resources to risk radical discipleship. People do not allow themselves to be thrown to the lions or burned at the stake for the sake of natural theology or philosophical arguments. Only a faith in the living Lord Jesus Christ, confessed to be the messiah of Israel and the Son of God, is sufficient for radical Christian discipleship. And only a truly trinitarian and Nicene faith is adequate to assure us that following Jesus in this world actually is possible.

Can These Typological Bones Live?

So far in this chapter, we have noted both the rhetorical strategies employed by Niebuhr to argue his case and the theological weaknesses found in the book. We have seen that Christendom is the unspoken assumption behind Niebuhr's typology

---

23. Thomas F. Torrance, *The Trinitarian Faith: The Evangelical Theology of the Ancient Catholic Church* (Edinburgh: T & T Clark, 1995), 204.

24. Ibid., 54.

25. Ibid., 203.

and that without this assumption the typology is not compelling. It has also become painfully apparent that, since Niebuhr's commitment to Christendom led him to water down orthodox Christian doctrine at many points, those who follow his lead will find it impossible to witness clearly to Jesus Christ in the postmodern world. So it might appear that it is now time to abandon this typology altogether.

But if we reject Niebuhr's typology as inadequate for a post-Christendom situation, does that mean we should stop thinking about the relationship of Christ and culture? Or should we embark on the constructive task of developing an entirely new typology, which beginning from the assumption that Christendom is over will base its evaluation of culture on orthodox, biblical Christology? If such a new typology is to be developed, should it start from scratch, or can some of Niebuhr's framework be salvaged? Since a great deal of confusion is caused by the mixture of taxonomy and typology in Niebuhr's method, should we move away from the ideal-type method to the method of taxonomy and try to classify all the major Christian responses to the problem over the centuries? Our choices narrow down to three at this point.

The first approach would be to abandon typology and move to taxonomy. This would mean doing historical theology in an attempt to classify all the possible approaches to the problem of Christ and culture advocated so far in the history of the church. Two things would be critical here: first, groups and individuals would need to be able to recognize themselves in the description of them given in the taxonomy; and, second, the taxonomy would need to be complete in that *all* the possible answers would be included. If these two conditions were met, then it would be possible to do what Niebuhr does in *Christ and Culture* and criticize individuals and movements for failing to conform to their types, and it might be possible to come to conclusions about the relative adequacy of the major types. This might open the way to genuine progress in understanding the proper relationship between Christ and culture.

However, this approach would be so complex that it might well be impossible for one scholar to synthesize all the information necessary to do it well. To the extent that a simplified range of types or families of types was created, which could be compared and contrasted, there would undoubtedly be accusations of oversimplification from groups whose positions were lumped with others or insufficiently analyzed. Yoder's taxonomy of varieties of religious pacifism delineates seventeen distinct types of pacifism plus twelve subtypes, and thus would come under just one of Niebuhr's original five types![26] Perhaps someone will attempt this daunting task in the future, but I do not think I could accomplish it.

The second approach would be to abandon both typology and taxonomy and give up on the idea of trying to classify answers to the question of how Christ

26. John Howard Yoder, *Nevertheless: The Varieties and Shortcomings of Religious Pacifism* (3rd ed.; Scottdale, PA: Herald, 1992).

should relate to culture. This would mean taking a case-by-case approach to practical problems as they arise in missiology, social ethics, church history, and theological method instead of attempting to think about the problem abstractly and globally. While this approach acknowledges the undoubted complexity of the problem and has the virtue of ensuring that theological discussion remains practical in focus, it seems to be a counsel of despair. The popularity of Niebuhr's book shows that tens of thousands of readers have found it helpful to think about the problem of Christ and culture, not only from a practical perspective while dealing with a particular problem, but also more generally. I can testify to being one of those who found the questions raised by Niebuhr to be interesting precisely after having myself come to apparently contradictory positions on different particular issues. I found it helpful to do both: think about specific issues *and* test my specific conclusions by applying them more generally at the same time.

In doing this type of analysis, one is engaging in the same kind of exercise as one engages in when doing systematic or dogmatic theology. Niebuhr's book is useful for the same reason as books of systematic theology are useful: not as a replacement for exegetical and historical theology, but as a second perspective on the same problems, one that considers various problems simultaneously so as to work out a consistent approach, which itself then needs to be applied to further problems and perhaps refined and altered and so on. We should be wary of replacing the task of grappling with particular problems simply by applying a general systematic approach to each situation, but we also should be aware of the dangers of not thinking our specific positions through systematically.

The third approach would be to stick with the typological approach and to revise Niebuhr's typology in a manner appropriate for a post-Christendom situation. This would involve creating new definitions for the terms *Christ* and *culture*, based on more biblical and orthodox doctrinal assumptions. It would also involve using the new typology in a purely heuristic manner and not confusing it with a taxonomy. This would mean not criticizing people for not conforming perfectly to an ideal type. The advantage of this approach would be to conserve (and improve) the heuristic value of Niebuhr's approach in a new cultural setting. Yoder writes that he had once set out to revise Niebuhr's typology but came to the conclusion that if one keeps asking the wrong question there is no hope of getting the correct answer.[27] But one would not necessarily still be asking the wrong question if one could redefine the key terms (Christ and culture) of the problem in a theologically adequate way.

In my view, it is not adequate simply to reject the whole enterprise of typology altogether. Nor is it feasible (though it perhaps would be ideal) to attempt a taxonomy of all the possible and historical answers to the problem. We need to face the fact that, inadequate as it is, Niebuhr's typology does address a real problem and that people are helped by engaging in the process of thinking that problem

27. Yoder, "How H. Richard Niebuhr Reasoned," 82–83.

through. Followers of Jesus really do have to struggle with the practical, everyday issues of how to relate to culture. On the one hand, we believe in Jesus Christ as the messiah of Israel and the Son of God, and we confess him as Lord of the cosmos. We want to be loyal disciples of the Lord Jesus Christ and bear a faithful witness to his lordship in this world. In my view, this is our main purpose in this life. However, we are born into a culture made up of a majority of people who do not share our faith. Along with other Christians we make up a countercultural minority within this larger culture, and we are faced with the dilemma of how to be "in the world" but not "of the world." Niebuhr's typology is not perfect—far from it. But it does wrestle with a real problem, and so the answer is not to give up on it, but rather to reformulate it.

In chapter 6 I will set out some of the difficulties any new typology will face and some of the conditions that must be met in order for it to overcome these difficulties. I will consider the terms of the problem, and I will propose new definitions of *Christ* and *culture*. I will also narrow the focus of the problem to reflect the real issues at stake in Niebuhr's book. I will argue that what really is at stake in Niebuhr's refutation of the radical position and endorsement of the conversionist approach is not culture in general, but specifically the controversial issue of how Christians should relate to the powers; that is, to the state and other power structures in society that rely on violence to maintain their position. Key to this whole discussion is the issue of the place of violence in Christian discipleship. I will propose a new typology, which addresses the issue of violence more directly than did Niebuhr's. This new typology will be appropriate for a post-Christendom situation because it will take exactly the opposite stance that Niebuhr took: whereas he took Christendom for granted, I will take as my starting point what Yoder calls "the disavowal of Constantine,"[28] the rejection of the whole Christendom project.

I mentioned in chapter 2 that the definition of terms is crucial in this whole discussion of Christ and culture. I also stressed that Niebuhr's definitions presupposed and functioned within the context of an assumption that Christendom both exists and ought to exist; that is, that Christendom cannot be challenged from a Christian point of view. In order for us to create a typology that is truly post-Christendom—that is, one that actually escapes the clutches of Christendom thinking—it is crucial that we understand what Christendom is and why Christendom thinking so radically deforms the gospel. This is not an easy task.

For one thing, we have to learn how to distinguish Christendom from the history of the church as a whole. Not everything in the last two millennia has been evil. Faithful witness has been rendered through proclamation of the gospel, healing of the sick, caring for the poor, and visiting prisoners. The church has often looked after widows and orphans in distress and kept itself from being

---

28. John Howard Yoder, *Royal Priesthood: Essays Ecclesiological and Ecumenical* (ed. Michael G. Cartwright; Grand Rapids: Eerdmans, 1994), 242–61.

polluted by the world. But these good things have been done in the context of Christendom, at least so far as European culture from the fourth to the twentieth centuries is concerned. I want to argue that a faithful witness has often been rendered in spite of and against Christendom, not because of it and through it. But this argument needs to be made.

In the next two chapters, we will prepare for the task of developing a post-Christendom typology by examining Christendom from a theological perspective. The goal is to determine how to identify and isolate that which corrupts, obscures, and contradicts the witness of the church to Jesus Christ and to distinguish it from the legitimate mission of the church as given to the church by its Lord. Only then can we hope to devise a new typology of Christ and culture that allows the church to imagine how to interact with culture in ways that avoid compromising our witness to the gospel.

In chapter 4 I will attempt to explain how and why Christendom arose in the first place, denying that it was either historically necessary or inevitable. I then will discuss what I call "the bitter fruits of Christendom." Here the intention is not to deny that many sincere Christians were doing many commendable things during the long centuries of Christendom, but rather to draw attention to the demonic features of a cultural system that denies the witness of those faithful servants of God. I conclude this chapter by considering possible responses to Christendom and by concluding that the only legitimate response is one of repentance for, and repudiation of, Christendom.

In chapter 5 I then move to a consideration of what the alternative would be to Christendom. If the church made a big mistake in the fourth century by joining in the Constantinian project of helping to govern the empire, what would have been the alternative? I argue that the church compromised its one, holy, catholic, and apostolic identity by aligning itself too closely with the political powers that be, and I imagine what it would have meant then (and now) to be truly one, holy, catholic, and apostolic church. I argue that a better reading of Scripture would have allowed the leaders of the church to avoid being coopted by the state. I then try to specify what the church that renounces Christendom would be like.

Only as we have in mind a vision of what Christendom is and what it would mean to be non-Christendom or post-Christendom do we stand any chance of succeeding in creating a post-Christendom typology that will be useful to the church in the coming years. The goal is to remove barriers to the church carrying out its true mission to bear witness to Jesus Christ until he comes again. We Western Christians have grown up in a culture that has been so deeply and profoundly shaped by the historical fact of Christendom that we find it difficult to imagine any other way of doing church and being the people of God. So imagination is the key. But where can we find nourishment for a sanctified imagination that can spring us free from the shackles of the Christendom paradigm? Scripture is the obvious answer, but our interpretation of Scripture itself has often been imprisoned within Christendom assumptions.

By the mercy of God, we do not have to approach the Scripture as isolated individuals. We have the promise of the Holy Spirit, and we have the examples of the martyrs and saints of the past to guide us. We need to read Scripture through the eyes of those who have stood for holiness, sanctification, and discipleship, rather than through the eyes of deeply compromised rulers, generals, and nobles. If we do so, we will find that the view from below brings the essence of Christendom clearly into focus. A commitment to wealth, power, and prestige leads us to imagine that there is no alternative to Christendom. But if we examine the lives of those who give up everything to follow Jesus, we will find that alternatives abound. The next two chapters will set the stage for rethinking church history from the perspective of disciples instead of from the perspective of worldly rulers.

What it comes down to is the problem that Jesus spent so much time dealing with in teaching his disciples: how to perceive the kingdom of God. Jesus taught them that the kingdom of God is very different from this world. Anyone who wants to enter it must become like a little child (Matthew 18:1–3). He explained that the values of this kingdom are "upside right" and that those of this world are upside down:

> You know that the rulers of the Gentiles lord it over them, and their high officials exercise authority over them. Not so with you. Instead, whoever wants to become great among you must be your servant, and whoever wants to be first must be your slave—just as the Son of Man did not come to be served, but to serve, and to give his life as a ransom for many. (Matthew 20:25–28)

The next two chapters constitute an exercise in learning to look at church history right side up, from Jesus's perspective.

4

Why Christendom Was a Bad Idea

In the previous chapter, I suggested that the major reason why *Christ and Culture* is inadequate as a guide to thinking about the problem of how Christ relates to culture in the twenty-first century is that it presupposes the existence and legitimacy of Christendom. However, I cannot assume that every reader of this book will be ready to agree that Christendom is dead and that we are better off without it. Many Christians, both liberal and conservative and both Roman Catholic and Protestant, still believe that Christendom should be restored and fervently pray to God that he restore it by means of a revival.[1] The purpose of this chapter is to make the case that Christendom was and is a bad idea. It is not an attempt to write a history of Christendom; rather, it is an attempt to interpret the theological and ethical meaning of Western Christendom from a post-Christendom perspective.

What Is Christendom?

To begin, let us recall the definition of Christendom given above in the introduction:

1. For examples of serious arguments for Christendom from Roman Catholic and Anglican perspectives, see Aidan Nichols, *Christendom Awake: On Re-energizing the Church in Culture* (Edinburgh: T & T Clark, 1999); and Oliver O'Donovan, *The Desire of the Nations: Rediscovering the Roots of Political Theology* (New York: Cambridge University Press, 1996).

Christendom is the concept of Western civilization as having a religious arm (the church) and a secular arm (civil government), both of which are united in their adherence to Christian faith, which is seen as the so-called soul of Europe or the West. The essence of the idea is the assertion that Western civilization is Christian. Within this Christian civilization, the state and the church have different roles to play, but, since membership in both is coterminous, both can be seen as aspects of one unified reality—Christendom.

In case anyone thinks that Christendom, as defined here, is innocuous, let me spell out what is wrong with this picture. The essence of Christendom is worldliness. In Christendom, the church is not only in the world; it is also of the world. In John 15, Jesus speaks to his disciples and through them to us:

> If the world hates you, keep in mind that it hated me first. If you belonged to the world, it would love you as its own. As it is, you do not belong to the world, but I have chosen you out of the world. That is why the world hates you. Remember the words I spoke to you: "No servant is greater than his master." If they persecuted me, they will persecute you also. If they obeyed my teaching, they will obey yours also. They will treat you this way because of my name, for they do not know the One who sent me. (John 15:18–21)

Christendom is a series of compromises made by the church with the world so that the offense of Jesus Christ is watered down, mitigated, and obscured to the point that the world is satisfied that the church is no longer foreign and dangerous. The world must be satisfied that the church no longer follows the Lord Jesus Christ to the exclusion of the gods of this world. Christendom means that Christianity is turned into a fit religion for natural, unconverted humanity and no longer poses a threat to the world.

In the New Testament, especially in the Gospel of John, the word *world* does not mean creation or planet earth. It means the organized system of authority that is in rebellion against God. It means fallen human culture interacting with the principalities and powers, which are fallen ideologies, forces, and cultural entities such as nations, religions, and so on. Jesus came to die for the world in order to redeem it, but the world crucified him and will continue to oppose him until the second coming. During this period of time, the purpose of the church is to witness to the lordship of Jesus Christ. Therefore, as Jesus warned us, we need to expect tension, resistance, and sometimes outright persecution. One thing we can never do is to settle down into a comfortable coexistence with the world by removing the offense of the gospel—the lordship of Jesus Christ.

Before Christendom

For the first three centuries (from Pentecost to 313) the Christian church was a small, sometimes-persecuted minority with virtually no political power. There were no cathedrals, no wealthy monasteries, no powerful Christian rulers, and no laws favoring the church. As the gospel spread around the Mediterranean basin, messianic synagogues/house churches were formed. When Paul went to a new city to preach the gospel, he went first to the synagogue. He often found a ready audience in the God-fearers, who were Gentile semiconverts to Judaism who believed in the one God and the moral law and participated in Jewish worship but were not circumcised. Because Judaism was very attractive to many people in the Roman Empire on account of its high moral standards and exalted idea of God, many people were in this category. As the Jewish community divided into those who accepted and those who rejected Jesus as messiah, messianic synagogues/house churches were often formed.

These churches gradually lost much of their Jewish character as the ratio of Gentiles to Jews increased, but their roots in the Old Testament and Jewish worship persisted. As pagans from the Greco-Roman world with no prior knowledge of Israel's God or Israel's law began to come into the church, they had to be discipled from square one, as it were, and even a basic knowledge of the Hebrew Scriptures could not be taken for granted. This led the church to institute a multiyear program of discipleship for new converts before they became full members (the process of catechesis). But the same things that had attracted Gentiles to Judaism also attracted Gentiles to the Christian church, and so, between the apostolic age and the fourth century, the church grew steadily and expanded its influence.

Gradually the church began to develop institutional structures, accredited leaders, a common liturgy rooted in Jewish forms of worship, and the canon of Scripture. Major theologians such as Irenaeus and Tertullian labored to expound Scripture. A form of the baptismal confession of the church at Rome, which later evolved into today's Apostles' Creed, was used from the second century on in Rome. Christians were known for rejecting violence, caring for abandoned children, looking after the poor, and having high sexual morality. Pagans were often attracted by the sense of community among Christians. A viable and healthy expression of Christianity existed prior to the rise of Christendom.

Beginning of Christendom

Christendom, like Rome, was not built in a day. Although scholars debate just how long it took to come into being, it certainly took a minimum of a century, and it would not be an exaggeration to speak of a 275-year-long process lasting from the middle of the third century to 528, when Emperor Justinian made it illegal for citizens not to be Christians. A key date was the Edict of Milan in 313, when coemperors Constantine and Licinius decreed the end of persecution of Christians and the beginning of religious liberty in the Roman Empire. But a major policy turn-around like that did not come out of nowhere. The great persecution under Diocletian had been brutal but brief, lasting from 303 to 312. Prior to that there had been half a century of peace for Christians, and during that period the church grew very rapidly. By 313, our best guess is that Christians made about 10 percent of the population of the empire, with heavier concentrations in Syria,

Asia Minor, and the cities around the Mediterranean.[2] During the last half of the third century, Christianity had become a powerful movement. Because of its numbers, its organization, the witness of its martyrs, the lucidity of its apologists, the attractiveness of its high moral standards, and its exemplary care for the poor, Christianity could not be ignored. Again, all this occurred before there was any such thing as Christendom.

The role of the so-called conversion of Constantine in the change in imperial policy toward the church can be overemphasized. Harold Drake points out that the question we should ask is not "did Constantine become a Christian?" but rather "what kind of Christian did he become?"[3] He was certainly an unusual one. Although he was not baptized until his deathbed, he presumed to interfere regularly in church affairs and called himself "the bishop of the bishops."[4] Constantine's moral behavior was basically no different from other emperors. He murdered friends, members of his own family, and political rivals. He constantly made war and exalted himself in pride and splendor just like any other emperor. While his policy clearly favored Christianity, his own personal convictions will never be known with certainty. All we know is that he would have had to live a very different life if he had wanted to be received into the church as an ordinary catechumen.

It is significant that Constantine did not persecute paganism, but rather pursued a policy of trying to bring together pagan monotheism and Christians into a kind of civil religion open to people with significantly different religious beliefs.[5] As Drake puts it, "Constantine's idea was to form a coalition of monotheists to support a vision of peace with the Emperor as the Divine representative on earth."[6] He was a devotee of *Sol Invictus*, "the Unconquered Sun," both before and after his "conversion." Gustavo Gutiérrez, commenting on the Edict of Milan, concurs: "Thus we find ourselves dealing with a text that grants freedom to practice the religion of one's choice in order to preserve the peace of the empire, resting on the acknowledgement of a supreme divinity that can be worshipped by Christians *as well as* by pagans. The actual acknowledgement of a religious truth is absent."[7] It is naïve to assume that Constantine's motives were religious and not political. They have to be described as both, but the evidence suggests that they were more political than religious.

It is important to understand that Constantine's reason for embracing Christianity was exactly the same as Diocletian's for persecuting it: "The premise that

---

2. Peter Brown, *The Rise of Western Christendom: Triumph and Diversity, A.D. 200–1000* (2nd ed.; Oxford: Blackwell, 2003), 63.

3. Harold Drake, *Constantine and the Bishops: The Politics of Intolerance* (Baltimore: Johns Hopkins University Press, 2000), 201.

4. John Howard Yoder, *Christian Attitudes to War, Peace, and Revolution* (Elkhart, IN: Goshen Biblical Seminary, 1983), 39

5. Drake, *Constantine and the Bishops*, 192.

6. Ibid., 199.

7. Gustavo Gutiérrez, *Las Casas: In Search of the Poor of Jesus Christ* (trans. Robert Barr; Maryknoll, NY: Orbis, 1993), 139.

proper regard for religion was vital to the security of the state."[8] The Roman emperors had always had the care of religion as one of their main tasks, and in the late empire of the third and fourth centuries the religious legitimizing of the emperor was very important. As the role of the Senate declined and the role of the army increased with regard to the making of emperors, the political challenge facing the emperors was how to avoid becoming totally dependent on the army for their position, lest the tail begin to wag the dog. The solution was to cultivate popular religious legitimacy, a kind of appeal over the head of the Senate and army alike to the population as a whole. If most people believed that the emperor was the choice of the gods, then his position was more secure. Thus the position of *pontifex maximus*, or high priest of Rome, became key to the emperors' political power. In an age when everyone believed that divine favor was key to winning battles, the responsibility of the emperor to make sure the gods were favorable to Rome was a crucial part of the emperor's job description.

Constantine ended the persecution of Christians because it was a failed policy. In fact, it was even unpopular with many pagans, who considered the attack on upstanding citizens, merely for refusing to compromise their monotheism, to be morally insupportable. Constantine saw the Christian church as a potential constituency, a source of support for an empire facing many challenges. One problem was that the emperor was dependent on local ruling elites to collect taxes and maintain public order. The empire was run through a huge patronage network and depended on local elites, rather than a professional class of civil servants. But in many places, these local elites were corrupt and, worse (from an emperor's perspective), ineffective. This is why, over the next twenty years, Constantine increasingly employed the bishops of the Christian church to distribute food to the urban poor, hold trials and settle disputes, and act as his network of advisors on matters of importance to the empire.[9] In some ways, they came to replace the Senate in terms of political influence. Most bishops at the end of the great persecution were honest and upright, although, of course, there were merely human and therefore increasingly susceptible to corruption as time went on and as they attained significant economic and political power. What is important to see is that Constantine had perfectly rational political reasons for making peace with the church. He was shrewd enough to seek a formula to reconcile "the imperial need for religious justification with the refusal of Christians to pay homage to any other deity."[10] Drake presses home the point that anyone who became emperor at the beginning of the fourth century would have been forced to at least consider the path Constantine chose: "Given the religious basis for legitimate rule, given a sizable group that could not recognize a legitimate ruler on that basis, given the failure of an effort to compel them to do so, what alternatives were open not merely to

8. Drake, *Constantine and the Bishops*, 215–6.
9. Brown, *Rise of Western Christendom*, 78.
10. Drake, *Constantine and the Bishops*, 190.

Constantine but to anyone who was going to rule Rome in 312?"[11] The point is that one does not need a conversion to explain Constantine's policy; in fact, one can explain the conversion by the need for the policy.

Constantine was a Roman monotheist who favored the Christian church rather than persecuting it. He never made Christianity the sole religion of the empire, but he was extremely interested in the unity of the church and the contribution it could make to help the empire remain unified. He never persecuted pagans. But he did set in motion forces that led to the persecution of non-Christians and the adoption of Christianity as the state religion. By the end of the fourth century, Constantine's successors found themselves dependent on the bishops for much of their legitimacy, and the power of the bishops increased accordingly. Constantine, however, considered himself to be the head of the church on earth. He presided over the Council of Nicea in 325 (despite not being a church member) and was buried, by his order, in the Church of the Apostles in Constantinople. The theological significance of this act was not lost on the Eastern church, which considers Constantine a saint and the thirteenth apostle.[12] It is fascinating to note that less than fifty years after Constantine's death one of his successors, Theodosius I, found himself on the receiving end of a form of ecclesiastical discipline. After punishing rioters who had destroyed a Jewish synagogue in 388 and after massacring the inhabitants of Thessalonica as punishment for a riot in 390, Theodosius found himself refused admission to communion by Bishop Ambrose of Milan until he did penance.[13] Drake comments on the amazing spectacle of Emperor Theodosius allowing himself to be disciplined by Bishop Ambrose:

> This growing strength of the bishops was an unintended consequence of Constantine's policies. Constantine himself would never have imagined a situation such as that in which Theodosius found himself. . . . The church, through its bishops, assumed the role of legitimator which had been played by the Senate during the Principate. This change meant that emperors now had to minister to the priorities and interests of the bishops at least as zealously as they had once done for the Senate.[14]

This story was retold endlessly throughout the Middle Ages and continues to be a staple of church-history textbooks as an example of the struggle for power between church and state. Certainly this incident would have shocked Constantine, who never intended the power of the bishops to get out of hand. But the ever-weakening political structure of the empire, combined with the ever-growing strength of the

11. Ibid., 158.
12. F. L. Cross and E. A. Livingston, eds., *The Oxford Dictionary of the Christian Church* (3rd ed.; Oxford: Oxford University Press, 1997), 405 s.v. "Constantine the Great."
13. Brown, *Rise of Western Christendom*, 80.
14. Drake, *Constantine and the Bishops*, 390.

church, led to a series of developments that turned powerless victims of persecution into powerful persecutors.

There were milestones along the way. Around 390 the pagan temples were closed and public pagan sacrifice was banned. During the next couple of centuries we see what Peter Brown aptly calls "a drift into respectable Christianity."[15] In 420 we find the first example of a bishop calling on the state to intervene with coercion against heretics, as Augustine calls in imperial troops against the Donatists.[16] After 436, non-Christians are excluded from the army.[17] In 438, under Theodosius II, the *Theodosian Code* was published. It contained all the legislation of the Christian emperors and ended with a section on religion, which for the first time in Roman history made heresy, in the sense of incorrect belief as opposed to outward practice, illegal. Brown puts it this way: "Now it was 'thought crime' itself—wrong views on religion in general, and not simply failure to practice traditional rites in the traditional manner—which was disciplined."[18] Hugh Trevor-Roper calls Theodosius I (a native of Spain) "the first of the Spanish inquisitors."[19] In 529 the philosophical schools in Athens were closed.[20] In 528 Emperor Justinian made it illegal not to be a Christian, and pagans were given three months to convert.[21] Christendom was fully established.

Why Did It Happen?

But why did it happen? Even if the political conditions of the late empire combined with the favor shown to the church by Constantine created an open door to a Christian empire, why did the bishops walk through that door? Some would regard this as a silly question, akin to asking a starving man why he ate the food.[22] But the reality of Christendom contradicted the plain teaching of Jesus at so many points that we have to wonder if all the bishops in office between 313 and 529 were so completely under Constantine's spell that they all forgot to read their New Testaments. For one thing, Jesus taught that Christian leaders were not to imitate the rulers of the Gentiles, who lord it over their subjects. Instead Christian leaders were to be servants of all (Luke 22:24–27). No greater

15. Peter Brown, quoted by R. A. Markus, *The End of Ancient Christianity* (Cambridge: Cambridge University Press), 27.

16. Yoder, *Christian Attitudes to War*, 40.

17. Ibid.

18. Brown, *Rise of Western Christendom*, 75.

19. Hugh Trevor-Roper, *The Rise of Christian Europe* (New York: Harcourt Brace Jovanovich, 1975), 36. I was directed to this quotation by James Carroll, *Constantine's Sword: The Church and the Jews* (New York: Houghton Mifflin, 2001), 207.

20. Kenneth Scott Latourette, *A History of Christianity*, vol. 1: *Beginnings to 1500* (New York: Harper & Row, 1975), 99.

21. Brown, *Rise of Western Christendom*, 178. See also Latourette, *History of Christianity*, 278–82.

22. In *Other Side of 1984* (Geneva: World Council of Churches, 1983), 34, even Lesslie Newbigin argues that the bishops had no choice; the Christendom experiment had to be made. This assessment comes from someone who came to recognize that Christendom is over and who does not lament it.

contrast between the ideal set forth by Jesus and the imperial swagger of "the bishop of the bishops" could possibly be imagined. The imitation of the emperor by the bishops in this regard is also perplexing; to this day they sit on "thrones." Why? Second, Jesus taught that his followers should turn the other cheek and refuse retaliatory violence (Matthew 5:38–39). If someone argues that Jesus was thinking only of private citizens in small-village society and never imagined his followers ever becoming generals and emperors, why is that not considered to be evidence that Jesus did not intend for his followers to become political rulers? After all, most of Jesus's contemporaries were looking for a messiah who would be a general and then become a king through holy violence. It was far from something he never imagined; in fact, it was something he consciously rejected.[23] Third, the gospel is good news, but how can it be perceived as good news when it is forced upon someone by the sword? In the second and third centuries, Christians understood this very well, and some eloquent pleas for religious toleration on the basis of the integrity of conscience came from Christians. For example, we hear Tertullian (145–220) saying: "It should be counted quite absurd for one man to compel another to do honor to the gods, when he ought ever voluntarily, and in the sense of his own need, to seek their favor."[24] Why were Christians in favor of religious liberty while suffering persecution, but not once they had attained power?

A reasonable question is to ask: At what point should the bishops have said no to the emperors? Surely they should have accepted toleration and the end of persecution? Yes, of course. Then where should the line be drawn? Should they have refused to come together at Nicea at the emperor's request? Well, probably not. Should they have refused to let him attend the council? Probably yes, but that would have created a confrontation and might have led to more persecution. Would that have been worth it? Maybe not. Perhaps he could have been allowed to attend but not dominate. Well then, should they have accepted the role he asked them to play in distributing food to the urban poor? Probably yes, although it did create problems and temptations for them. What about gifts of churches and other buildings for Christian use? What about accepting the duty to pray for the empire? And on it goes. It is easy to say that Christendom should not have happened, but it is not so easy to put oneself in the place of a bishop attending the Council of Nicea and say exactly what should have happened then and in the half century that followed Nicea. However, this is exactly what we must do, or else we must give up and admit that the Bible and the Spirit cannot reveal to us God's will for the church. But before we attempt to answer these thorny questions, it is necessary to pause and look ahead to the results of the bishops' decision to collaborate in the creation of Christendom.

23. See John Howard Yoder, *The Politics of Jesus: Vicit Agnus Noster* (2nd ed.; Grand Rapids: Eerdmans, 1994), chap. 2, for a discussion of the temptations that Jesus faced throughout his career in this regard.
24. Tertullian, "Apology" (Ante-Nicene Fathers 3; repr. Peabody, MA: Hendrickson, 1994), 41.

The Bitter Fruits of Christendom

Between the fall of Rome in 410 and the sixteenth-century Reformation, Christendom became an "oppressive, a totalitarian religious system, in which the church became phenomenally wealthy and seriously corrupt."[25] We might tend to be more charitable today, but one would be hard pressed to find a reformer of any stripe in the sixteenth century who would disagree with that assessment. Let us consider some of the characteristics of Christendom as it developed in Europe during this time.

First, there were the attempt to enforce faith and the suppression of all dissent. Infant baptism was the means by which it was ensured that everyone would be a Christian. There was no religious liberty and no freedom of conscience.

Second, tithes were ruthlessly exacted from the population, which gave the church a financial incentive to support the civil order and suppress political dissent. Anybody who dissented from church doctrine automatically was a threat to the civil order and, therefore, to the economic order, which enabled a small nobility and clergy hierarchy to have a high standard of living while the vast majority of the population endured a subsistence level of existence. Heresy, in this regard, was an economic and political issue, and both church and state had a stake in it. This dynamic eventually made possible the Inquisition.

Third, the political and legal framework of Christendom was based on oaths, just as the pagan Roman Empire had been, even though oath-taking had been renounced by the early church on the basis of the teaching of Jesus. Taking an oath was seen as calling down God's judgment if one failed to keep one's word, and divine judgment was taken very seriously and feared, at least by pious people of this period.

Fourth, war was sanctioned as the right of rulers, and Christians were expected to fight and kill for their sovereigns. Once again, this went against the New Testament and the practice of the early church up to approximately the third century. The just-war theory, derived from pagan Greco-Roman writers like Cicero, justified by certain passages in the Old Testament, and developed by Augustine and Thomas Aquinas, replaced the Sermon on the Mount. Ultimately, in Christendom, the ideology of war became absolute. The Crusades were holy wars, inspired by the wars of conquest under Joshua.

Fifth, there was a general tendency to justify Christendom from the Old Testament, especially where the New Testament was not amenable to Christendom practices. Scripture was read in an ahistorical manner, rather than as progressive revelation with the New Testament serving as the lens through which the Old Testament was understood. To a great extent, Jesus's teaching was marginalized. His radical teaching was called the "counsels of perfection" and applied to the

25. Stuart Murray, *Post-Christendom: Church and Mission in a Strange New World* (Carlisle, Cumbria: Paternoster, 2004), 110.

clergy only, in particular, to the monks. Jesus as an object of devotion became detached from the teachings of Jesus, with the result that Jesus could be thought of as Savior (religion) without necessarily being thought of as Lord (morality).

Constantine never had much to say about Jesus, and throughout the long ages of Christendom this became the pattern. A monotheistic civil order made room for those who wanted to follow Jesus (like monks and nuns, for example), as long as they did not challenge the overall civil order. It was similar to the modern toleration of conscientious objectors to war. Since the number of such people was small, there was no threat to the overall raising of funds or recruiting of armies, and so it was easier to tolerate them than to persecute them. The radical teachings of Jesus were ignored or domesticated in a variety of ways. Nevertheless, they were always there, threatening to break out as a result of someone reading the Gospels and being convicted of their truth. What could never be tolerated was the message that the way of Jesus is for everyone from the emperor and pope on down. From time to time, various people came to this very conclusion, and they always were regarded as a threat by the rulers of Christendom.

A religious system that denied freedom, exploited the lower classes, sanctioned violence, and marginalized Jesus was bound to lead to demonic injustices, and that is what happened. We will look briefly at three of the worst injustices, although we could easily list dozens equally worthy of consideration.

Hating God's People in the Name of God: Christian Anti-Judaism

One of the most ironic and clearly evil disasters of Christendom was the anti-Judaism and anti-Semitism perpetrated by both church and state, which prepared the ground on which the Holocaust happened. The Jews of Europe were barely tolerated most of the time in Christendom. Because there was no religious liberty, their position was always precarious. Continuous anti-Jewish preaching by the church encouraged scapegoating and pogroms.

Anti-Jewish prejudice and violence predated Christendom, but, during the late Roman Empire and the Middle Ages, Christian anti-Judaism merged with popular superstition and the general human tendency to fear and hate outsiders. The really shameful thing, from a Christian perspective, is that Christian clergy and other leaders provided fuel for the hatred of Jews with their writing and preaching. Even though the Romans put Jesus to death, the Jews were blamed, and they were blamed as an entire religion (and later as an entire race). Even Jews who were born centuries later were blamed for killing Jesus. Since Christianity was identified with the power structures of society and since the Jews were resident aliens or pilgrims within the empire/tribes/early nation-states of European Christendom, Christians joined in and even took the lead in persecuting God's people. Blood libels were myths that accused Jews of kidnapping and using Christian children in an evil ceremony of ritual murder as part of their religion. The poisoning of wells was often blamed on Jews. Jews were often suspected of having magical and occult powers. Banned from most occupations, Jews often became moneylenders in order to survive. This, in turn, led to the stereotype of Shylock, the greedy and cruel Jew. Frequently, Jews were expelled from various European countries and then allowed back in only if they paid a bribe or tax. This was an easy way for kings to raise money for war or other purposes. Beginning in the eleventh century, mobs accompanying the first three Crusades attacked Jewish settlements in England, France, and Germany on their way to the Holy Land. Jews were slaughtered like cattle by ordinary people and by soldiers, urged on by preachers and priests.

The Jews of the Middle Ages survived as a people without having national sovereignty and without using violence to ensure their survival. Thus, as John Howard Yoder puts it, "Judaism through the Middle Ages demonstrated the sociological viability of the ethic of Jesus."[26] After the fall of Jerusalem, the rabbinic tradition renounced revolutionary and nationalistic violence. Yoder elaborates: "The ethics of the Jews can be generally characterized as never justifying violence, as making much of frequent nonviolent martyrs who would not fight back against their persecutors, because it might be that God himself is the one who is chastising them at the hand of the persecutors, and because only God can save."[27] In a contest over who followed the teachings of Jesus best—the Jews or the Christians who preside over Christendom—the Jews win hands down. This is more than irony; it is mystery.

In the novel *The Last of the Just*, we read of a conversation between a Jewish boy and girl who have fallen in love just in time to fall victim to Hitler's murderers:

"Oh, Ernie," Golda said, "you know them. Tell me why, *why* do the Christians hate us the way they do? They seem so nice when I can look at them without my star."

Ernie put his arm around her shoulders solemnly. "It's very mysterious," he murmured in Yiddish. "They don't know exactly why themselves. I've been in their churches and I've read their gospel. Do you know who the Christ was? A simple Jew like your father. A kind of Hasid."

Golda smiled gently. "You're kidding me."

"No, no, believe me, and I'll bet they'd have got along fine, the two of them, because he was really a good Jew, you know, sort of like the Baal Shem Tov—a merciful man, and gentle. The Christians say they love him, but I think they hate him without knowing it. So they take the cross by the other end and make a sword out of it and strike us with it! . . . Poor Jesus, if he came back to earth and saw that the pagans had made a sword out of him and used it against his sisters and brothers, he'd be sad, he'd grieve forever. And maybe he does see it. . . . And it's true, he and your father would have got along together. I can see them *so* well together, you know. 'Now,' your father would say, 'now my good rabbi, doesn't it break your heart to see all that?' And the other would tug at his beard and say, 'But you know very well, my good Samuel, that the Jewish heart must break a thousand times for the greater good of all peoples. *That* is why we were chosen, didn't you know?' And

26. Yoder, *Christian Attitudes to War*, 125.
27. Ibid.

your father would say, 'Oi, oi, didn't I know? Didn't I know? Oh, excellent rabbi, that's all I *do* know.'"[28]

The irony is that it is true that the Hasidic rabbi mentioned here likely *would* have gotten along fine with Jesus, precisely because they were so much alike. The contrast between the bloodthirsty and violent Germans, on the one hand, and both Jesus and his fellow Jews, on the other, is heartbreaking and should cause us as Christians to be ashamed to be called by the same name as those who hate God's people in God's name. How it could have happened is almost beyond comprehension.[29] That the Holocaust could have taken place in a Christian nation places a giant question mark beside the whole concept of a supposedly Christian nation.[30]

Persecuting Those Most Like Jesus: Sixteenth-Century Anabaptists

Christendom was in a constant state of change for the millennium between Constantine and Luther, but the continuity is substantial. An example of the continuity is the basis for the persecution of the Anabaptists. When the Anabaptists of the sixteenth century began to practice believers' baptism, they were arrested and tried in civil courts on the basis of laws that date back to the codifications of Theodosius and Justinian. The specific law that made "rebaptism"[31] a crime originated in the Donatist controversy.[32] The Donatists originated in the third century in North Africa as a result of a dispute within the church over whether church leaders who had handed over copies of Scripture and in other ways collaborated with the persecutors during times of persecution should be barred from church leadership. The Donatists felt that sacraments (such as baptism) performed by such bishops were not valid, and they were in the habit of rebaptizing those who had been baptized by such clergy. So a law was passed that forbade rebaptism, and twelve hundred years later this law was dusted off and used to justify the burning and drowning of evangelical Christians whose

28. Andre Schwarz-Bart, *The Last of the Just* (trans. Stephen Becker; New York: Atheneum, 1960), 324–25.

29. For a study of how anti-Judaism turned into anti-Semitism, see Jacob Katz, *From Prejudice to Destruction: Anti-Semitism, 1700–1933* (Cambridge: Harvard University Press, 1980). I thank Rebecca Carter-Chand for drawing my attention to this work.

30. Note the insightful words of Katz: "As Christianity became more diluted, it often came to represent a more extreme contradiction to Judaism" (ibid., 159).

31. In fairness to the Anabaptists, "rebaptism" must be placed in quotation marks, since they did not accept the validity of infant baptism and, therefore, did not believe that they were rebaptizing people when they administered the New Testament ordinance in the New Testament manner; that is, at the request of the believer. In the case of the Donatists, people were rebaptized regardless of the manner of their first baptism. The Donatists' issue was the authority of compromised persons to act on behalf of the church in administering the sacrament.

32. C. Arnold Snyder, *Anabaptist History and Theology: An Introduction* (Kitchner, ON: Pandora, 1995), 1.

only crime was trying to live according to the New Testament. Christendom was an enduring institution.

We must never forget how simple biblical Christians, whose only crime was to believe the Scriptures, share the gospel, be baptized in the New Testament manner, and meet together to sing praises to God, encourage one another, and read the Bible were ruthlessly hunted down and killed. A typical story is as follows:

> In this year 1538, in the month of August, ten, or seventeen persons, male and female, were apprehended in the town, who were accused of rebaptism. These were principally of the poorer classes, except one, a goldsmith, called Paul von Drusnen, of whom it is reported that he was their teacher. Paul, and three others, were put to death at Vucht, in the theatre, then afterwards burnt on the 9th of September.[33]

The account continues with a description of an attempt to coerce the Anabaptists into recanting.

> Paul's wife said: O Lord! Enlighten these who inflict such sufferings upon us, that they may see what they are doing. I thank thee, O God! That thou didst think me worthy to suffer for your name's sake.
>
> The Dominican said to another woman: Will you not stay with the holy church? She replied: I will remain with God; is this not a sufficient holy church?
>
> Then spoke the Dominican to a man, John von Capelle: Pray that he may forgive you, because you have set a bad example. He replied: I did not err, but I have been engaged in the word of God and I am sorry that I remained so long in darkness. I entreat you, brothers, read the gospel, and live according to its precepts, and leave off your debauchery, roguery, and cursing, and the crossing of yourselves, etc.
>
> The third woman said: O, Almighty God! Lay no greater burden upon me than I can bear, etc. Thus they died cheerfully.[34]

The martyrs were not violent revolutionaries; they were pacifists. They were not immoral; they lived exemplary lives, for the most part. They were not heretics; rather, they tried to live out the New Testament to the best of their ability. They shared their personal faith with their circle of acquaintances and formed house churches. How could a so-called Christian society perceive such people to be such dangerous threats to the social order that they had to be hounded, tortured, and killed? Like the Jews, the Anabaptists attempted to live out the nonviolent lifestyle of Jesus and were persecuted by those who called themselves Christians. This is a great mystery.

Anabaptists are often criticized for being separatists, for isolating themselves from the rest of society. Niebuhr, as we saw in chapter 2, joined in this chorus. But, as Stanley Hauerwas and William Willimon point out, "the early Anabaptists

---

33. *Martyr's Mirror*, quoted by William Estep, *The Anabaptist Story* (rev. ed.; Grand Rapids: Eerdmans, 1975), 48.

34. Ibid.

had no desire to withdraw from world. . . . They were murdered by Calvinist, Lutheran and Roman Catholic societies because they attempted to be the church. . . . The Anabaptists did not withdraw. They were driven out."[35] The experience of the Anabaptists should alert us to the reality that not every society is willing to be transformed by Christ and that sometimes attempts to transform society will be met with persecution, violence, and martyrdom. Christians are witnesses to a living Lord who does not change to suit the whims of non-Christians of various times and places, and so we cannot change the gospel to fit the preconceptions of those to whom we preach. This means that, even if we do not believe in taking a Christ against culture position, sometimes we will be confronted with the fact of culture against Christ.

Murder and Theft Disguised as Evangelism: Invasion of the Americas

In 1492 Christopher Columbus thought he found a way to India by going west, but of course it turned out that he had actually bumped into the Americas. Spain promptly launched a series of wars of invasion against the native civilizations of the West Indies, Central America, and South America in which millions of people were killed, enslaved, and made to work in gold mines for their new masters. Incredibly, this was done in the name of evangelization!

The excuse for Spanish adventurers seeking their fortune by grave robbing and enslaving the native peoples in the Indies was the supposed Christianizing of the natives. A story related by Dominican Father Bartolomé de Las Casas, a champion of Indian rights in the years immediately following the conquest, illustrates the situation:

> A Franciscan Friar was seeking to persuade Cacique Hatuey to become a Christian before he died. The latter asked "why must one be like the Christians, who were wicked." The Father replied, "Because those who die Christian go to heaven, ever to behold the face of God, and take their ease and enjoyment." [Hatuey] inquired once more whether Christians went to heaven; the Father said yes, those that were good did. The other finally said that he had no wish to go there, since they [the Christians] went there, and were there. This occurred at a moment when it had been decided to burn him alive, so then they extended him over a slow fire and burned him alive.[36]

Who can blame Hatuey? Would you want to go to the place where such barbarians claimed to be going? Las Casas was a lonely, prophetic voice in condemning

---

35. Stanley Hauerwas and William Willimon, *Resident Aliens: A Provocative Christian Assessment of Culture and Ministry for People Who Know That Something Is Wrong* (Nashville: Abingdon, 1989), 41–42.

36. Las Casas, *Historia de las indias* 2.25, quoted by Alberto L. Garcia, "Christological Reflections on Faith and Culture," in *Christ and Culture in Dialogue* (ed. Angus J. L. Menuge; Saint Louis: Concordia, 1999), 68.

what was done during those years in the name of Christ, but his writings continue to this day to witness against those who called themselves Christians but who really worshiped gold.

Las Casas originally went to the Indies as part of the system only ten years after Columbus's first voyage and was given land and owned slaves himself in Cuba. But his life was changed by the witness of some brave Dominicans on the island of Hispaniola headed by Pedro de Cordoba. Nineteen years after the arrival of the Spanish, the population of the island was decimated, and the few remaining Indians were enslaved and dying young due to the hardships of mining gold for their masters. A former conquistador, Juan Garces, had repented of his crimes and become a Dominican lay brother. He gave a remarkable account of the cruelties that he and others had committed against the Indians. The consciences of the Dominicans were pricked, and after much prayer and consideration they decided to act. They worked together to compose a sermon to be delivered by Friar Anton Montesino, which they all signed. They picked the fourth Sunday in Advent to deliver it to a church full of the notables of the island, including Admiral Diego Colon. In the sermon they said:

> You are all in mortal sin! You live in it and you die in it! Why? Because of the cruelty and tyranny you use with these innocent people. Tell me, with what right, with what justice, do you hold these Indians in such cruel and horrible servitude? On what authority have you waged such detestable wars on these people, in their mild, peaceful lands, where you have consumed such infinitudes of them, wreaking upon them this death and unheard-of havoc? How it is that you hold them so crushed and exhausted, giving them nothing to eat, nor any treatment for their diseases, which you cause them to be infected with through the surfeit of their toils, so that they "die on you" [as you say]—you mean you kill them—mining gold for you day after day? And what care do you take that anyone catechize them, so that they may come to know their God and Creator, be baptized, hear Mass, observe Sundays and Holy Days? Are they not human beings? Have they no rational souls? Are you not obligated to love them as you love yourselves? Do you not understand this? Do you not grasp this? How is it that you sleep so soundly, so lethargically? Know for a certainty that in the state in which you are you can no more be saved than Moors or Turks who have not, or wish to have, the faith of Jesus Christ.[37]

After the service, Diego Colon and the other royal officials descended on the Dominicans' residence and demanded to see the preacher. Pedro de Cordoba, the Dominican Superior, explained that the sermon had been the responsibility of the whole community but called the preacher down. Montesino, the preacher, explained that the friars, after much deliberation, had decided to preach "the gospel truth necessary for the salvation of all the Spaniards of the islands, as well as of the Indians."[38] Gutiérrez rightly comments: "This evangelical perspective . . . is the key to an understanding

37. Quoted in Gutiérrez, *Las Casas*, 29.
38. Ibid., 32.

of the Dominicans' mighty challenge."[39] Here we see the biblical gospel, taking the plain teaching of Jesus at face value, confronting the evil of Christendom's espousal of violent coercion in the service of so-called Christian evangelism.

Repentance as the Proper Response to Christendom

Christendom was a bad idea. It was not an honest mistake made by people who did not know better. It was a perversion of the gospel and a twisting of Christianity into an ideology that served the interests of power brokers. It was the forsaking of mission and the embrace of evil in the name of God. At least three possible responses can be made at this point in history to the reality of Christendom: rationalization, reform, and repentance.

First, it is possible to respond to the horror of what has gone on in Christendom in the name of God by rationalizing it all. One can argue that the twisting of religion in the service of power elites is no reflection on the religion, but only on those who do the twisting. Violence can be justified as the necessary reaction to what others do first. The coexistence of evil motives mixed with good ones can be viewed as unavoidable in this world of sin. And on it goes. The bottom line is that it is always someone else's fault, not the fault of Christianity itself or Christians themselves. Rationalization is always a possibility.

Second, it is possible to respond to the horror of what has gone on in Christendom in the name of God by vowing to reform it. Reformers of Christendom call for more—not less—Christian involvement in government and other positions of power. But there are always compromises to be made along the way to those positions of power, and it is easy to forget one's purpose in seeking the power along the way. Reform usually involves some form of coercion. Typically, however, the call is for a new approach that involves less violent forms of coercion than before, which justifies the minimal forms of coercion being advocated. Reformers seek to reform society all at once from the top down. Yet, the human heart needs to be reformed one at a time from the bottom up. So the illusion must be sustained that changing social, legal, economic, or other structures and conditions of life will result in justice being done by those who inhabit those structures. But what if the whole basic approach of trying to force people into being Christian is wrong in the first place? Does it then matter all that much if it is done loudly or quietly, forcibly or gently, violently or by persuasion only? Reform is good whenever it is possible. But if the problem is violent coercion, then that problem cannot be remedied by further applications of violent coercion. And, at bottom, that is so often what reform amounts to.

Third, it is possible to respond to the horror of what has gone on in Christendom in the name of God by repenting of it and forsaking it utterly. The hatred,

---

39. Ibid., 30.

persecution, and destruction of Jews, dissenting Christians, and non-Western native peoples is not a peripheral flaw in the Christendom system; it is the normal, natural, inevitable outcome of forcing Christianity on the population and using it as the ideology that justifies the ruling powers that be. The only adequate response, in the final analysis, is repentance. Yet repentance must involve not only feeling sorry for what has happened in the past, but also a turning away from the sin so that the future will not be a repetition of the past. But how can this happen? What is the alternative to Christendom? Supposing one wanted to repent of it, how is one supposed to do so? That is the question we take up in the next chapter.

5

The Alternative to Christendom

Having examined some of the bitter fruits of Christendom and having concluded that the only adequate response to it as disciples of Jesus is repentance, we now turn to the question of what repentance could mean in this situation. No quick fixes are prescribed here. We need to realize that the poison that needs to be drawn from the body of Christ has been spreading itself throughout the body for over fifteen hundred years, and it may take another fifteen hundred years for it to be eliminated completely. Modern people are conditioned to expect that every problem can be solved overnight or at least in seven easy steps. God took approximately two millennia between the call to Abraham and the coming of Jesus to reveal himself fully, and it may very well take the church centuries to overcome the sad legacy of Christendom and learn how to bear a more adequate witness to Jesus Christ. We need to start by returning to the crucial moments in the fourth century when the die was cast.

Was there really an alternative to Christendom in the fourth century? Many people could not see it then, and many people cannot see it now. Christendom forms such a huge part of our cultural heritage as Westerners that it is a feat nearly beyond our power to imagine what it would be like to have no Christian past in our heritage. And it is equally difficult to imagine a future that is so unlike the past—a future without Christendom. Perhaps Asians, Africans, and Christians from the former Soviet Union can help us with the challenge of learning how to think from the perspective of a minority without prestige, status, wealth, or privilege. What would it mean frankly to acknowledge Western culture as dominated by polytheistic paganism and to see Christianity as an odd little group of people who actually take Jesus seriously, as opposed to the majority of the culture that does not? This is a question worth wrestling with.

However, as I mentioned in the first chapter, the church has been here before. For the first three centuries of its existence, the church was just a minority group in a large, pluralistic, pagan society with no power, no prestige, no wealth, and no status. And the church thrived. The church grew, flourished, and spread all around the Greco-Roman world. Ironically, the legal props that the church grew so used to depending on during the Christendom period were not necessary in order for the church to grow so strong as to become a threat to the empire in the first place! Maybe the dissolution of Christendom will lead not to the extinction of Christianity, but to the renewal of the faith. Maybe we should spend less time clinging to the levers of cultural power and relax a bit. "Except a seed fall to the ground and die."

In order to chart a course for the future, we must return to our roots. We must return to the past. What really were the options in the fourth century during those crucial moments when the synthesis of church and state we call Christendom was being forged? How could and should it have been different? Was there really an alternative to Christendom? Armed with these questions, we return to the question of what should have happened in the fourth century.

The Myth of Christendom's Inevitability

As we look at the situation in the fourth century, we have to conclude that there was an alternative to Christendom and that the bishops could have, and should have, chosen it. Would it have taken courage? Of course it would have, but these bishops were courageous; concerted Roman persecution had been unable to break them. Had Constantine chosen the opposite path, there is every reason to believe that he would have been broken upon the rock of the church. The persecutor would have been frustrated and perhaps destroyed by the passive resistance of a church that would not stop calling Jesus Lord. However, as the devil has discovered over and over again, you catch more flies with honey than with vinegar, and history certainly shows that, while the church can seldom be crushed by violent coercion, it often can be corrupted by power and comfort. So when persecution fails, establishment is the next strategy.

But if the bishops could have resisted social pressure, legal sanctions, and the sword, could they also not have resisted flattery, monetary inducements, and high social status? Let us consider first what the alternative to Christendom would have been and then consider the question of whether the bishops could reasonably have been expected to choose it.

There is a widespread myth, on which, as we have seen, Niebuhr traded heavily in *Christ and Culture*, that the church of the fourth century really had no alternative but to try the Christendom experiment. Highly respected early church scholar Robert Louis Wilken, in an interview for a popular church history magazine, expresses this myth in a typical manner. When asked if the bishops were not coopted by the state at Nicea, he says: "The simple answer is this: what does the church do when it winds up convincing most of the society to become Christian? That's what was happening by the fourth century. I don't think the church was co-opted by the state. It was the other way around: It's Constantine who changes."[1]

But there are real problems with this perspective. First, most of the society had not become Christian. In 325 the church made up about 10 percent of the population plus one semiconverted emperor. That does not make the Roman Empire Christian; it merely tempts the church to use force to compel people to conform to its religion. Second, Constantine did not actually change. His moral behavior was exactly the same as pagan emperors. He still murdered political rivals (including his own son), built monuments to himself, and made war at will. He did not become a catechumen and was not baptized until his deathbed. Therefore, he could not have partaken of the Eucharist during almost the whole of his reign. He was the poster boy for a new way of being Christian: no ethical or lifestyle change necessary, just shower beneficence on the church. Eleven centuries later Martin Luther's protests against indulgences would be a protest against this very same logic! Constantine was the first of a type of character we meet again and again throughout church history from this point on: pagan in substance and yet officially Christian in religion. Third, two things are confused here: on the one hand, the obvious opportunity for the church to use influence in the public square, which was not to be refused, and on the other, the temptation to utilize the violent, coercive, top-down methods of the world (i.e., fallen created powers, both human and demonic, arrayed in rebellion against God), which was to be refused. Have influence—yes. Use typical imperial methods—no. The influence could have been utilized to promote religious liberty and increase respect for human life and dignity.

Above all, it should have been impressed upon the emperor that his duty was to rule justly and to permit the Christian church to pursue its mission to carry out the Great Commission in the empire. If he wished to become a Christian, the same rules should have applied to him as to any other convert: true repentance and a demonstrably changed life, instruction in Christian teaching, baptism, and following Jesus as one of the faithful. Whether Constantine actually converted, merely became favorably inclined toward the church, or continued the failed policy of persecution, the church could have avoided being coopted.

Rejecting Christendom by Being the Church

In a nutshell, the alternative would have been for the church simply to *be the church*, rather than allowing itself to be coopted as the religious arm of the

1. Robert Louis Wilkin, "Why a Creed? A Conversation with Robert Louis Wilkin," *Christian History and Biography* 85 (winter 2005): 16.

empire. The Nicene Creed teaches that the church is one, holy, catholic, and apostolic. These are universally agreed-upon characteristics of the true church. Let us consider what would have happened if the bishops of Nicea had decided to concentrate on ensuring that the church really was truly one, holy, catholic, and apostolic.

Being Truly One: Unifying in a Christian, Rather Than an Imperial, Way

Constantine wanted the church to be unified for his own political reasons. Those reasons were likely a mixture of a desire to buttress his own personal dynasty and altruistic concerns for the well-being of the empire and public justice. Portraits of Constantine as either a saint or a monster serve only to confuse the issue. Like most Roman emperors, he was somewhere in between. But the bishops were not wrong in wanting unity in the church too. After all, Jesus prayed that his followers would be one in his high priestly prayer in John 17. Unity is a worthy goal, but there is more than one way of seeking unity.

Constantine's method of obtaining unity was a combination of allowing time for rational discussion in hopes of the bishops coming to an agreement and then, after a certain amount of time, lowering the boom on the minority who did not conform. In other words, the long-term plan was still the persecution of heretics—which was Diocletian's strategy between 303 and 312. Only the identity of the heretics had changed—from Christians in general to those Christians who disagreed with the theology currently in imperial favor. But what right does the emperor have to banish bishops who disagree with the currently favored imperial theology, whether that theology was Nicene (as it was from 325 to 337 when Constantine died) or Arian (as it was from 337 to 361 under his sons) or pagan (as it was from 361 to 363 under Julian the Apostate) or Nicene again (as it was after 363 under various emperors)? The point is that the emperor does not have the right to define Christian orthodoxy; nor does he have the right to force Christian orthodoxy on anybody, regardless of whether he or the bishops define it.

What then is the alternative to enforced orthodoxy? It is Christian patience. Christians should have kept on talking to one another for as long as it took. Even if some heretics eventually had to be excommunicated for the sake of the purity of doctrine, so be it. But those heretics should be welcomed back when they repented and, in any case, never attacked or harmed physically. Christian patience is the alternative to imperial violence: patience with long, drawn-out conversation to avoid schism if there is any way possible and patience even with excommunicated heretics, for whom we should pray, just as Jesus instructed us to pray for enemies.

Being Truly Holy: Refusing to Persecute Others

The bishops should have been more worried about the holiness of the church than about its material prosperity. After the fourth century, we see a growing concern within Christendom about the worldliness of the church and a corresponding rise in monasticism and asceticism. The issue was a gospel-fed drive toward holiness, which seemed to be missing from the imperial politics in which bishops and secular clergy were increasingly caught up. But the holiness is not something for which responsibility should be delegated to one division of the church; holiness is something fundamental to the identity of the church as a whole. The Nicene Creed itself testifies against the bishops who framed it at this point.

One thing is certain: whoever wants to be holy must abandon the way of violence and power politics and follow Jesus in the way of peace. If we are to love our enemies, how can we persecute those who presume to disagree with us? How can we be holy except we renounce violence? This is the unshakeable testimony of apostles, martyrs, confessors, mystics, and holy men and women down through the ages. Confessing our faith in Jesus Christ makes us vulnerable to those who choose to take the way of bloodshed and worldly power. But this very renunciation of violence has a strange power of its own, which is not understood by those who have chosen the other way. Tertullian says: "The oftener we are thrown down by you, the more we grow; the blood of Christians is seed."[2]

Being Truly Catholic: Putting Christian Fellowship above Political Loyalties

Very few people consider that the Roman Empire was not the whole civilized world in the fourth century. The church had spread out from Jerusalem after Pentecost, not just all over the Roman Empire, but much farther. Samuel Moffett's magisterial *A History of Christianity in Asia* shows that by the fourth century Christianity had spread beyond Greco-Roman Asia to Persia, India, and China.[3] The kingdom of Edessa, a small buffer state between the Persian and Roman empires, became largely Christian very early, perhaps by the second century.[4] Christians were allowed to operate freely in Persia and grew rapidly during the very period—the second and third centuries—when Christianity was persecuted in the Roman Empire.

But after Constantine's conversion, the rulers of Persia began persecution of Christians in the Persian Empire, and it is clear that the identification of Christianity with the emperor of Rome was one of the main causes of this persecution, along with the hostility of Zoroastrianism to Christianity.[5] For 250 years, Persia had been a refuge for Christians persecuted by Rome, partly because Christians

2. Tertullian, "Apology" (Ante-Nicene Fathers 3; repr. Peabody, MA: Hendrickson, 1994), 55.
3. Samuel Hugh Moffett, *A History of Christianity in Asia*, vol. 1: *Beginnings to 1500* (San Francisco: Harper, 1991), chaps. 1–7.
4. Ibid., 56–57.
5. Ibid., 137.

were considered enemies of Rome and thus friends of Persia. An ill-advised letter
from Constantine to his Persian counterpart, Shapur II, recommending protection for Christians, probably sparked this persecution.[6] When, a few years later,
Constantine gathered his forces for war in the east, Christian bishops were not
only praying for a Roman victory over the Persians, but also were willing to ac-
company their emperor to battle![7] This was the beginning of Christians killing
other Christians in the name of national/imperial allegiances, an act of disobedience to Christ that continues today.[8] Only after the crushing defeat of the pagan
Roman Emperor Julian in 363 by Persian forces did the persecution of Christians
in Persia gradually peter out.[9]

The ancient Romans were fond of arrogantly referring to their empire as the
whole of the civilized world, and the church in the Roman Empire picked up this
bad habit—as if the church of the Roman Empire was really catholic. In fact, it
was provincial—the state religion of one powerful political entity among others.
And the failure of the bishops in the Roman Empire to look at the Christian
faith as a worldwide, universal faith, which by definition therefore could never
belong to one political ruler or to one empire, was a failure to be truly catholic.
Maybe the Nicene bishops could have done nothing to stop the persecution of
Christians in Persia once Constantine wrote his unfortunate letter, but what
they could have done was to ensure that history would show that there was no
real substance to the charge that Christianity was merely the court religion of
the Roman emperor. They could have maintained a distance from identification
with any one political entity, no matter how powerful and seductive it was, for
the sake of being truly catholic.

Being Truly Apostolic: Preaching the Gospel to Rulers Also

The bishops could have decided to preach the gospel to Constantine like
Pedro de Cordoba and his fellow Dominicans did on Hispaniola approximately
twelve hundred years later. They could have asked what it would mean to preach
the gospel truth necessary for Constantine's salvation. That would have been
the apostolic thing to do. The church cannot remain apostolic when it fails to
declare the gospel to the political authority. And declaring the gospel does not
mean simply saying what the emperor wants to hear; it is a matter of spiritually
discerning how to present the truth of Scripture under the guidance of the Holy
Spirit so as to convey to the emperor what it might mean for him, in his situation,
to acknowledge the lordship of Jesus. Just as the Dominicans of Hispaniola had
spoken "the gospel truth necessary for the salvation of all the Spaniards of the

6. Ibid., 138.

7. Ibid.

8. Ironically, as I write these words in 2005, recent news reports tell of the growing persecution of
Christians, not in Iran, but in Iraq as the United States, a latter-day Roman Empire, prepared to invade.
The more things change, the more they stay the same.

9. Ibid., 142.

islands, as well as of the Indians,"[10] it was the responsibility of the bishops of the fourth century to speak truth to power.

The bishops might have done the things that Stuart Murray imaginatively suggests:

- They might have recognized that all Roman emperors had used religion to impose order on the empire: Constantine was acting in a typically Roman (not Christian) way.

- They might have questioned his continuing allegiance to the Unconquered Sun and the nature of his allegiance to Christ.

- They might have challenged him to become a catechumen earlier and to have prepared for baptism before he became terminally ill.

- They might have encouraged him to behave as a true Christian, rather than a normal emperor, accepting that this might have resulted in his reign being brief.

- They might have reflected on their survival and growth through 250 years of intermittent persecution and decided that they did not need imperial protection or patronage.

- They might have differentiated between toleration and imperial endorsement, welcoming the former and courteously but firmly refusing the latter.

- They might have explained to Constantine that massive basilicas and lavish bequests were inappropriate for followers of Jesus.

- They might have insisted that the cross symbolized sacrificial suffering and was inappropriate as a military standard, explaining that Jesus's followers were a peaceful people who would not fight to defend the empire.

- They might have recalled their own experience of persecution and historic commitment to religious liberty and refused to persecute or pressure others.

- They might have listened to dissenting voices warning that the theological reinterpretations of Augustine and others were leading them away from their roots and core values.[11]

Unfortunately, the bishops seemed more interested in what Constantine could do for them than in evangelizing him. While this judgment may seem harsh, so were

10. This was the friars' explanation for why they had felt compelled to preach their sermon (see discussion in chap. 3), quoted from Gustavo Gutiérrez, *Las Casas: In Search of the Poor of Jesus Christ* (trans. Robert R. Barr; Maryknoll, NY: Orbis, 1998), 32.

11. Stuart Murray, *Post-Christendom: Church and Mission in a Strange New World* (Carlisle, Cumbria: Paternoster, 2004), 104. See also John Howard Yoder, *Christian Attitudes to War, Peace, and Revolution* (Elkhart, IN: Goshen Biblical Seminary, 1983), 53–54.

the results of bishops allowing the church to be coopted by various emperors and other rulers during the long, sad, bloody history of Christendom.

Should the Fourth-Century Bishops Have Known Better?

But to say this is to beg the question. Should we really expect the bishops to have been able to foresee the consequences of bowing to the will of the emperor to intervene in church affairs? It is fair to remember that "fourth-century Christians were evidently taken by surprise when Constantine decided to favour the church and responded without thinking through the implications of their grateful acceptance."[12] While this is a valid point, it can excuse only so much. Perhaps the bishops needed some time to consider the problems, and we could understand if it took them a few years or decades to draw some distinctions and take a stand. But they were not exactly without resources. They had the life and teachings of Jesus, the Holy Scriptures, and the guidance of the Holy Spirit in understanding how to follow Jesus in these new circumstances. And they had recent experience of standing up to Roman persecution with great courage, faithfulness, and dedication.

Eighth-Century Jewish Prophets

The bishops could have read the Old Testament, not as a justification for a theocratic kingdom, Christian kings, state violence, and war, but rather as a cautionary tale about the incompatibility of the exercise of power politics with divine justice. The eighth-century Jewish prophets (Amos, Isaiah, Micah, Hosea) stood up to the kings of Israel and held them to the standard of justice found in the Torah. The two main sins denounced by the prophets were idolatry and oppression of the poor. The kings had their own court prophets who rationalized and justified everything they did and even denounced the true prophets of God who spoke the truth. But the true prophets proclaimed judgment on the Jewish state.

Samuel had warned the people of Israel that if they persisted in wanting a "king like all the other nations" (1 Samuel 8:6–18), then they would suffer high taxation, a military draft, and the centralization of wealth and power in the hands of an elite. In the days of David and Solomon, Israelite society became divided into classes, with much of the power and wealth in the hands of an elite. Contrary to the teaching of the Torah, many families permanently lost their ancestral lands, and a whole class of landless poor was created. The kings created standing armies and formed military alliances with pagan nations, which led to idolatry and syncretism. The distinctive witness of a people entirely dependent on Yahweh and dedicated to worshiping Yahweh gradually disappeared. This is when the prophets arose in Israel and predicted the exile—the judgment of God on a people who forgot their

---

12. Murray, *Post-Christendom*, 105.

unique mission to witness to Yahweh and worship Yahweh alone. Finally, in 586 BC the Babylonians destroyed Jerusalem, the temple, and the political structure of the nation. God then allowed his people to become his witnesses in the Diaspora, and the hope of the messiah gradually arose to sustain them.

The bishops could have drawn from this history the lesson that the way for the people of God to witness to God is not by aligning itself with a political state and using violence to sustain itself, as all the other nations do. They could have concluded that this had been tried and had failed. They could have realized that the calling of the people of God in this world is the Jeremian vision of being resident aliens, pilgrim witnesses to God, citizens of heaven living on earth (Jeremiah 29), as Peter advocates in his letter (1 Peter 1).

Jesus's Rejection of Nationalism and Violence

This interpretation of the Old Testament is certainly different from the one we have come to view as normal after fifteen hundred years of Christendom, but it was not one that should have been difficult for the bishops to come to, because it was the way that Jesus himself interpreted the Old Testament. Jesus was born into a situation in which the exile was still going on, even though some of the Jews had returned to the land of Israel. Most Jews still lived in the Diaspora, and the Jews did not rule their own land. Jerusalem and Judea were part of the Roman Empire and, after AD 6, were ruled directly by a Roman procurator. The Sanhedrin, the council of Jewish religious leaders headed by the high priest, had real, but limited, powers over the Jewish population of Jerusalem and the surrounding area. Most pious Jews in this era yearned for deliverance from foreign rule and oppression. They longed for the messiah and conceived of the messiah as a warrior-king who would drive out the hated Romans, purify the land, and extend his rule and power until the kings of the Gentiles would come to give homage to the Lord.

Jesus read the same Old Testament as his contemporaries but interpreted it differently. He fused the concepts of Isaiah's Suffering Servant (Isaiah 42:1–7; 49:1–6; 50:4–9; 52:13–53:12) and Daniel's Son of Man (Daniel 7:13–14) and apparently came to the conclusion that, since Israel had not repented of its sin, the calling of the messiah was to preach repentance to the nation, confront the Gentile religious and political rulers (as well as the dark, demonic forces behind them), and to suffer and die at their hands. This pure, innocent suffering by one who kept the Torah perfectly and lived in perfect harmony with God would somehow be used by God to redeem his people. So he told his disciples that he "must suffer many things and be rejected by the elders, chief priests and teachers of the law, and that he must be killed and after three days rise again" (Mark 8:31). He then set his face toward Jerusalem and set out to confront the leaders of the nation like an eighth-century prophet walking off the pages of history.

Jesus also founded a new community headed by twelve apostles, apparently representing the twelve tribes of Israel. In a radical departure, individuals entered this community voluntarily, even though ancient Palestine was a society based on kinship bonds. This new community was one in which there is mutual care for one another, love, forgiveness, and the living out of what it would mean to observe the spirit of Torah. In the Sermon on the Mount, Jesus spells out the contrast between the wider society and his new countercultural people of God. This remnant or nucleus of the new, redeemed people of God was intended by Jesus to be a concrete, living example of what it means to live in the kingdom of God even while surrounded by the kingdom of darkness. The fourth-century bishops were the stewards of this new community of faith, responsible for guiding it under the guidance of the Holy Spirit.

Resurrection and Politics

The difference between an irresponsible, utopian fantasy and the actual in-breaking of God into history is the reality of resurrection. Apart from the resur-rection, Jesus could be dismissed as a loveable, but unrealistic, dreamer. He could have been summed up as a person who witnessed against the evils of this world, but who had no real alternative to power politics and the use of force to achieve even a minimum of justice in a fallen world. But the resurrection changes the equation. First, it means that Jesus is alive and reigning right now, and so everyone is called to bow the knee to him as Lord. Second, it means that those who follow him in faith can look forward to a day of resurrection. Therefore, we do not need to fear those who can kill only the body. Third, resurrection means that this life is not all there is—there will be a day of judgment when all the evils of history will be known and punished and all injustices made right. Paul quotes Scripture: "'It is mine to avenge; I will repay,' says the Lord" (Romans 12:19). The God who raised Jesus from the dead will also raise us from the dead. This means that even when justice is denied in this life, as it so often is, there is still hope for the gospel of resurrection in that injustice is always temporary, in that evil had a beginning in the past and will have an end in the future, and in that innocent sufferers in this life will be rewarded in the next. The resurrection makes politics an eternal, rather than a temporal, affair.

The Church after Christendom

The church of Jesus Christ must renounce Christendom and seek to live as a pilgrim people bearing witness to the kingdom of God and proclaiming the resurrection hope of the gospel. Christendom is a declaration of faith in power, violence, and coercion as the only way justice can be done. The state replaces God as the highest authority in the life of the individual, and the church becomes an arm of the state. The problem with Christendom is that the church is gradually absorbed by the state. Karl Barth puts it this way: "Uninterruptedly absorbed in progress toward its own deification, the state feels less and less the need that God should be spoken about. The tasks of popular instruction and education seem to depend less and less on the theologians."[13] In Christendom, the church was gradually drawn into acts of intolerance, pogroms, persecution of heretics, war, inquisition, invasion, murder, theft, and violence in the name of national security. In order to avoid this fate, the church must do five things.

Keep Church and State Separate

Christians should do today what the fourth-century bishops should have done and ensure that church and state are kept separate. In the modern world we think we already have the separation of church and state in most Western nations, but actually we do not. Nation-states are religious entities, even though they are seldom acknowledged as such. Lesslie Newbigin explains:

> The nation-state replaces the holy church and the holy empire as the centerpiece in the post-Enlightenment ordering of society. Upon it devolves the duty of providing the means for life, liberty, and the pursuit of happiness.... If—for modern Western people—nature has taken the place of God as the ultimate reality with which we have to deal, the nation-state has taken the place of God as the source to which we look for happiness, health and welfare.[14]

The nation-state demands the absolute sacrifice from us. Just as Jesus demands that we make ourselves ready to die for him, the nation-state also demands that we make ourselves ready to die for it. But there is a key difference. Although the nation-state also demands that we kill at its command, Jesus does not.

Insofar as the nation-state calls on all citizens to fight in wars at the command of the government, Christians must say no to this demand. Although many Christians give lip service to the just-war theory, hardly anyone puts it into practice. The dominant view of war in our time is the patriotic-duty theory, which says that citizens have an obligation to fight for their nation and that it is up to the rulers to determine the justice of the war. According to the patriotic-duty theory, the Christian is acting in a way pleasing to God if he or she fights, regardless of whether the war is just or unjust. The patriotic-duty theory puts the nation-state in the place that only Jesus Christ can occupy in the life of a Christian. It also makes the nation-state into one's real church and privatizes the faith to such an extent as to nullify the concrete lordship of Christ. Christians are part of nation-states in terms of their earthly citizenship, but their real citizenship is in heaven (Philippians 3:20), and their heavenly citizenship must take precedence whenever there is a clash. Peter confirms

13. Karl Barth, *Church Dogmatics* I/2 (trans. Geoffrey W. Bromiley et al.; ed. Geoffrey W. Bromiley and Thomas F. Torrance; Edinburgh: T & T Clark, 1957–77), 759.

14. Lesslie Newbigin, *Foolishness to the Greeks: The Gospel and Western Culture* (Grand Rapids: Eerdmans, 1986), 27.

this: "Judge for yourselves whether it is right in God's sight to obey you rather than God" (Acts 4:19).

Follow Jesus in Rejecting Violence

Christians must follow Jesus in the rejection of violence as the solution to the problems of life. This has broader ramifications than just refusing to take part in war. It means rejecting and opposing the so-called culture of death in all its forms and espousing a consistent ethic of life. To follow Jesus means very concretely to step into the struggle between the demonic forces that drive human beings to believe the lie that violence solves problems and to witness to the truth—that violence solves nothing. Whether it is a matter of an unplanned pregnancy, the invasion of a nation, the punishment of criminals, or the care of the dying, to kill is always the temptation, but never the way Jesus calls us to go.

The church knows that it has succumbed to worldliness whenever it crosses the line that marks off the taking of human life. This should be our guideline to what kinds of practices, institutions, and vocations we as Christians can be involved in. From the very earliest days of the church it was clear that, in order to become members of the church, seekers would need to abandon certain professions. The only debate in church history has been over which ones are on the list. One of the problems in Christendom has been that, in order to bless the social order and hallow the state, the church has been tempted to put its seal of approval on all professions, even ones that go against Jesus's commands, such as executioner, soldier, and abortionist. The church may not be able to convince the majority in a democracy that abortion should be banned, but the church can insist that no unrepentant abortionist be counted among the faithful. The church may not be able to stop war, but the church can ensure that those who profit from war are challenged to choose between their church membership and their business opportunities.

Rejecting violence and following Jesus means drawing visible lines between the church and the world. The point is not that the church is made up of perfect people who never sin, but rather that it is made up of sinners who confess their sin and seek forgiveness. The issue is not self-righteousness, but precisely the opposite: self-condemnation and testimony that the Lord alone is righteous.

Renounce Natural Theology

The church needs to renounce natural theology and make use of the God's self-revelation in Jesus Christ, as attested in the Holy Scriptures, as the criterion of all truth. Constantine wanted to create a civil religion that is extremely similar to the contemporary civil religion of the United States. It was a vague monotheism that deemphasized Jesus and the Bible in favor of general doctrines of providence and that moved the empire/nation-state into the place of the church. A respectable, rational religion is what he wanted—one that blesses and hallows the state and has no prophetic edge. That is what rulers always want. From the ancient kings of Israel to the Roman emperors to modern politicians—everyone wants tame court prophets who preach a message of how God has elected and blessed this nation for special things. Barth asks the question of why natural theology has persisted so stubbornly throughout church history, in spite of all that can be said against it from a biblical perspective, and he comes up with this answer:

> The triumph of natural theology in the Church, described as the absorbing and domesticating of revelation, is very clearly the process of making the Gospel respectable. When the Gospel is offered to man, and he stretches out his hand to receive it and takes it into his hand, an acute danger arises which is greater than the danger that the man not understand it and angrily reject it. The danger is that he may accept it peacefully and at once make himself its lord and possessor, thus rendering it innocuous, making that which chooses him something which he himself has chosen, which therefore comes to stand as such alongside all the other things that he can also choose, and therefore control.[15]

Barth here names the theological source of the political danger of natural theology: the danger of human beings owning or possessing the gospel and thus domesticating it for their own selfish purposes.

Challenge the Powers

Only when the church abandons the project of natural theology is the gospel unleashed in all its power. Only then can the church name, unmask, and denounce the powers. The term *the powers* is shorthand for what the apostle Paul calls "authorities," "powers," "principalities," and "thrones" (e.g., 1 Corinthians 15:24; Ephesians 3:10; Philippians 2:10–11; Colossians 1:16). New Testament scholars debate whether supernatural, personal, demonic forces or simply human social, economic, and political forces are in view here.[16] But a third approach sees these forces as more than human, yet not simply demons. There is a sense in which institutions, revolutions, and ideologies can pass from the control of human beings and take on a life of their own. The powers can become demonic, as in the case of the ideology of Marxist-Leninism in Stalin's Soviet Union, yet the difficulty with calling them demons is that government, for example, is not simply and totally evil. Even evil governments often provide peace and order. The

---

15. Barth, *Church Dogmatics* II/1, 141.

16. See G. B. Caird, *Principalities and Powers: A Study in Pauline Theology* (Eugene, OR: Wipf & Stock, 2003 [orig. 1956]); Hendrikus Berkhof, *Christ and the Powers* (trans. John Howard Yoder; Scottdale, PA: Herald, 1977); John Howard Yoder, *The Politics of Jesus: Vicit Agnus Noster* (2nd ed.; Grand Rapids: Eerdmans, 1994), chap. 8; and the trilogy by Walter Wink: *Naming the Powers: The Language of Power in the New Testament* (Philadelphia: Fortress, 1984); *Unmasking the Powers: The Invisible Forces That Determine Human Existence* (Philadelphia: Fortress, 1986); and *Engaging the Powers: Discernment and Resistance in a World of Domination* (Philadelphia: Fortress, 1992).

powers are not simply demonic and not simply human; they are what Barth calls "the lordless powers"—created aspects of the world that have been created good by God, but that have been caught up in the rebellion of the world against God and thus spiraled out of control.[17]

The problem with all natural theology is that it is based on reading God's intentions for creation from the observation of fallen human beings and the lordless powers. This means that natural theology cannot be trusted as the foundation of our understanding of right and wrong or the will of God. Only revelation can be trusted as the source of truth, and so theology becomes an act of prayer as we submit our minds to the influence of the Holy Spirit as we study the Holy Scriptures. Natural theology tends to be inherently conservative, so far as the established social order is concerned. To mount a challenge to the powers, it is necessary to move beyond natural theology and root our theology in revelation.

Learn to Think Like Jews Instead of Like Romans

The church needs to learn survival skills from the Jews. One of the most ironic facts about the history of Christendom is that the majority of Jews rejected Jesus as messiah and then went on to live a lifestyle that largely conformed to the lifestyle Jesus laid out for his followers in the Sermon on the Mount. Up until the Enlightenment, the Jews of Europe were resident aliens and pacifists. They lived in communities (ghettos) in which they cared for one another and took care of widows, orphans, and the poor. They were persecuted by the world and hated because they remained faithful to God and Torah. On the other hand, the Christians, who professed to accept Jesus as messiah, lived like Gentiles and persecuted the Jews. Christians fought their enemies, immersed themselves in the power struggles of the world, and lorded it over others just like Roman emperors. Of course, one could argue that the Jews were powerless by no choice of their own and that their adoption of a pacifist, minority stance was a matter of survival rather than virtue. Still, they did survive, and that seems to be the point that is often overlooked when people claim that the way of Jesus is unrealistic.

All that I wish to claim here is that the Jews are living proof that it is possible to be the kind of community that Jesus founded and commanded his disciples to be. They lived for two and a half millennia (from the sixth-century BC exile to the twentieth century AD) surrounded by pagans but never losing their faith, their identity, and their hope. They were a wandering people: often expelled, often on the move to escape persecution. They established urban networks and helped each other in amazing ways. They mixed in with the nations in some ways but maintained visible differences as well. Christians need to learn to live in these ways, giving a witness to Jesus Christ rather than simply being absorbed into the nation-states we temporarily call home. We need to learn from the Jews the secrets of surviving

17. Karl Barth, *Church Dogmatics: Lecture Fragments* (trans. G. W. Bromiley; Grand Rapids: Eerdmans, 1981), 213–33.

in a pagan environment without becoming completely isolated, yet without losing our identity.

Christendom marginalized Jesus, put the state in the place of the church, and replaced the clarity of revelation with the mists and fog of natural theology. Christendom was a reversion to the ancient Israelite monarchy, rather than a messianic community witnessing to the lordship of Jesus Christ. Christendom was a bad idea. Thankfully, it is now over, although its vestiges will take centuries to fade away. The church, however, is far from dead. The center of Christian faith has moved to the southern hemisphere, and the church is growing rapidly in Africa and gaining strength in Latin America. The challenge in the global village of the twenty-first century is to figure out how to be the church that Jesus wants us to be after Christendom.

Part 2

A Post-Christendom Typology
of Christ and Culture

Blessed are you when people insult you, persecute you and falsely say all kinds of evil against you because of me. Rejoice and be glad, because great is your reward in heaven, for in the same way they persecuted the prophets who were before you.

Matthew 5:11–12

There is only one relation to revealed truth: believing it. The fact that one believes can only be proved in one way: by being willing to suffer for one's faith. And the degree of one's faith is proved only by the degree of one's willingness to suffer for one's faith.

Søren Kierkegaard, *Attack Upon Christendom*

The real *civitas dei* on earth, which is invincible, and can therefore be proclaimed with confidence, is not the rule of the Church, but the rule of Him who in this world had to be nailed to the cross. . . . Obedience to this cannot mean a triumph at the point where prophets and apostles were defeated and slain and where Jesus died on the cross.

Karl Barth, *Church Dogmatics*

It is often said that the failure of the Western churches is of the first kind: irrelevance, failure to make contact. I want to suggest, on the contrary, that it is a failure of the second kind, that the Christian churches of the West have been so co-opted into our culture that we have lost the power to challenge it.

Lesslie Newbigin, *Signs amid the Rubble*

6

Introducing a Post-Christendom Typology of Christ and Culture

As I argued in part 1, the root problem with Niebuhr's typology is that it presupposes both the existence and legitimacy of Christendom. However, both his criticism of the Christ against culture type and his endorsement of the Christ transforming culture type lose their cogency in our post-Christendom context. Not only does he assume that the church should make the compromises necessary to retain influence with the culture, he also assumes that the wider culture is ready and willing to be transformed by Christians. Both assumptions are highly dubious in the post-Christendom context. We have examined examples in which Christians who challenge entrenched cultural practices can be persecuted by the wider society to the point where it can fairly be said that culture is against Christ (a type Niebuhr never considers). There always has been and always will be cultural pressure on the church to compromise and to deny the lordship of Jesus Christ. The problem with Niebuhr's approach is that it leads to Christians accommodating themselves to the society around them. That was bad enough in a Christendom society that was supposedly Christian, but in a post-Christendom society that is increasingly non-Christian it is a recipe for Christianity losing its biblical and historical identity completely.

What would a post-Christendom typology look like? What, exactly, would it mean to remove Christendom as the basic assumption? In this chapter, I propose that the church joining in state-sponsored violent coercion of heretics and other enemies of the state is a key sign that a Christendom mentality is at work. The sword will always be utilized by the state, whether Christians like it or not. But the variable is the degree to which the church identifies itself with the state and whether the church actually justifies, endorses, or joins in state-sponsored violence. The sword is for the state; the church renounces all swords except the sword of the Spirit, which is the Word of God.

In the last chapter, we saw that the bishops of the fourth century compromised the unique identity of the church when they allowed it to be coopted by the emperor for his own political purposes and made into the religious arm of the empire. The state persecution of heretics led to a false ecclesial *unity* based on state coercion and political considerations. The church of the martyrs became the church of the persecutors, which compromised the *holiness* of the church. The *catholicity* of the church was compromised by the provincialism of the church becoming the court religion of the Roman emperors, which led to the persecution of Christians in Persia. Finally, we saw that the failure of the bishops to preach the gospel to Constantine represented a failure of the church to be truly *apostolic*. A new typology of Christ and culture should aid us in the task of discerning how the church can engage culture without compromising its unity, holiness, catholicity, and apostolicity.

In response to these failures, I suggested that the church today needs to keep church and state separate, follow Jesus in rejecting violence, renounce natural theology, challenge the powers, and learn to think like Jews instead of Romans. In analyzing the problem of how to conceptualize the essence of these five mandates, I have come to believe that the core issue is the temptation to join the state in violent coercion. This is always a central temptation, and when the church endorses, requests, or joins in violent coercion with the state, it is utilizing a Christendom strategy—it is presupposing Christendom. When it refuses to be coopted into rationalizing violent coercion, the church retains its integrity and maintains a distance from the state sufficient to keep its own separate identity from being absorbed into that of the state. Engaging culture is not a bad thing, but becoming worldly is. So the question is this: How can the church influence culture and avoid becoming violent? How can the church be in, but not of, the world?

Violent Coercion and the Church-World Distinction

The typology introduced here distinguishes between Christendom and non-Christendom types of solutions to the problem of Christ and culture by separating those that accept the necessity of the church endorsing, requesting, or joining in violent coercion from those that do not (see table 2). Types 1–3 are Christendom types, and types 4–6 are non-Christendom types. This way of looking at the problem avoids forcing all people and movements who reject violence into one mold. It also demonstrates that approaches that reject violence can be as transformational as the ones that employ or sanction it.

Table 2. Post-Christendom Typology of Christ and Culture

	Christendom Types (accept violent coercion)			Non-Christendom Types (reject violent coercion)		
	Type 1: Christ legitimizing culture	Type 2: Christ humanizing culture	Type 3: Christ transforming culture	Type 4: Christ transforming culture	Type 5: Christ humanizing culture	Type 6: Christ separating from culture
Examples	• Theodosius I • Crusades • German Christians	• Luther • pietism • revivalism • Billy Graham	• Augustine • Columbus • Cromwell	• William Penn • Martin Luther King Jr. • Desmond Tutu	• Mother Teresa • Mennonite Central Committee • Brethren in Christ	• Antony of Egypt • Benedictines • Amish
View of Christ	symbol of ruling powers of society	unattainable yet relevant ideal	Lord of the cosmos	Lord of the cosmos	unattainable yet relevant ideal	Lord of the church
Biblical support	• conquest of Canaan under Joshua	• NT call to personal faith in Jesus (John 1:12; 3:16)	• Colossians 1:15–20 • OT Israel as theocracy	• Colossians 1:15–20 • Sermon on the Mount	• Jesus's parable of sheep and goats • early church in Acts	• OT exilic community • Revelation
Teaching of Jesus	denial of, even while using Christ as a cultic symbol to unify society	applicable only to private life (person/vocation dualism)	for all society and therefore should be imposed by force if necessary	for all society but should not be imposed by force, but preached by word and deed	for the church only, but motivates loving service to society	for the church only
Christology	docetic	partially docetic	inconsistently Nicene	Nicene	Nicene	Nicene

Duane Friesen proposes an alternative typology to Niebuhr's in an article entitled "A Discriminating Engagement of Culture."[1] Building on John Howard Yoder's critique of Niebuhr, he proposes a sixfold typology of church and society. His typology is similar to mine in some ways and different in others. He speaks of "church and culture," while I follow Niebuhr in speaking of "Christ and culture." He divides his typology into what he calls the "church as an alternative cultural model to the dominant culture" (non-Constantinian stream) and the "church in collaboration with the dominant institutions of society" (Constantinian stream). This approach avoids Niebuhr's error of lumping a whole array of different approaches to the relationship of Christ and culture into the "against" category and exposes the Constantinian presuppositions driving Niebuhr's book.

1. Duane K. Friesen, "A Discriminating Engagement of Culture: An Anabaptist Perspective," *Journal of the Society of Christian Ethics* 21 (2003): 145–56.

My typology follows Friesen's lead at this point. However, I differ from Friesen in that I am not willing to label my approach "an Anabaptist perspective." I want to position myself within the mainstream theological tradition as a Nicene theologian who acknowledges that the Anabaptists have sometimes been more truly Nicene in their emphasis on the lordship of Christ than those who most loudly proclaim their fidelity to Nicea. Unlike Friesen, I wish to trace various approaches to the problem of Christ and culture back to christological convictions and in so doing expose the non-Nicene nature of Christendom (or what he calls Constantinianism).

Violent coercion is the key to dividing Christendom from non-Christendom types because it at this point that the dividing line between the church and the world is either maintained or blurred. For the church to embrace violent coercion is for it to become worldly and to obscure the church-world distinction, which is crucial for evangelism and missions. This is also the key point of testing in whether or not the church will follow its Lord in the path of suffering service; that is, discipleship. The rejection of violent coercion is what it means to heed the call of Jesus to "take up your cross and follow me." The cross is the alternative to the sword, which is why it was such a perversion for Christendom to put the cross on its shields and banners as a symbol of war. Jesus rejected the zealot option, the pressure on him to be a military messiah who would drive out the Romans and mount the throne of Israel in Jerusalem. Jesus knew that this way had been tried before and would not work; evil must be challenged at a more fundamental level. So he allowed the principalities and powers to put him to death and then rose in triumph, putting their defeat on display for all to see. He chose the path of suffering violence, rather than inflicting it, and calls his disciples to do the same. And he offers us the hope of resurrection after the suffering of the cross.

The followers of Jesus make up the church, the body of Christ, and are thereby a distinct society in tension with the world. The existence of the church as church makes it possible for the world to know itself as the world; that is, as unredeemed and in need of grace. The existence of the church and the world makes conversion possible; that is, passing from one to the other by an act of faith in Jesus Christ and commitment to following him (baptism). The gospel cannot be experienced as good news unless response is voluntary, and it cannot be experienced as a concrete claim on our lives without the possibility of church membership, which is differentiated from citizenship.

In viewing the acceptance or rejection of violent coercion as a major dividing line between types, I actually am in agreement with Niebuhr. He puts Tertullian into the Christ against culture type—despite his education, his career as a lawyer, and his theological influence on the catholic church's development of the doctrine of the Trinity—for only one reason: he rejected military service for Christians. Niebuhr apparently sensed that to refuse to join in state-sanctioned violence creates a gulf between the person and the state, which prevents a complete harmony with the culture. A key difference in my proposed new typology is that the Christ against culture type is expanded into three distinct ways of relating to culture without taking up the sword.

There is no doubt that any Christian who denies the right of the state to order him or her to kill whenever the state orders him or her to do so is thereby denying the lordship of Caesar. Christendom has been a search for a way to confess the lordship of Christ without denying the lordship of Caesar, but this is impossible when it comes right down to the brutal matter of taking human life. Since culture consists of citizens who are acknowledging the lordship of Caesar, this means that there is a separation or a gulf between the one who acknowledges the lordship of Jesus and other citizens. As much as the advocates of Christendom wish it were so, it is just not the case that one can simultaneously confess both Jesus and Caesar as Lord.

This is not the case only with absolute pacifists. If the just war theory is taken seriously as a guide to Christian discipleship, then it effectively dethrones Caesar and puts Jesus above the state. Assuming that the purpose of the just-war theory is to determine whether Christians can participate in a given war (which not everyone would admit), the just-war theory is just as politically subversive as pacifism and, in some ways, even more so. The just-war theorist who reserves the right to refuse participation in unjust wars is implicitly rejecting the absolute lordship of the state and exalting Jesus to a status above the state. The state may be able to tolerate the pacifist who refuses to fight because of a religious conviction that all war is evil, but the person who says that violence is sometimes a justified last resort, but not in this case, is an even greater threat to the sovereignty of the state. The state needs to be able to presume that in time of war it can mobilize the full strength of its population to fight. This is seen as the basis for national security, both in terms of actual fighting strength and also in terms of morale and national unity. If individual citizens challenge the right of rulers to make decisions regarding going to war, then the power of the state is undermined and the ability of the state to deter would-be aggressors and to cow other states that resist its policies is in question. This is why conscientious objectors can be assigned noncombat service, but just-war theorists who refuse to take part in an unjust war are usually jailed.

These reflections bring to light the considerable confusion about the proper Christian attitude toward war in the modern church. The confusion begins with the categories: just war, crusade, and pacifism. Often it is thought that the largest divide is between pacifists and everyone else, but I contend that the largest divide is between pacifists and those who take the just-war theory seriously as a guide to discipleship on the one hand and everyone else on the other hand. In the Roman Catholic Church, pacifism is required of the clergy and of all those who choose a religious life (i.e., monks and nuns), while the laity is allowed to fight in wars only under certain conditions. Outside the Roman Catholic Church, pacifism is the official position of the historic peace churches (Brethren, Mennonite, and

Quaker), but most other denominations accept war as a regrettable necessity and bless their members' participation in it. Most Christians today reject the crusade as an appropriate Christian approach to war, although in times of war we note that crusade language quickly creeps into Christian discourse. When challenged, most Christians who participate in war tend to fall back on the just-war theory.

The just-war theory seems to function in two distinct ways. On the one hand, it serves as a blanket justification for war for the vast majority of Christians. All they seem to hear from their religious leaders is that war is sometimes justifiable, and from that point on the whole issue revolves around whether one's country is going to war. The usual assumption is that if one's country does go to war, it is an individual's moral duty to fight regardless of his or her personal belief that war is the best course of action in this situation. Of course, ethics textbooks indicate that there is far more to the just-war theory than this stripped-down version. But one would never know that from an examination of sermons, Christian education materials, articles, editorials, speeches, and so on. We need to distinguish between the just-war theory of the textbooks and the just-war theory of church practice.

Leaving the crusade category aside, as a clearly sub-Christian view of war, we can clarify our understanding of the real beliefs of modern Christians about war by distinguishing between at least three different forms that the just-war theory takes in the modern world.[2] First is what could be called the "academic just-war theory." This is a philosophical theory that functions in the world of universities, military academies, and law courts. Its purpose is to distinguish between relatively more and relatively less civilized methods of making war and to nudge political and military leaders toward a more humane and civilized approach to war wherever possible. The moral actor it has in mind is not the Christian, but the political and military leaders who make war.

Second is the "discipleship just-war theory." This is an honest attempt to use the just-war theory to evaluate the moral choices facing Christians in a time of war so as to determine whether a Christian should participate in a given war. It is important to see that this is not the purpose of the academic just-war theory, which is not focused on participation or nonparticipation, but only on mitigating the worst features of a war that is seen as inevitable. The discipleship just-war theory is something that a few individual Christians and pastors wrestle with, but it is not usually taken seriously by denominational leaders. During the twentieth century there was some attempt by the Roman Catholic Church and by a few Protestant denominations to address the morality of nuclear war, but even here it was assumed that war itself is both inevitable and morally supportable. The recent stand of Pope John Paul II against the American war on Iraq is a rare and courageous stand taken on the basis of the discipleship just-war theory, for which we should

---

2. My thinking about the categories of justifiable war has been stimulated greatly by John Howard Yoder's analysis of the just-war theory in *When War Is Unjust: Being Honest in Just-War Thinking* (Minneapolis: Augsburg, 1984). My categories do not exactly mirror his, however.

give thanks. But the degree to which American Catholics have ignored the clear moral teaching of the united voice of their bishops in this matter demonstrates the higher loyalty that many American Catholics feel toward the United States, as compared to their loyalty to their church. Very few Catholics refused to fight in Iraq, even though the just-war criteria clearly demonstrated that this was an unjust war and that their pastors clearly said so.[3]

This brings us to the third form of the just-war theory, which could fittingly be called the patriotic-duty theory. This is a popular-level moral and political theory that functions in the public square. Its purpose is to rouse popular support for the nation's war effort and to reassure ordinary people (both Christian and non-Christian) that their participation in the brutal matter of killing their fellow human beings is a noble and unselfish act of loyalty to their nation, tribe, state, empire, or civilization, as the case may be. The patriotic-duty theory says that it is the national leaders' responsibility to decide whether war is just in a given situation. It is the individual citizen's duty to fight for his or her country when called upon to do so. The individual is morally praiseworthy or blameworthy depending on how faithful he or she is to doing his or her duty. But questioning the moral judgment of the nation's leaders is not the duty of the individual citizen.

A major source of confusion is the lumping of all three attitudes toward war under one label: the just-war theory. The patriotic-duty theory removes the duty of making moral judgments from the church and gives it over to the state. This has the practical effect of allowing the state to determine what is morally acceptable for the church. Once it has been conceded that the abstract possibility of war in general is morally supportable, the specific decision of whether a particular war is morally supportable is removed from the purview of the church. This means that the lordship of Jesus has been ceded to Caesar on this particular (and very important) moral issue (see table 3).

The patriotic-duty theory is frequently used to justify the duty of soldiers on both sides to fight in the same war against each other. But how can a war be just for both sides—for both the aggressor and the side defending itself? This stretches the terminology too far. If a war is just because it involves repelling the aggressive invasion of one's country by another country, how can it be just for the soldiers involved in doing the invading? If it was just for the Poles in 1939, then it must have been unjust for the Germans. To use the just-war theory to justify both sides of a war is to empty the concept of what many people unreflectively think it contains; namely, a moral judgment that one is doing the right thing and opposing injustice by fighting in a given war. If one side is unjust, one cannot be doing the right thing by supporting it, unless the just-war language is merely rhetoric or propaganda, as one fears it very often is in wartime. It would be clearer and more

---

3. See William T. Cavanaugh, "At Odds with the Pope: Legitimate Authority and Just Wars," GodSpy: Faith at the Edge website: http://godspy.com/faith/At-odds-with-the-pope-legitimate-authority-and-just-wars.cfm (accessed August 20, 2005).

Table 3. Christian Attitudes to War

Theory	Description	Adherents
Academic just-war theory	Academic, theoretical, legal-philosophical form of discourse. Purpose is to mitigate the violence and injustice associated with war-making where and when possible. Does not usually penetrate to the popular level. Taught to military officers, but penalties for not following it strictly are often not enforced after the fact.	• Oliver O'Donovan • Michael Walzer
Patriotic-duty theory	Popular discourse in newspapers, school textbooks, churches. Associated particularly with military ceremonies and Memorial Day events. Purpose is to build up patriotism through civil religion by glorifying killing and dying for one's country. Responsibility for determining the morality of a given war is moved from the church to the state.	• George Weigel • Billy Graham
Discipleship just-war theory (practical pacifism)	Theological and ethical discourse usually more academic than popular. Used by scholars who regard the just-war theory as a guide to Christian discipleship. Does not usually penetrate to the level of sermons, Sunday school, catechism classes, small-group Bible studies, but in theory it should.	• Karl Barth • Pope John Paul II
Pacifism	Theological and ethical discourse used at both the academic and popular levels within the historic peace churches, but in very few other places in society.	• John Howard Yoder • Stanley Hauerwas

honest to use the term *patriotic-duty theory* instead of *just-war theory* in most of the contexts in which the just-war theory is discussed.

The discipleship just-war theory is a possible form of Christian discipleship. Although I am personally a pacifist and think that pacifism is biblically justified, I can see that a conscientious application of the discipleship just-war theory would result in what Karl Barth calls "practical pacifism" and would bring its practitioner extremely close to my position.[4] As a pacifist, I can disagree with my fellow Christians' assessments of the morality of war as a last resort in a given tragic situation without questioning his or her sincere desire to follow Jesus as Lord. The academic just-war theory also probably has a place, as long as one does not hope for too much from it or confuse it with Christian morality. One can only hope and pray that the nations of the world would attempt to mitigate the worst effects of their war-making. But the patriotic-duty theory of war is wrong and inadequate as a path of Christian discipleship. It clashes forcefully with the Christian commitment to the lordship of Jesus Christ.

What I want to stress here is that the common factor between a strict discipleship just-war theory and pacifism is that the state's claim on my obedience is made

---

4. This was Barth's position on war; see *Church Dogmatics* III/4 (trans. Geoffrey W. Bromiley et al.; ed. Geoffry W. Bromiley and Thomas F. Torrance; Edinburgh: T & T Clark, 1957–77), 450–70. See John Howard Yoder's study of Barth's approach to war: *Karl Barth and the Problem of War and Other Essays on Barth* (ed. Mark Thiessen Nation; Eugene, OR: Cascade, 2003).

subservient to the lordship of Jesus Christ. There must always be a presumption against violence for the Christian, and whether we say that there are no exceptions or only a few, in both theories the authority of the state to order Christians to kill is undermined in some instances. The issue is whether Jesus is concretely Lord. Unfortunately, history shows that it is probably unrealistic to expect Christians to practice the discipleship just-war theory as a guide to Christian participation or nonparticipation in war. Hardly any nonpacifist Christians actually refuse to fight even in unjust wars.[5] The patriotic-duty theory of war appears to be well entrenched in the nonpacifist churches, and it apparently rules the actions of the vast majority of Christians in times of war.

The patriotic-duty theory of war, I suggest, makes sense only within a Christendom mindset and needs to be set aside now that Christendom is over. The assumptions in the development of the patriotic-duty theory were that the rulers are just as much Christians as the pastors and theologians and that the rulers have access to more relevant facts about the situation than do those outside of government. It is claimed that the informed Christian ruler should make the decision, assuming that Christian rulers would not knowingly violate Christian morality in this important matter. But if a ruler is caught up in a system that requires violence and depends on violence, then the personal morality of the ruler will not determine what takes place. In fact, if a Christian president of the United States failed to act to defend the interests of the United States by authorizing the use of military force, how long would that person remain in office? Depending on how serious and imminent the threat was, the president might be voted out of office or even in an extreme situation deposed. The president takes an oath to defend the Constitution of the United States, and this is usually interpreted as defending the country's interests in general. So there is some logic to saying, "If you don't want to do the job, don't apply for it." This raises the serious question of whether a Christian can be the leader of a modern nation-state in good conscience. But it also shows that just being a Christian, as far as one's personal beliefs go, should not be overestimated as a guide to how that person will be different once in office in a democratic political system. It is very different from the historical situation when the ruler was a hereditary monarch who was deemed to own the realm and was seen as put there by God. When the people put you there to do a job for them, it is quite a different matter.

In a post-Christendom situation, it is even more incumbent on those who advocated the patriotic-duty theory to rethink their position. Christians killing at the command of pagan rulers and thinking themselves automatically justified, even if the war is unjust, clearly involves Christians in the service of other gods (i.e., the gods worshiped by those rulers). How can we place decisions about what is moral and immoral in the hands of those who do not even profess to believe in Jesus Christ and biblical morality? And how can we place such decisions in

5. The latter stages of the Vietnam War perhaps constitute the exception that proves the rule.

the hands of those who are not really free to act Christianly under the terms of their oath of office?

The issue at stake here is larger than simply the issue of war and pacifism. While it is true that the types to the right of the dividing line in table 2 are pacifist, they also reject the persecution of heretics and discrimination against non-Christians and maintain a clear distinction between church and state in general. Since violent coercion is at the heart of every human government in a fallen world, a church that refuses to participate in violence will never be able to identify completely with any government, and conversely no government will ever be able to identify completely with such a church. Such a church could never be a department of the state, and it could never even be a state church. A church that refuses to participate in killing people will never be viewed as being patriotic enough to be endorsed by the state without qualification. Such a church will always have a somewhat alien character as far as the state is concerned, it will always place a question mark beside the actions of the state.

Since it will be impossible for a church that rejects violence ever to merge with the state, there will be no confusion of the distinct nature and task of the church with those of the state. The state will not do evangelism, and the church will not provide rationalizations for state behavior, which involves breaking Jesus's commands yet seems (to the state) to be necessary for national security. The church will be free to preach the gospel, and the state will not pretend to have any role in preaching the gospel except to ensure that the church is free to do it. The state is responsible for maintaining justice and public order. Individuals should be free to accept or reject the Christian message without thereby gaining or losing their status as citizens of the state.

The New Testament clearly expects that disciples of Jesus who bear a clear and consistent witness to his lordship will not be embraced completely by the world. Sometimes there will merely be tension between the church and the society in which it is embedded. Sometimes there will be milder forms of persecution such as discrimination or mockery. Sometimes there will be violent persecution resulting in imprisonment and even martyrdom for Christians. This tension between church and world is not pleasant for the church, and it is not desirable in and of itself (Christians are not masochistic), but it is a necessary condition for carrying out the church's mission in the world (Christians are realistic).

The visible church-world distinction is absolutely necessary for the preaching of the gospel. The gospel cannot be preached faithfully if it is privatized and turned into a purely internal matter of one's inner disposition toward God. The gospel requires public discipleship; it calls men and women to follow Jesus in the way of peace in the context of the kingdom of God. Without a church to enter, full conversion is impossible. And without a church-world distinction, there is no visible church. The core of Christian discipleship, according to the New Testament, is acknowledging the cosmic lordship of Jesus, a lordship that comes into direct conflict with the absolute claims of modern nation-states, just as it used to come into conflict with the absolute claims of monarchs. In the ancient church, the focal issue was the question of whether Christians would burn a pinch of incense to Caesar, thus acknowledging his claims to divinity and therefore indicating the unquestioning obedience of the citizen. The modern equivalent is the claim of the modern nation-state to have the right to demand of its citizens that those citizens kill enemies of the state in the name of national security. This puts the state above morality and makes its will absolute in much the same way as did the ancient claim that the emperor is divine. The issue of violent coercion was at the center of the process by which Christendom came into existence in the third to fifth centuries, and it is still central to differentiating between Christendom and non-Christendom ways of relating Christ and culture today.

Description of the Types

The result of Niebuhr's failure to distinguish between Christendom and non-Christendom approaches to the problem of Christ and culture was that all those movements that reject violent coercion are dismissed as being "against culture," when in reality there is a wide range of cultural engagement or nonengagement within such movements. In the context of Christendom, any church that does not join the state in violence is labeled as being against culture and therefore irresponsible and irrelevant. By lumping all the non-Christendom types together into one, Niebuhr makes it easy to dismiss them all as irrelevant and irresponsible simply by highlighting the weaknesses of the weakest examples, as if they implicated all the people and movements that Niebuhr chose to put into this category. All the reasonable choices thus appear to presuppose some form of Christendom, which means that the legitimacy of Christendom cannot be challenged within Niebuhr's typology. This typology makes it clear that the church always has a range of both Christendom and non-Christendom choices in all cultural situations. The church often has rejected violence and yet still engaged culture in highly creative and important ways.

At one extreme (type 1), the church takes over power in society completely, and Christ becomes the legitimating symbol of the social powers that be. At the other extreme (type 6), the church withdraws from (or is pushed out of) the center of society and becomes an alternative community, in which case Christ is viewed as Lord of the church. There are, it must be stressed, no pure types, and all examples are only impure incarnations of them. There never has been any Christian community completely cut off from culture; in fact, the world frequently has beaten a path to the door of monastic communities, from the Dark Ages to the present. On the other hand, Christianity has never been completely and totally reduced to a political symbol of power and coercion even in the midst of the most horrible and shameful episodes of Western imperialism and conquest. Faithful missionaries ministered to, defended, and loved the native peoples of North America even while invasion, conquest, and genocide were occurring (e.g., the case of Bartolomé de Las Casas noted in chapter 4).

The proposed post-Christendom typology shows that a similar range of engagement is possible by those movements that reject violence as well as by those that embrace it. Both Christendom and non-Christendom approaches can be described as humanizing and both can be described as transforming. The Christendom humanizing type (type 2) focuses on individuals and humanizes through sensitizing individuals to the ideal of Christian love and hoping that indirectly some restraints will be imposed on power politics (e.g., by means of the honesty of Christian politicians), while the non-Christendom one (type 5) also focuses on individuals but works primarily through social service rather than through politics. In both of these types, Christ is seen as an unattainable yet relevant ideal. But for the Christendom type, this ideal is unattainable for both Christians and non-Christians, while in the non-Christendom type, the ideal is attainable for Christian communities but not for the world.

The only difference between the Christendom transforming type (type 3) and the non-Christendom one (type 4) is that the latter rejects violent coercion as a method of transforming society. Both types affirm the cosmic lordship of Jesus Christ. When examples of the two transforming types are studied side by side, it is not at all obvious that type 3 is actually any more effective in changing society than is type 4. Despite its renunciation in advance of any recourse to violent coercion, type 4 has exerted great influence on Western society down through the centuries. Thus, the division of the transforming type into two distinct types accounts for a major anomaly in his theory, which Niebuhr himself recognized, namely, that radical Christians throughout the centuries have transformed society, even though that was seldom their primary goal. He puts it this way: "In social reform they accomplish what they did not intend" (67). Recognizing that transformation of society occurs through the witness of both Christendom and non-Christendom movements helps clarify both the history and the options facing the church today.

Biblical Basis

All of these types claim some degree of foundation in the biblical text. Type 1, Christ legitimizing culture, claims the precedent of the invasion of Canaan as an example of God approving violent aggression. The Crusaders claimed to be doing God's work as they persecuted Jews and annihilated Muslims.

Type 2, Christ humanizing culture, emphasizes the New Testament call to personal faith in Jesus Christ within a Christendom context. From the Magisterial Reformers to the pietistic and revivalist traditions to Rudolf Bultmann and Billy Graham, this individualistic interpretation of the Christian life has flourished both in liberal democracies and in totalitarian states. The belief is that when individuals are converted, they will provide a "salting" effect as individuals working within the structures of society, even though they continue to live by the rules of society, including the utilization of violence.

Type 3, Christ transforming culture, tends to equate Christendom with the Old Testament theocracy of Israel. The precedents of God being with the kings of Israel when they exhibited faithfulness to Torah is invoked as a basis for assuming that God will bless conquest undertaken in the name of Jesus. Thus the Spanish conquistadors claimed that evangelizing the aboriginal peoples of the New World was justification for conquest, genocide, torture, and theft.

Type 4, Christ transforming culture, rejects Christendom and bases itself in the Sermon on the Mount and the preaching of Jesus concerning the kingdom of God and the Year of Jubilee. Both transforming types (3 and 4) would also typically appeal to the New Testament's proclamation of the cosmic lordship of Jesus Christ as exemplified in Colossians 1:15–20. They disagree on whether this lordship should be witnessed to by the use of violence by Christians in this present age. The difference between type 4 and type 3 is that in type 4, transformation occurs through witness, persuasion, and nonviolent political action. With regard to slavery and race issues in the United States, the Civil War is an example of type 3, while the early civil-rights movement, a century later, is an example of type 4.

Type 5, Christ humanizing culture, bases itself on passages such as Jesus's parable of the sheep and goats in Matthew 25 and looks to the example of the apostolic church in the early chapters of the book of Acts and the ministry of Paul for validation of its sense of call to serve the sick, weak, prisoners, and poor. Pietism, which could be considered an example of either type 2 or type 5, emphasizes services, such as schools and hospitals, as well as personal conversion. The only difference between the movements mentioned in type 2 and those in type 5 is that those in type 2 sanction the use of violence. Thus, the concept of a pietist chaplain in an army is perfectly consistent, whereas type 5 movements typically operate outside military structures. The call to offer the cup of cold water in Jesus's name is seen as the uniquely Christian form of ministry.

Type 6, Christ separating from culture, would resonate with the book of Revelation and its apocalyptic imagery and sense of conflict between the church and the world. Some Roman Catholic monastic orders fit here, but not those with a highly developed sense of mission to the world, such as Dominicans, Jesuits, and so on. The desert fathers and some orders that have a nearly exclusive focus on the salvation of the souls of their members also fit here, as do some branches of the Anabaptist movement, such as the Amish.

Just because all the types appeal to the Bible in some way, however, does not necessarily mean that all have an equally solid exegetical basis in Scripture. In many cases, the Christendom context in which the exegesis was done seemingly influenced the interpretation. We need to reexamine several biblical passages and themes in a post-Christendom context in order to see if interpretations of certain passages need to be reworked. We cannot conclude merely because a type appeals to Scripture that it therefore has a legitimate basis in Scripture.

Life and Teachings of Jesus

Each type relates to the life and teachings of Jesus in its own way. The three Christendom types need to find ways to affirm the authority of Christ without actually following his teachings. The life and teachings of Jesus are regarded as irrelevant by the Christ legitimizing culture type (type 1). The teachings of Jesus are replaced (by, for example, muscular Christianity), and the Christ of the Gospels is replaced (by, for example, the Aryan Christ). In the Reformation (type 2), which saw a revival of personal faith in Jesus Christ, Christendom was maintained by means of the person/vocation distinction, which allowed people to be committed Christians on the personal level, while still contradicting their discipleship in their public roles as executioners, soldiers, and rulers. In the transforming type (type 3), war in the name of the Prince of Peace causes a confusion of categories. To assert that Jesus is Lord, not just of the inner life of individuals, but of all of society, is biblical, but then to impose the worship of Jesus by force creates a major contradiction. Peace cannot be imposed by force without becoming something other than peace.

By contrast, the life and teachings of Jesus are affirmed as normative by the non-Christendom types. One way to explain the differences in the degree of influence on society is to shift attention from the intention of the Christian communities to the degree of receptivity in the society in which various Christian communities are located. For example, the receptivity of Russian society to Christian influence has undergone a seismic shift during the last third of the twentieth century from the hostility to the church exhibited by the Marxist Soviet regime to the relative openness of the 1990s. Maybe yesterday's Irish monk in a monastery on the edge of Europe is today's labor activist in Chicago. Perhaps Desmond Tutu would have been martyred as a young man if he had been born Chinese. Perhaps the Chinese church is destined to be embraced by the leaders of China and become the main religion of China. If so, then underground house churches may no longer be necessary. When it comes to the issue of how Christ and culture relate, history matters. This question can never be decided abstractly or in general terms.

It is also necessary to take into consideration that the church itself can also be transformed from one historical period to another. The Roman Catholic Church in Latin America has undergone a significant transformation from type 1 to type 3 or 4, with 1968 being the symbolic hinge year. Today, much of the debate within much of the Latin American church is over whether it is more appropriate for Christians to attempt to change society by means of a type 3 or a type 4 approach. The need for a commitment to social transformation is not debated, but the validity of the use of violence is.

Christians may well come to the conclusion that the teachings of Jesus are only for the church because of the rejection of those teachings by the wider society. The non-Christendom transforming type (type 4) sees the teachings of Jesus as valid for all of society in principle and is undoubtedly right to do so. But before condemning the humanizing and separating types for viewing the teachings of Jesus as being only for the church, one should ask if the difference is more than semantic. When type 4 says that the teachings of Jesus are for the entire world, it really means that the call of Jesus to follow him is addressed to all, not that all actually will respond to that call. But sometimes enough people do respond to the call that an entire society is affected by the gospel. On the other hand, to expect that those who reject Jesus will take up their crosses and follow him is unrealistic, and this is the truth embodied in types 5 and 6. So the teachings of Jesus are for the church, but the church is open to all who believe. Since all the non-Christendom types would agree with that statement, the extent to which they are relevant and responsible should not be underestimated.

Christology

Ultimately, the difference between the two categories of types (Christendom and non-Christendom) is rooted in Christology. Niebuhr's Christ is docetic and can never become embodied in history. He points away from history to the absolute will of the Father, which Niebuhr seems to locate above and beyond the earth. Despite Niebuhr's deployment of the orthodox doctrine of the Trinity against the sectarians, the irony is that his typology justifies an unorthodox view of Christ, a view that Nicene Christology was formulated to rule out as unbiblical. If Christ is "the Son of God" who "points away from the many values of man's social life to the One who is alone good"[6] then he is not the embodiment of the good in history, but instead the one who points away from himself to God, who alone is absolute. To the extent that Jesus is truly human, he is unable to embody the will of God. To the extent that he is God, he is unable to function as a real human. So the response called for is not discipleship, participating in Christ's body by cross-bearing, and loving fellow believers, but rather, regarding this world (and all worlds) as relativized by the absolute God. In typically Niebuhrian fashion, then, the Father is played off against the Son, which leads to a foggy night in which all the typological cats are gray. The ultimate result is that radical Christians who believe that concrete discipleship means following Jesus by renouncing violence are portrayed as one-sided and fanatical.

But it is far from one-sided and fanatical to refuse to abandon the unity of God. The idea of *perichoresis* originally was put forward in trinitarian theology as a means by which the unity of the persons of the Godhead (and thus monotheism) could be preserved. *Perichoresis* means the mutual interpenetration or coinherence of the persons of the Godhead and is a concept designed to guard against tritheism by insisting that whatever one person of the Trinity does, all do. Thomas F. Torrance puts it this way:

6. H. Richard Niebuhr, *Christ and Culture*, with a new foreword by Martin E. Marty, a new preface by James M. Gustafson, and an introductory essay by the author (New York: Harper, 2001), 28.

Its application to the doctrine of the Trinity . . . enables us to recognize that the coinherent relations of the Father, the Son and the Holy Spirit, revealed in the saving acts of God through Christ and in the Spirit, are not temporary manifestations of God's nature, but are eternally grounded in the intrinsic and completely reciprocal relations of the Holy Trinity. In this way the concept of *perichoresis* serves to hold powerfully together in the doctrine of the Trinity the identity of the divine Being and the intrinsic unity of the three divine Persons.[7]

There simply is no way to play off the work of one member of the Trinity against the work of another in orthodox trinitarian thought, because God is truly one being. Niebuhr's manipulation of the doctrine of the Trinity fails to be governed by the principle of *perichoresis* and therefore swerves dangerously close to tritheism, if it does not actually advocate it.

In order to do justice to the humanity of Jesus Christ, our response to him must include discipleship, cross-bearing, and public witness as part of his body, the church. Our discipleship and our ecclesiology must be as embodied and historical as the incarnation. In addition, the authoritative character of Jesus's life and teachings is sealed forever by his divinity and by the hypostatic union of humanity and divinity in one person—Jesus Christ. So then, only those movements of Christianity that follow Jesus in rejecting violence, practicing reconciliation, and witnessing to the triumph of the Lamb can be said to be truly Nicene in character. All others deny the incarnation, to one extent or another, by denying that Jesus lived a life of obedience to the will of God and calls us to follow him in the path of discipleship. To deny that it is possible to follow Jesus is to deny that he was really human in his divinity.

No one type is considered to be right for all times and places, but the argument of this book is that the church should pursue the strategies to the right of the vertical dividing line demarcating violent coercion. Type 3 presents special problems in that it is trying to witness to the incarnation, but it inconsistently attempts to witness to Jesus by means that Jesus clearly rejected. Dialogue is needed between those adhering to type 3 and type 4.

In the next four chapters, we will flesh out the types in order to make the usefulness of this new typology as clear as possible. I will begin with type 1 (Christ legitimizing culture) in chapter 7 and then look at type 6 (Christ separating from culture) in chapter 8. A careful look at table 2 shows that both type 2 and type 5 are named Christ humanizing culture and that both type 3 and type 4 are named Christ transforming culture. In chapter 9 I discuss types 2 and 5 together, and in chapter 10 I examine types 3 and 4 together. It is important to see the reason

---

7. T. F. Torrance, *The Christian Doctrine of God: One Being Three Persons* (Edinburgh: T & T Clark, 1996), 102.

for this procedure. My point is that there are both violent and nonviolent ways of engaging culture and that rejecting violent coercion does not condemn one to helpless irrelevance. This is where Niebuhr's typology really is inadequate. It groups all who reject violence into the Christ against culture type and assumes that they are equally irrelevant to the culture. This move basically was a way of classifying his opponents out of existence. I have been very hard on Christendom in this book, but as we go along I hope it will become increasingly clear that I see a lot of faithful witnessing and relevant cultural engagement in the history of Western Christianity, in addition to the compromise and worldliness of the accommodated, official church. We will examine a wide variety of ways in which Christians have witnessed to the lordship of Jesus Christ in various cultural settings.

7

Christ Legitimizing Culture (Type 1)

We begin our survey of the six ways in which Christ relates to culture by examining type 1: Christ legitimizing culture. Type 1 is located to the far left side of the left half of table 4. The three types on the left side of the centerline presuppose and accept the existence and validity of Christendom. It is possible to support Christendom either actively or passively: type 1 defends Christendom, which it imagines is already established and so simply needs defending; type 2 supports Christendom passively; while type 3 is active in seeking to establish the kingdom of God by force.

In type 1 the Christian religion either already has become the state religion or is diligently trying to impress the rulers with its patriotism, nationalism, and utility to the state. Either way, the result is that Christianity has become deeply committed to the goal of supporting the goals and national security of the state. Believing that whatever is good for the state is good for the church, the church is gradually coopted into the service of the state and sometimes becomes a department of government. However, the structure is not crucial; a church that is technically free of state control can still be fervently nationalistic, uncritically patriotic, and adroitly exploited by the government for its own ends. We often see this kind of situation in the United States, where the power elites of both political parties (but especially the Republicans) have become adroit at manipulating Christians. It should also be noted that the state is not the only cultural entity capable of coopting the church. Nationalistic movements in political opposition or ideological constructs—such as individualism, when embodied in artistic, media, educational, and literary institutions—can also coopt the

Table 4. Post-Christendom Typology of Christ and Culture

	Christendom Types (accept violent coercion)			Non-Christendom Types (reject violent coercion)		
	Type 1: Christ legitimizing culture	Type 2: Christ humanizing culture	Type 3: Christ transforming culture	Type 4: Christ transforming culture	Type 5: Christ humanizing culture	Type 6: Christ separating from culture
Examples	• Theodosius I • Crusades • German Christians	• Luther • pietism • revivalism • Billy Graham	• Augustine • Columbus • Cromwell	• William Penn • Martin Luther King Jr. • Desmond Tutu	• Mother Teresa • Mennonite Central Committee • Brethren in Christ	• Antony of Egypt • Benedictines • Amish
View of Christ	symbol of ruling powers of society	unattainable yet relevant ideal	Lord of the cosmos	Lord of the cosmos	unattainable yet relevant ideal	Lord of the church
Biblical support	• conquest of Canaan under Joshua	• NT call to personal faith in Jesus (John 1:12; 3:16)	• Colossians 1:15–20 • OT Israel as theocracy	• Colossians 1:15–20 • Sermon on the Mount	• Jesus's parable of sheep and goats • early church in Acts	• OT exilic community • Revelation
Teaching of Jesus	denial of, even while using Christ as a cultic symbol to unify society	applicable only to private life (person/ vocation dualism)	for all society and therefore should be imposed by force if necessary	for all society but should not be imposed by force, but preached by word and deed	for the church only, but motivates loving service to society	for the church only
Christology	docetic	partially docetic	inconsistently Nicene	Nicene	Nicene	Nicene

church. In Western culture, the state often has a complex interrelationship with these kinds of cultural powers, and very often the issue comes down to whether Christians will subordinate their loyalty to Jesus Christ to their loyalty to such interests.

The key issue is not the formal structure of how church and state are related, but whether the church is focused on preaching and bearing witness to the gospel. As long as the church is highly focused on preaching the biblical gospel, it can never be completely manageable so far as the state or other cultural forces are concerned. Such a church will always be pursuing an agenda that is foreign to them and that they cannot fully grasp. To the extent that the church's focus on the gospel wavers, however, it becomes easy prey for the spirit of the age, for example, ideologies of empire and unity in fourth-century Rome, nationalism and racism in Europe in the 1930s, and liberal democracy today.

To make matters even worse, the church that loses its focus on the gospel often retains enough vestiges of Christian idealism about human redemption to make it naïve about power politics and enough trace memory of apocalyptic imagery to make it susceptible to revolutionary rhetoric. Cut off from the true gospel, the church is insufficiently critical of false gospels and false messiahs. So the church that has veered away from the gospel of the Lord Jesus Christ quite often is led into embarrassing alliances with wild-eyed nationalists and revolutionary zealots and finds itself compromised and discredited. Think of any bloody battle, high-minded intervention turned disaster, or utopian fantasy gone horribly wrong in the history of Western civilization, and usually Christians may be found cheering on the perpetrators. Like the Israelite kings of old, Western generals, emperors, and kings have always had their court prophets assuring them that absolutely nothing can possibly go wrong and that God definitely is on their side.

Examples of Type 1

The most obvious example of type 1 is Theodosius I, Roman emperor from 379 to 395. A native of Spain, he was baptized in 380, a year after gaining control of the whole Roman Empire, and gave up the pagan title *pontifex maximus*, which all Roman emperors up until then had borne. Theodosius was the first emperor to make it a crime not to be a Christian of the right sort, which is why British historian Hugh Trevor-Roper calls him "the first of the Spanish inquisitors."[1] In 381 he outlawed heretical churches and sects, including the Arians, and handed their property over to the orthodox churches. Theodosius I called the First Council of Constantinople in 381, at which the creed we know today as the Nicene Creed was adopted. Technically, it should be called the Niceno-Constantinopolitan Creed of 381 because the text of the Creed of Nicea, which was approved at the Council of Nicea in 325, was expanded somewhat in the 381 version, but with no change to the essence of the Nicene faith, embodied in the oneness (*homoousios*) of the Father and Son, which had been developed over the three centuries since the apostles.

Theodosius I went further than Constantine in making Christianity (specifically catholic, orthodox Christianity) the official religion of the empire. Whereas Constantine had been content to show imperial favor to Christianity and tolerate paganism, Theodosius moved to establish Christianity as the state religion. To get a sense of what it must have been like for pagans and non-Nicene Christians, one could imagine the United States adopting Presbyterianism as the state religion and then persecuting all other denominations. There are evangelicals alive in Canada today who remember the persecution of Protestant groups in staunchly Roman Catholic Quebec before the so-called quiet revolution of the 1960s. In the postmodern West, it is increasingly hard for us, for whom pluralism is second

1. Hugh Trevor-Roper, *The Rise of Christian Europe* (New York: Harcourt Brace Jovanovich, 1975), 36.

nature, to imagine what it would be like to have one official religion with one hierarchy favored enormously by laws and given official government protection. But most of us would not want to live in such a situation.

A second example of type 1 is the Crusades.[2] The Crusades were a series of seven major and many minor invasions of the Middle East by Western Europeans between 1095 and 1291. Pope Urban II responded to an appeal from the Byzantine emperor for help against the Muslim Turks. The result was a holy war in which preachers exhorted soldiers to die and kill for the faith, and the whole affair was conducted in the context of a frenzy of religious enthusiasm. Persecution of Jews was part and parcel of the general ethos of fighting for Christendom by violent means. Semimonastic orders of knights like the Templars and the Hospitalers fought to protect pilgrims and holy places. Although Jerusalem was conquered initially and several small Crusader kingdoms were set up in Palestine, the Muslims regrouped and eventually pushed the Christian forces out by 1291.

Modern liberal educators and intellectuals—even those who loudly proclaim their commitment to moral relativism in other matters (e.g., sexual morality)—display an almost universal repugnance toward the Crusades. No matter how relativistic such people are, they nevertheless usually find some way to morally condemn the Crusades in absolute terms. Now I have no interest in defending the Crusades as morally good, but I suspect that my reasons for condemning them are very different from those of most modern liberals. I think the Crusades are incompatible with the teachings of Jesus in the Sermon on the Mount. They are a contradiction in terms: Christian violence perpetrated in the name of the Prince of Peace. I think they are wrong because all violence done in Jesus's name is wrong. Yet, many of those who condemn the Crusades say that World War II was a just war. But how different were they?

Some say that the moral problem with the Crusades was that they were an invasion of another country rather than being defensive wars. But the Muslims themselves had invaded and conquered the Holy Land in 638, so it was plausible for the Europeans to speak of liberating the holy places four centuries later. In World War II British, Canadian, and American forces invaded Europe in order to liberate it. Others say that the Crusades were evil because they were fought in the name of religion, as if religion is so unimportant that it should never be allowed to provoke strong reactions. But World War II was fought in the name of ideals like democracy, freedom, and human rights. These concepts are just as religious in nature as the ideals of Christian Europe that motivated the Crusaders. Also, not far below the surface were strong undertones of the Christian West fighting against non-Christian Nazism and the Japanese emperor, who was worshiped in pre–World War II Japan. James Carroll points out that "not for nothing was Dwight Eisenhower's book about World War II entitled *Crusade*

2. For what follows in this paragraph, see Robert G. Clouse, "The Crusades," in *The International Dictionary of the Christian Church* (ed. J. D. Douglas; Grand Rapids: Zondervan, 1974), 273–74.

in Europe."[3] In that book, Eisenhower makes a claim that reflected the view of many of his day: "This war was a holy war, more than any other in history this war has been an array of the forces of evil against those of righteousness."[4] Certainly these words reflect the attitude of many veterans of this war.

Some give as their reason for finding the Crusades to be morally repugnant the barbaric behavior of the Crusaders. For example, the attacks on the Jews on the way to the Holy Land were horrible and wanton.[5] But the murder of the population of Jerusalem in 1099 is often cited as the reason for our revulsion toward the crusading mentality. The Crusaders determined to slaughter every inhabitant of the city, Jew and Muslim, including every man, woman, and child. The slaughter went on for days, and modern readers feel nauseated as they read the account. However, the wholesale destruction of men, women, and children in the cities of Hiroshima and Nagasaki by the Americans was no more civilized than the Crusaders' murder of the inhabitants of Jerusalem; it was simply high tech. In Jerusalem, the Muslims were shocked by the ferocity and barbarism of the European conquerors. A millennium later, the atomic bomb was used even though the war was almost over. The Japanese were looking for ways to surrender, and the impending shock of the Soviet Union's entry into the war, combined with an assurance that the emperor would not be tried as a war criminal, would likely have induced them to surrender without an allied invasion of the homeland.[6] Not only uninformed, idealistic, antiwar people believe this to be true, but so did military personnel, as is demonstrated by the blunt assessment of Admiral William Leahy, head of the U.S. Joint Chiefs of Staff from 1942 to 1949:

> Once it had been tested, President Truman faced the decision as to whether to use it. He did not like the idea but was persuaded that it would shorten the war against Japan and save American lives. It is my opinion that the use of this barbarous weapon at Hiroshima and Nagasaki was of no material assistance in our war against Japan. The Japanese were already defeated and ready to surrender. . . .
>
> My own feeling was that in being the first to use it, we had adopted an ethical standard common to the barbarians of the Dark Ages. I was not taught to make war in that fashion, and wars cannot be won by destroying women and children.[7]

Even Eisenhower went public in 1963 with his regret that the bomb had been used against Japan and his conviction that it had not been necessary to end the

---

3. James C. Carroll, *Constantine's Sword: The Church and the Jews* (Boston: Houghton Mifflin, 2001), 255, referring to Dwight D. Eisenhower, *Crusade in Europe* (Garden City, NY: Doubleday, 1948).

4. Dwight D. Eisenhower, quoted in Max Hastings, *Victory in Europe: D-Day to V-Day* (Boston: Little, Brown, 1985), 187.

5. For a lurid account, see Carroll, *Constantine's Sword*, 246–67.

6. Gar Alperovitz makes an overwhelmingly convincing case for this assertion in his meticulously documented and exhaustively argued *The Decision to Use the Atomic Bomb* (New York: Random, 1995).

7. William D. Leahy, *I Was There: The Personal Story of the Chief of Staff to Presidents Roosevelt and Truman, Based on His Notes and Diaries Made at the Time* (New York: Whittlesey, 1950), 441.

war. Upon being informed by Secretary of War Henry Stimson that the United States was preparing to drop an atomic bomb on Japan, Eisenhower writes:

> During his recitation of the relevant facts, I had been conscious of a feeling of depression and so I voiced to him my grave misgivings on the basis of my belief that Japan was already defeated and that dropping the bomb was completely unnecessary, and secondly because I thought that our country should avoid shocking world opinion by the use of a weapon whose employment was, I thought, no longer mandatory as a measure to save American lives. It was my belief that Japan was, at that very moment, seeking some way to surrender with a minimum loss of "face." The Secretary was deeply perturbed by my attitude, almost angrily refuting the reasons I gave for my quick conclusions.[8]

Even if it had been necessary to win the war and even if it had saved the lives of hundreds of thousands of Allied soldiers, it would still have been morally evil according to any fair interpretation of the historic just-war theory. Michael Walzer, who for many years defended the just-war theory against pacifists like John Howard Yoder, writes of the decision to drop the bomb: "I can find . . . no way of defending such a procedure."[9] Interestingly, given our twenty-first-century context in which terrorism is a major preoccupation of the American people, Walzer spoke in 1977 of the use of terrorism by British and Americans: "The Americans had adopted in Japan the British policy of terrorism: a massive incendiary raid on Tokyo early in March 1945 had set off a firestorm and killed an estimated 100,000 people."[10] What else can the fire-bombing of German and Japanese cities be called other than terrorism? The goal was to terrify the population into giving up on the war. Clearly, Hiroshima and Nagasaki were of minimal military importance; if they had been militarily important they would have been bombed long before August 6, 1945.[11] The killing of civilians was not an unintended side effect of an attack on a military installation; it was the whole point of the attack.

It is sobering to remember that, at the outbreak of World War II in 1939, the President of the United States had asked for assurances from the belligerent nations that civilian populations would not be attacked.[12] The world had been outraged at the attack on civilians by German planes in the Spanish Civil War. (Picasso's great antiwar painting *Guernica* was created as a furious response to the attack on a village of that name by Hitler's air force.) The reason commonly given why civilized nations like the United States had to go to war to defeat Nazi barbarism

8. Dwight D. Eisenhower, *Mandate for Change, 1953–56* (Garden City, NY: Doubleday, 1963), 312–13.

9. Michael Walzer, *Just and Unjust Wars: A Moral Argument with Historical Illustrations* (New York: Basic Books, 1977), 264.

10. Ibid., 266.

11. See Alperovitz, *Decision to Use the Atomic Bomb*, chap. 42, especially 520ff.

12. Elizabeth Anscombe, "Mr. Truman's Decree," in *War in the Twentieth Century: Sources in Theological Ethics* (ed. Richard B. Miller; Louisville: Westminster/John Knox, 1992), 237.

was morally outrageous acts like this one. The horror of ordinary people at the atrocities of Hitler is justifiable; nothing excuses Nazi evil. But, just six years later Truman took a page from Hitler's book by ordering the cold-blooded killing of over one hundred thousand men, women, and children with one bomb. By the end of World War II, the Western allies were complicit in war crimes on a par with anything Hitler had done, with the exception of the Shoah, which cannot be compared with anything else that happened in the war.

Whether one does it with axes and swords or with planes and bombs makes very little difference. In both cases innocent civilians were ruthlessly killed. In both cases the just-war theory was flaunted. In both cases the so-called Christendom powers were not restrained or governed by Christian morality. The Crusades were a perfect example of Christendom at work. The church preached the need for the war, and the kings and nobles who governed Europe answered the call. Church and state joined together in one purpose, which was deemed to be the will of God. Violent conquest was seen as a perfectly legitimate way to expand the faith, and the Turks were viewed as evil, devilish, beyond the pale of God's grace and thus worthy of death. A thousand years later, the same kind of killing in the name of God was still going on, and Christendom had still not managed to fight wars according to the sub-Christian criteria of the just-war theory—let alone follow Jesus in the way of peace. World War II was the last crusade, although radical Islam considers the U.S. invasion of Iraq to be another crusade. If we are to have a "clash of civilizations,"[13] the wars between the West and Islam will be a continuation of the Crusades of the Middle Ages.

A third example of type 1 is the prehistory, rise, and rule of the Nazis in Germany and the support offered to the Hitler regime by the majority of the Protestant state churches in Germany. Particularly noteworthy in this regard are the German Christians, a party within the national church that supported the Nazi Party, attacked the Old Testament as Jewish, substituted hymns to the German *Volk* for hymns to Christ, and led the way in purging the church of clergy of Jewish descent. The important thing to understand is that the German Christians did not spring out of nowhere the day Hitler became chancellor in 1933. From Luther to Protestant Scholasticism to nineteenth-century culture-Protestantism, the German church was always anti-Judaism and nationalistic. Famed church historian Adolf von Harnack helped to write the kaiser's speech when he declared war in 1914.

Throughout the centuries, from the first time that Luther appealed to German nationalism for support for the Reformation, there was a linkage between German religion and German nationalism. The nation that perpetrated the Shoah was 95 percent baptized Christian. From Luther to the German Christians, the flames of German nationalism were fanned and the hatred of Jews was promoted. The blessing of Hitlerism, therefore, by conservative, nationalistic, Roman Catholic

---

13. See Samuel P. Huntington, *The Clash of Civilizations: Remaking of World Order* (New York: Simon & Schuster, 1996).

and Protestant German politicians and military leaders was an extension of the continual subordination of the message of the gospel to the supposed needs, priorities, and agendas of the German nation.

The rise of Nazism was the rise of an anti-Christian neopagan religion that certainly would have turned to the destruction of the Christian church following a successful war.[14] This makes it all the more ironic that Christendom in Germany helped pave the way for the rise of such an anti-Christian movement. It also makes the German Christian movement, composed of those church leaders who tried to conform the church to Hitler's wishes, look foolish and deceived, as well as unfaithful to Christ, by attempting to meet the Nazis halfway.

The Shoah and the use of the atomic bomb in World War II by so-called Christian nations are the end results of the historical decision of the bishops of the fourth century to accept the offer of the Roman emperors to force adherence to Christianity and to punish deviance from Christianity by means of coercive violence. These events are the extremes to which violent coercion in the name of the gospel can be taken, but the differences between events occurring throughout the history of Western civilization from the fourth century to the twentieth and the incredibly evil culmination of such ideas in the human catastrophe that is called World War II are differences of degrees only and not differences in kind. Once it is accepted that such religious hatred and violence is justifiable in principle, it is impossible to put the genie back into the bottle, as we Western Christians have learned to our everlasting shame and horror.

View of Christ Entailed by Type 1

Type 1 views Christ more as a symbol of the dominant forces of a given culture than as an historical person. To accomplish this move, the idea of Christ as an object of devotion is detached from the Jewish rabbi and his radical teachings. The shift of emphasis from historical person and Lord to symbol and Savior makes it possible for new meaning to be poured into the empty shell of the Christ symbol. To the Germanic tribes in the early middle ages, Christ was a warlike king and his disciples were a band of warriors. To the German Christians of the 1930s, Christ was a strong, muscular Aryan figure. To the peasants of the Middle Ages, Christ was a judge who was so exalted that Mary and the saints were needed as intermediaries. To liberation theologians of the twentieth century he was the symbol of the revolution—the peasant guerilla fighter.

If Christ becomes a symbol of whatever is deemed to be highest and best in a given culture, he can become a symbol of anything. A symbol points to something other than itself; otherwise it would be the thing signified, rather than a

14. Arthur C. Cochrane, *The Church's Confession under Hitler* (Philadelphia: Westminster, 1962), 22.

symbol of it. What a symbol means is socially constructed, at least in part, by common agreement. What was previously understood to be a symbol of one thing can become a symbol of something quite different. Type 1 uses Christ as the symbol of whatever that culture deems to be highest and best, whether that is liberal individualism or blood and *Volk*. Christ can thus become the symbol of a police state, an absolute monarchy, a revolutionary ideology, libertarianism, an authoritarian religious organization—the possibilities are limitless. In the modern West, Christ has been turned into the symbol of the forces of civilizing progress and the state power that pushes progress forward.

Biblical Support for Type 1

Since type 1 usually means Christ legitimizing the power structures of a society, this means that the biblical idea of the kingship of Christ is utilized in such a way as to authorize human kingship or other power structures that claim to give allegiance to Christ. Of course, the allegiance given in this case is not literally allegiance to the teachings of Jesus Christ, which he commanded to be spread throughout the world in the Great Commission (Matthew 28:19–20); rather, it is allegiance to Christ as a symbol of the ideals of the culture in question. This is how the teaching of the Jesus of the Gospels is evaded and the prerogatives of Christ's own kingship, as described in the apocalyptic literature, are assumed by the state power of that culture. The Old Testament is mined for examples of kingship that can serve as justifications for the exercise of human political power by those who claim Christ as the symbol of their culture. The wars of conquest under Joshua and the later wars of the kings of Israel and Judah are especially emphasized by those wishing to find a biblical justification for the use of worldly power and violent coercion by Christendom.

The use of the Old Testament involves the appropriation of a failed tradition of religious zealotry, which was repudiated by Jesus when he told Pilate that his kingdom is not of this world, else his followers would fight for it (John 18:36). The followers of a Maccabean messiah would, of course, have fought.[15] We are told that in the Garden of Gethsemane Jesus struggled in prayer and surrendered to the will of God even though, as he told Peter, he could have called twelve legions of angels to help him fight if that had been his choice instead (Matthew 26:53). Jesus specifically chose to embrace the identity of the Suffering Servant of Isaiah instead of the popular Maccabean conception of a military/political messiah. The use of apocalyptic imagery to justify warfare and political kingship

15. The Maccabees were a family of priests who led a Jewish revolt against the occupying Ptolemaic rulers, which resulted in an independent Jewish state from 142 BC to 63 BC, when the Romans conquered Judea. They served as heroes and examples to those Jews who yearned to rise up and expel the occupying Roman forces in Judea.

involves the appropriation of a role reserved to Jesus in his second coming. Yes, it is right for God to fight against his enemies and execute judgment on them, but the followers of Jesus in this present age are not called to take up arms as if we were Jesus Christ. We are to bear witness to the messiah by suffering persecution without retaliating against those who hate both us and our Lord. By so doing, we make visible the means by which God is redeeming the creation—the redeeming suffering of Jesus Christ. We are people of the new covenant, and we live between the times, between the first and second comings of the messiah.

Critique of Type 1

The use of the Bible by type 1 involves a peculiarly flat and literalistic reading of the Bible, as if every part and section were equally valid as stand-alone prooftexts. The Anabaptists of the sixteenth century read the Bible as a witness to Jesus Christ. They did not dismiss the Old Testament, but they did read it in the light of the New Testament. They distinguished between revelation that had been given prior to Christ and revelation given through Christ, and they interpreted the former in the light of the latter. The Old Testament examples of kingship, war, and worldly kingdoms are not to be imitated today. By contrast, the Reformers read the Old Testament account of the kingdom of David and Solomon as if such writings were to be imitated literally and directly today—as though the coming of Jesus Christ were irrelevant! If ancient Israelite kings did it, then the contemporary rulers of Zurich or Geneva or Germany can do it too. This kind of Bible reading is often dismissed as fundamentalist and naïve when it comes to anything *except* the project of justifying Christendom from the Old Testament.

It is important to maintain our belief in the Old Testament as God's self-revelation through the prophets, for two reasons. First, the identity, actions, and teachings of Jesus can be understood only insofar as he is placed within the tradition of the people of Israel and if he is understood as the representative Israelite fulfilling the covenant and suffering unjustly as a witness to the incompatibility of the justice of Yahweh and the sinfulness of humanity. The Old Testament is the absolutely crucial historical, theological, and literary context in which Jesus must be understood. Second, to reject the Old Testament is to make faith in God impossible. If we throw out the Old Testament and assume that God is starting over in Jesus and a Gentile church, that means that the old covenant that God made with Israel failed. It means that God did not keep his promise to be faithful to the covenant no matter what Israel did or did not do. It means that Israel's unfaithfulness, documented by the prophets, resulted in God abandoning his people forever. If so, how confident could we ever be that at some point in the future God will not abandon us? Is our security dependent on how good, faithful, and obedient the church of Christendom has been? If so, we have no real hope. Life is a tragedy and not a comedy.

Paul wrestled with these very questions in Romans 9–11. The problem revolves around most of Israel rejecting Jesus as the messiah and the gospel now being received enthusiastically by the Gentiles. He asks: "Did God reject his people?" (Romans 11:1) and replies: "By no means," which is a rather weak English translation. "Not on your life!" would be more like it. He also denies that God's word has failed (9:6). For God to reject his people would mean he had not kept his covenant. For his word to fail would mean that divine election was a failure. But, Paul argues, the covenant has not failed because God has not permanently rejected his people. He has merely temporarily given them "eyes so that they could not see and ears so that they could not hear" (11:8), and this blindness and deafness is part of God's plan to allow the Gentiles to come into the covenant (11:11–12). The Gospels record Jesus as condemning Israel's failure to reach out to outsiders, sinners, and those who need God's grace. Paul is convinced that Israel's failure to take the grace of God to the nations is being rectified by God through Paul's ministry. Calling some from every tribe and nation to come into the covenant and glorify God is the fulfillment of the Great Commission given by the risen Lord Jesus to his church. This is the mission of the church. But Israel will not be cast aside forever; Paul's fervent hope and firm belief is that in the end "all Israel will be saved" (11:26).

The Old Testament thus has both a preparatory and a permanent value. It can never be set aside without the church and the gospel being destroyed in the process. Yet, the Old Testament is not simply to be read as a program for contemporary discipleship. We need to discern how Jesus sets aside nationalism, dependence on violence and war, and worldly power politics in order to advance a more important agenda: the spread of the gospel throughout the world and the coming into the kingdom of disciples from every tribe and nation. The church is the firstfruits of the kingdom, and its nonviolent nature sets it apart from worldly kingdoms.

The teachings of Jesus, which he commanded the apostles in the Great Commission to teach to the disciples they were to make from all the nations, are systematically ignored by those who exemplify the Christ legitimizing culture type. Dozens of ways of evading the teachings of the Sermon on the Mount and related passages have been devised. Some say that the sermon is meant to be a way of showing us how we fall short of God's perfect law and that its only purpose is drive us to repent and ask forgiveness; it was not given to be literally followed because it would be impossible to do so anyway. But the Ten Commandments are as hard to obey perfectly as the Sermon on the Mount, and there has been no setting aside of them within Christendom. In fact, the Ten Commandments, along with the Apostles' Creed and the Lord's Prayer, have typically formed the core of catechetical teachings throughout the Christendom era. This is curious, since the Sermon on the Mount is Jesus's interpretation of the law for his followers. One would have thought that the Sermon on the Mount would be the basic catechetical material for the Christian church. Instead, the Lord's Prayer has been lifted out of its context, and the Ten Commandments have replaced the rest of the sermon. Jesus's intention was that the Ten Commandments be understood in the context of the sermon, yet that they have not been read in this way accounts for the many unresolved tensions between the Old and New Testaments in Christendom.

Others argue that we will follow the Sermon on the Mount only in a future kingdom age, but not now. However, this approach goes against the grain of the strong biblical witness that the kingdom came in the person of Jesus and that he rules at the right hand of God right now. Of course, the fullness of the kingdom will not be revealed until the second coming, when every knee will bow and every tongue confess that he is Lord. But the point of the New Testament seems to be that this is exactly what his disciples are to do here and now while awaiting his return. This is the core of our witness—that Jesus, not Caesar, is Lord. The ascended Lord has already begun to rule the world, but only when he comes again will this rule be universally acknowledged.

The Christology of type 1 is the fundamental problem with this approach. Since the life, ministry, and teachings of the historical Jesus, as presented in the Gospels, is supplanted by an understanding of Christ as a symbol of what the culture views as highest and best, I call this approach to Christ docetic. I am not using the word *docetic* in the strict historical sense as if all Christendom cultures were self-consciously gnostic or necessarily believed that the historical Jesus was more of a wraith or a ghost than a flesh and blood man. There are more and less sophisticated ways to be docetic. But I do mean to say that all Christendom Christologies share one important feature in common with the historical heresies called docetic; namely that the incarnate Jesus is not allowed to be decisive for one's conception of Christ. When the humanity of Jesus Christ is not permitted to be authoritative for Christian humanity, then we have a form of Docetism even if the historical christological heresy is formally rejected.[16]

Only a Christology that takes seriously the human Jesus as the incarnation of God, and thus as authoritative for us in his life, ministry, and teachings, can really be said to be Nicene in character. Nicea, in opposition to all gnostic schemes, which found a place for Christ within some complex of ideas, symbols, and religious leaders, identified the one true God, creator of heaven and earth, with the Jew from Nazareth in the strongest way it could. Those who accuse the creeds of replacing biblical narratives about Jesus with Greek metaphysical constructs have actually gotten it completely backward. By holding together in an unbreakable bond the historical particularity of Jesus's humanity and the complete and total deity of this same Jesus, Nicene theology ensures that the historical Jesus of first-century Palestine can never be detached from the Christ symbol, and thereby it ensures that Christ can never be reduced to being merely the symbol of whatever

16. Historically, Docetism was a heresy associated with Gnosticism and rooted in Greek dualism, which viewed matter as intrinsically evil. Docetists said that Jesus was only apparently fully human. They could not really conceive of the full union of the divine and human, as orthodox teaching on the incarnation insisted had occurred.

human ideas or ideals that a given culture chooses to worship under the guise of Christianity. It ensures that acknowledging Jesus Christ as Lord can never mean less than taking up one's cross and following Jesus in the way of discipleship. Nicene Christology is antidocetic.

Christendom, on the other hand, is docetic and therefore never has really been Nicene in character. The adoption of the *homoousios* of Jesus and the Father in the Nicene Creed by the Councils of Nicea and Constantinople was determined by the worship practices of the church, not the imperial will.[17] The legend that Constantine himself intervened on behalf of the term *homoousios* may or may not be rooted in fact. But if he did do so, it could not possibly have been done out of a deep theological understanding of the implications of that word because Constantine would have been a complete novice theologically at that point. His interest was unity and his specialty was politics. If he observed that the clear majority of the bishops wanted this particular term and if he saw no way to get to unity without this term being imposed, despite its not being biblical language, he may well have pushed for it to be adopted. But to imagine that he had any idea of the real meaning of the *homoousios* and its ethical implications would be to give him far more credit that he deserves. The point is that Constantine did not specifically support or oppose the Nicene doctrine of the oneness of Christ and God because it was deeper theology than he cared about. He simply wanted unity.

It would be highly surprising, given that Jesus was clearly worshiped in the liturgy of the early church, if the fourth-century church would have been able to win a clear majority of bishops to a christological position that lowered Jesus Christ to a status below that of deity. If we recall that the compromise that created Christendom did not occur all at one specific point in time, we will not be surprised that the Nicene Creed as a symbol of Christendom in terms of its use to suppress heresy and enforce political unity nevertheless contained a theology that supports the pre-Christendom church, rather than Christendom. We need to bear in mind that the Nicene Creed as a tool of imperial, political unity is not simply and solely the same thing as the theology of the Nicene Creed. One can reject the former and embrace the latter, as the entire free-church movement of the past five centuries and many movements during the previous millennium have done. At this point in history there is no need to suppose that one has to reject the doctrines of the Trinity and the deity of Jesus Christ in order to oppose Christendom, any more than one has

---

17. The word *homoousios* means "same being" and was designed to counter the Arian teaching that Jesus is only similar to the Father in being; that is, not fully God. The debate in the fourth century centered on the status of Jesus. Is he one with the Father and thus to be worshiped as God? If he is a second, lesser god, would that not be polytheism? If he is not God, then would not worshiping him be idolatry? These were the issues that Nicea intended to resolve by affirming the *homoousios* of Jesus and the Holy Spirit with the Father. Thus, the orthodox doctrine of the Trinity, which is only implicit in the New Testament, was defined explicitly.

to reject the canon of Scripture, which was finalized around the same time as the Nicene Creed.[18]

The anti-Christendom theology embedded within the Nicene Creed has inspired individuals and groups throughout the history of Christendom to draw the natural conclusion that following Jesus in the path of discipleship means rejecting violence. The official churches of Christendom, which have officially endorsed Nicene theology, have also endorsed the canonical Scriptures of the Old and New Testaments, which contain the Sermon on the Mount. So, both Nicene theology and the Sermon on the Mount remained officially authoritative, even while the teachings and implications of both were being undermined and ignored. This ironic situation is no more astounding with regard to the Nicene Creed than it is with regard to the Sermon on the Mount.

The radical witness of following Jesus in the way of peace has never been completely eradicated during the long centuries of Christendom, even though Christianity has been twisted into an ideological justification for the violence of the state and turned into a religion of rituals instead of a path of discipleship. There was always tension between Christendom and the monastic movement, which often caused problems. And there have always been small groups of earnest believers who have attempted to follow Jesus in a more literal and peaceful manner than the official state religion. The witness to the historical Jesus has never been completely eclipsed by the symbolic Christ of Christendom. In the post-Christendom situation, the need is to call all Christians to follow Jesus in the way of peace and to become a minority suffering church that is capable of bearing witness to the good news that Jesus, not Caesar, is Lord.

18. The first list of the twenty-seven canonical books of the New Testament as we have them today is found in Athanasius's Easter Letter of 367. See Kenneth Scott Latourette, *A History of Christianity*, vol. 1: *Beginnings to 1500* (rev. ed.; New York: Harper & Row, 1975), 134. For a copy of the letter, see Athanasius, "Letter XXXIX (for 367)" (Nicene and Post-Nicene Fathers 2/3; repr. Peabody, MA: Hendrickson, 1994), 551.

8

Christ Separating from Culture (Type 6)

In this chapter we examine type 6: Christ separating from culture. Type 6 is located to the far right side of the right half of table 5. The three types on the right side are non-Christendom types; that is, they do not presuppose the existence and validity of Christendom. They may exist in pre-Christendom situations (such as the early church before Constantine), post-Christendom situations (such as present-day Canada), or non-Christendom situations (such as China). Type 6 embodies a desire on the part of Christians to obey the biblical injunction to "come out from them and be separate."[1] Many Christians of various types have attempted to take this command in more or less literal fashion, including hermits, monks, nuns, Hutterites, Diggers, Amish, Protestant fundamentalists, Jesus People, and members of many different kinds of communes. Some have been called to a solitary existence, some live celibate lives in community, and others have founded small communities where families work together as a small village.

Three points—which are largely obscured in Niebuhr's one-sided polemic against the Christ against culture type—about the exemplars of this type need to be kept in mind as we think about this issue. First, many separatist individuals and groups have had considerable influence on the wider society because members of the wider society have come to them for confession, counsel, and approval. The narrative of Scripture affirms that the church, although it is called out of the world,

1. This is the apostle Paul's command to the church at Corinth (2 Corinthians 6:17), echoing Second Isaiah (Isaiah 52:11). The primal call to God's people to come out from the nations is that of Abraham (Genesis 12:1), and it is connected immediately with blessing for the whole world (12:3).

Table 5. Post-Christendom Typology of Christ and Culture

	Christendom Types (accept violent coercion)			Non-Christendom Types (reject violent coercion)		
	Type 1: Christ legitimizing culture	Type 2: Christ humanizing culture	Type 3: Christ transforming culture	Type 4: Christ transforming culture	Type 5: Christ humanizing culture	Type 6: Christ separating from culture
Examples	• Theodosius I • Crusades • German Christians	• Luther • pietism • revivalism • Billy Graham	• Augustine • Columbus • Cromwell	• William Penn • Martin Luther King Jr. • Desmond Tutu	• Mother Teresa • Mennonite Central Committee • Brethren in Christ	• Antony of Egypt • Benedictines • Amish
View of Christ	symbol of ruling powers of society	unattainable yet relevant ideal	Lord of the cosmos	Lord of the cosmos	unattainable yet relevant ideal	Lord of the church
Biblical support	• conquest of Canaan under Joshua	• NT call to personal faith in Jesus (John 1:12; 3:16)	• Colossians 1:15–20 • OT Israel as theocracy	• Colossians 1:15–20 • Sermon on the Mount	• Jesus's parable of sheep and goats • early church in Acts	• OT exilic community • Revelation
Teaching of Jesus	denial of, even while using Christ as a cultic symbol to unify society	applicable only to private life (person/vocation dualism)	for all society and therefore should be imposed by force if necessary	for all society but should not be imposed by force, but preached by word and deed	for the church only, but motivates loving service to society	for the church only
Christology	docetic	partially docetic	inconsistently Nicene	Nicene	Nicene	Nicene

is, like Israel before it, God's instrument for the salvation of the world, and most separatist groups do not forget this truth, regardless of how much emphasis they place on separation. Second, most separatists are not against culture; they are just against the majority culture. In fact, many separatist groups have a culture of their own and often develop certain aspects of culture to a very high level. Just because they reject some of the values and practices of the majority culture does not mean that they necessarily reject culture as such. In fact, for some such groups having their own preferred culture is a far more important motivation for being separate than the mere avoidance of contamination by the majority culture. In other words, they have a positive, rather than a negative, reason for separating from the wider culture. Of course, a few hermits actually attempt to renounce all human society totally; but this is a comparatively rare phenomenon. Third, separatists do not always start out necessarily wanting to be separatists. Quite often in the history of the church, dissident groups were persecuted so ferociously that they were forced to keep to themselves and maintain a low profile just to have a hope of surviving.

The existence of a separated minority may say more about the character of the wider culture than about the minority group itself.

Adherents of Type 6

In 270, the year in which Constantine the Great was born, Antony of Egypt (251?–356), went out into the desert.[2] If he was not the first Christian hermit, he certainly was the most famous one. He was a comfortable Egyptian farmer from a Christian family who lost both parents as a young man and who then decided to sell all that he had and adopt an ascetic lifestyle. His decision to devote himself to a life of prayer and purification, which eventually led him to a solitary life of spiritual warfare in the Egyptian desert, began as an act of obedience to the gospel reading in church: "If you would be perfect, go and sell that you have and give to the poor; and come follow me and you shall have treasure in heaven."[3] Immediately upon hearing these words, Antony obeyed them by giving away his property to the poor.

Having committed his sister to a convent, he began to work with his hands to provide his daily food and began to visit and observe holy men. As he persevered in discipline, the devil attacked him, but without success. Antony resisted the devil's temptations and trickery and grew closer and closer to God. Eventually he moved out of town into some nearby tombs.[4] There he fought with demons in a physically exhausting battle, which left him in pain and weakened. Then he had a vision of the Lord, and when Antony asked him where he had been during Antony's struggles, the Lord answered that he had been there all along invisibly, but had been waiting to see if Antony would endure.[5] At this point in his life, Antony was about thirty-five years old, and from this time on he had continuous victory over demons. He moved farther and farther out into the desert, finally coming to rest at Mount Colzim, near the Red Sea. Yet many worldly people beat a path to his door. He was able to exorcise evil spirits from people; he had only to rebuke demons and command them to do his will. He even had a visit from Satan himself, who confessed to Antony that he was losing his power and had become extremely weak because of the rapid spread of Christianity, even in his traditional stronghold in the desert![6]

Antony's life is described in *The Life of Antony*, which was published soon after his death and is traditionally attributed to the great defender of Nicene orthodoxy,

2. Peter Brown, *The Rise of Western Christendom: Triumph and Diversity, A.D. 200–1000* (2nd ed.; Oxford: Blackwell, 2003), 81.

3. Athanasius, "Life of Antony" (Nicene and Post-Nicene Fathers 2/4; repr. Peabody, MA: Hendrickson, 1994), 196.

4. Ibid., 198.

5. Ibid., 199.

6. Ibid., 207.

Athanasius of Alexandria. This work portrays Antony as a holy man with great wisdom and spiritual power. He is said to have performed many miracles, including healings and exorcisms, and to have attracted to himself many followers. He is said to have stood firmly for Nicene orthodoxy and repudiated heretics like the Melitians and Arians.[7] He is also said to have been respectful (unlike some holy men) of the clergy and bishops of the catholic church.[8] He is depicted as refuting Neoplatonist philosophers with great spiritual wisdom, even though he was untutored and could neither read nor write.[9] He is said to have sought martyrdom, going so far as to leave the desert during a time of persecution to go into the city of Alexandria in order both to comfort the confessors and to defy the Roman general in charge of the persecutions.[10] He is also said to have received letters from Emperor Constantine and two of his sons seeking advice. After living to an old age, he died peacefully.[11]

The Life of Antony was written in Greek soon after Antony's death in 356 and was translated into Latin soon afterward. It had a great influence not only on the development of monasticism in the West, but also on many individuals who did not become monks but who were attracted to Christianity or to a more devout Christian life by "tales of the desert."[12]

Perhaps the most outstanding example of one who was powerfully influenced by Antony's life is Augustine of Hippo, who recounts the influence of *The Life of Antony* on his conversion in his *Confessions*. Augustine tells us that a friend named Ponticianus, a fellow African with a high position in the emperor's household, recounted to the then-unconverted Augustine a story revolving around this work about Antony.[13] Ponticianus related the account of how he and three friends were out walking one day in a garden in Trêves while the emperor was busy watching chariot races. Two of his friends, who had become separated from Ponticianus and his companion, came to a house of some Christians and found a book: *The Life of Antony*. One of them began to read it, and before finishing it he looked at his friend and said:

> What do we hope to gain by all the efforts we make? What are we looking for? What is our purpose in serving the State? Can we hope for anything better at court than to be the Emperor's friends? Even so, surely our position would be precarious and exposed to much danger? We shall meet it at every turn, only to reach another danger which is greater still. And how long is it to be before we reach it? But if I wish, I can become the friend of God at this very moment.[14]

7. Ibid., 214–15.
8. Ibid., 214.
9. Ibid., 215–16.
10. Ibid., 208.
11. Ibid., 220.
12. The phrase is Brown's in *Rise of Western Christendom*, 83.
13. Augustine, *Confessions* (trans. R. S. Pine-Coffin; New York: Penguin, 1961), 165–67 §8.6.
14. Ibid., 168 §8.6.

The man determined in very short order to abandon his career and begin to serve God. His friend was so impressed that he stated that he would stand with his friend, "for such service was glorious and the reward was great."[15] At this moment, Ponticianus and his companion found their two separated friends and listened to their story, culminating in their joint decision to renounce the world and become monks. Although Ponticianus and his friend were not convinced to enter into the monastic life themselves, they were moved to the point of tears by the noble resolution of their two friends.

Augustine tells us what a tremendous impression this story of Ponticianus made upon him: "All the time that Ponticianus was speaking my conscience gnawed away at me like this. It was overcome by burning shame."[16] This restlessness, guilt, and sense of conviction of sin did not leave Augustine until he finally experienced his conversion by reading Scripture. Remembering the story of Antony and how a text he had heard read in church had become the very word of the Lord to Antony when he chanced to hear it, Augustine picked up a book of Paul's Epistles and read the first text upon which his eye fell. Amazingly, it was one that spoke directly to his struggle against lust and fleshly pleasures: "Not in reveling and drunkenness, not in lust and wantonness, not in quarrels and rivalries. Rather, arm yourselves with the Lord Jesus Christ; spend no more thought on nature and nature's appetites."[17] In that instant, Augustine was converted. And he would not be the last to be led to conversion by the testimony of one who had renounced culture, withdrawn to the desert, and sought only to find salvation for his or her own soul. Yet he must be counted as an extremely significant convert, one whose thought would influence both the Roman Catholic and Protestant streams of Western civilization decisively.

By withdrawing from the world and practicing a solitary life of asceticism, prayer, and spiritual combat, Antony exerted a great influence on the world. The thesis of *The Life of Antony* appears to be that there is an inverse proportion between the holy man's degree of rejection of the world and his actual effect on the world. Precisely because he became indifferent to the material world and totally attuned to the unseen spiritual reality around him, he grew powerful, wise, and admirable. Certainly, down through church history many people have been influenced to become monks by Antony's example and even more have been drawn to faith. When one stops to think about it, this is a very strange phenomenon. Why should those who renounce human society end up influencing it? R. A. Markus gives one reason: "Asceticism was coming to be the mark of authentic Christianity in a society in which to be a Christian no longer needed to make any visible difference in a man's life."[18] As lines between the church and Roman society in

---

15. Ibid.
16. Ibid., 170 §8.7.
17. Ibid., 178 §8.12.
18. R. A. Markus, *The End of Ancient Christianity* (Cambridge: Cambridge University Press, 1990), 36.

general were increasingly blurred, an acute need was felt by many people to define true Christianity in some way that could not be imitated by those who merely accepted the outward forms. The ascetic life not only did that; it also established a connection with the age of the martyrs, whose lives continued to inspire the faithful. Genuine faith influences the world.

A second example of the Christ separate from the world type is the Benedictine Order. In the very same year (529) as Roman Emperor Justinian closed down the academy in Athens, which was a descendent of Plato's academy, Saint Benedict founded his monastery at Monte Cassino in Italy. It seems symbolically significant that at the moment of the official birth of Christendom, the closing of pagan philosophical schools and the birth of monasticism would occur in the same year. The significance of both of these events for the creation of Christendom is profound.

The Benedictines are founded on the basis of *The Rule of Saint Benedict*, the rule written by Saint Benedict (ca. 480–ca. 550) for his monastery at Monte Cassino. The simplicity, wisdom, and practicality of this rule are evidenced by thousands of congregations or monastic communities having lived under it for a millennium and a half so far. (The U.S. constitution, by contrast, has had a mere 230 years to prove itself.) Each congregation is autonomous; there is no overall hierarchy over the order. There is, however, a fraternal bond between those who live under the same rule. Each monastery has an abbot elected for life, and each monk takes vows of perpetual poverty, chastity, and obedience to the abbot. Benedictine monasteries are economically self-supporting communities whose focus is the life of prayer. Life consists of a balance of prayer, manual labor, and rest.

A recent edition of *The Rule of Saint Benedict* defines monasticism in this tradition as "the quest for union with God through prayer, penance and separation from the world, pursued by men sharing a communal life. The energy generated by this kind of living produces effects within the individual member, within the community and to some extent upon the world at large."[19] What is intriguing about this definition is the matter of fact manner in which the authors speak of the "energy" generated by these monasteries, which have also been referred to as "powerhouses of prayer."[20] As Peter Brown explains, a belief arose in sixth-century Europe that entire convents and monasteries "possessed a collective power of prayer that was somehow stronger that the prayers offered by any one person."[21] In addition to the unmeasured spiritual influence of the prayers offered in Benedictine monasteries, there were other, more tangible, effects on society as well.

One visible effect of monasteries on the wider society around them was the provision of monastery-trained leaders for the church—monk bishops and missionaries. One example is the island monastery of Lérins. Located off the Mediter-

---

19. Benedict of Nursia, *The Rule of Saint Benedict* (trans. and ed. Anthony C. Miesel and M. L. del Mastro; New York: Bantam, 1975), 9.

20. Brown, *Rise of Western Christendom*, chap. 9.

21. Ibid., 226.

ranean coast of Gaul, it became a virtual school for bishops during the fifth century. Young men of noble families were sent to this holy place and then emerged, years later, completely transformed. The main administrative center of Gaul, Arles, was governed by a succession of monk-bishops trained at Lérins. By 434 eight episcopal sees in Gaul were led by bishops from Lérins.[22] The reality was that the worldly church of the late Roman Empire was unable to spiritually form effective future leaders by itself, and monasteries, which were minority countercultures, were able to do so.

Another example is Pope Gregory the Great, an admirer of Saint Benedict, who founded monasteries and became an abbot but was called back into the world to become bishop of Rome. He sent one of his monks to Britain as a missionary, Augustine of Canterbury.[23] Of course, one must remember that the vast majority of monks entered the monastic lifestyle with no thought of ever leaving, and indeed most never did. Also, not all monks were highly educated. But out of the total population of Europe's monasteries, a leadership group was produced that exerted influence beyond all proportion of its size in European society. The life of prayer produced tangible as well as intangible results in terms of influencing the world around it.

A third example of this Christ separating from the world type is the Anabaptists and their modern descendents such as the Mennonites and the Hutterites. Niebuhr mentions the Mennonites briefly in *Christ and Culture*. In speaking of the Christ against culture motif, he says: "The Mennonites have come to represent the attitude most purely, since they not only renounce all participation in politics and refuse to be drawn into military service, but follow their own distinctive customs and regulations in economics and education" (56). In this section, the Mennonites get one sentence and monasticism gets one paragraph; Niebuhr then goes on to talk about Tolstoy for nearly ten pages as his main example of the Christ against culture type. But it simply does not work to lump together such disparate movements as desert hermits, Benedictines, Jesuits, several varieties of Mennonites, Hutterites, and other small Brethren movements together with Tolstoy (who really requires a category of his own). Niebuhr's decision to do so constitutes a fatal weakness in his book, not because it distorts the historical reality of who these groups were and are, although it does that, but rather, because it makes one type do at least triple or quadruple duty and thereby makes the type mean so much that it means nothing. It destroys the integrity of the type. Niebuhr's Christ against culture type simply covers too many different individuals and movements to be a real type. This problem can be illustrated by both monasticism and Anabaptists.

The hermit's ideal of renouncing all human society completely is very different from the Benedictine ideal of a disciplined community, which is separated from the wider society, but in a very real sense is dedicated to the well-being of

22. Ibid., 112.
23. Ibid., 210–11.

Table 6. Types of Monasticism

	Anchoretic Monasticism		Cenobitic Monasticism		
	Hermit	**Holy man**	**Brothers**	**Missionary orders**	**Monk/bishop**
Asceticism	extreme, including near starvation and mortification of the flesh	extreme, including near starvation and mortification of the flesh	basically strict, including vows of poverty, chastity, obedience, stability	moderate, including vows of poverty, chastity, obedience	moderate, including vows of poverty, chastity, obedience, but can be wealthy and powerful
Relationship to the world	• renounces all human contact • sees all human society as harmful, including religious society • no emphasis on learning or scholarship • preference for self-support but no desire to rise above subsistence-level diet	• does not renounce all human contact • usually supported by monastic community or laypeople • available for advice, confession, healings, absolution • may be learned but is always considered to be especially wise	• living together in community is positive help in spiritual life • service is part of sanctifica-tion • simple internal economy, which may interact with outside world and lead to cultivation of certain arts and sciences	• a community with a mission to the world • education is necessary as preparation for mission • may be employed in secular contexts as part of mission	• form, train, and send out leaders to wider church community, especially bishops and missionaries, who serve God in the world even though they remain monks • such men normally retire to monasteries
Examples	• desert fathers • Simeon the Stylite (390–459)	• Antony of Egypt (251?–356)	• Benedictines • Cistercians	• Dominicans • Franciscans • Jesuits	• Basil the Great (327–79) • Augustine of Canterbury (died 604?) • Gregory the Great (540–604)

that wider society. Certainly monks entered Benedictine houses to save their own souls. But the monastery itself had a dual purpose: to facilitate the salvation of the individual monks and to pray for the world around it. This is why many medieval monasteries became wealthy; laypeople endowed them generously in the expectation that the monks would pray for them, their communities, and their loved ones. This second purpose of prayer for the wider society, in many cases, also morphed into the training and preparing of leaders for the wider society (especially missionaries and bishops). Benedictine monasticism thus developed into something very different from the ideals of hermits like Antony. Monasticism is usually divided into two types: anchoritic (solitary living like Antony) and cenobitic (communal living as in the rule of Saint Benedict). But it is actually far more complicated than one neat and tidy division.

Although it is still an oversimplification, it is more accurate to think of monasticism as a spectrum moving from the hermit who renounces all human contact to the leader prepared by the monastery for service to the wider society (see table 6). The first two categories are expansions of the anchoretic ideal, while the last three are expansions of the cenobitic ideal.

Although all forms of monasticism involve some form of asceticism, the degree of asceticism varies widely. The extremes are the hermit who practically starves himself to death, while sleeping on the ground and cutting himself off from all human contact, to the monk/bishop sitting on a throne who needs to wear a hair shirt under his luxurious robes in order to remind himself of the ascetic ideals he professes. There is wide variation in terms of service. The hermit seeks to serve no one other than God and seeks no one's service. The holy man serves by hearing confessions, praying for people, and speaking words of wisdom and, in turn, has his physical needs provided for by others. (Antony, as described in *The Life of Antony*, was a combination of hermit and holy man.) The Benedictine brothers see their mutual service of each other as part of working out their salvation. The missionary orders and the monks who leave the monastery to serve the church in the world take the further step of viewing the service of outsiders, as well of each other, as being part of what it means to work out their own salvation. There is also wide variation in the attitude to scholarship, culture, arts, and sciences. The hermit renounces them all, while the holy man is usually known for his wisdom, even though he may not be highly educated. The Benedictines evolved an ethos in which the arts and sciences were developed both for their utility (e.g., in improving crops) and for their own sake. In the missionary orders, education is highly regarded as preparation for effective mission in the world. The word *monasticism* means so many things that one type cannot possibly cover it. Typical Protestant rhetoric, which tends to paint all monasticism as anticultural, is inadequate and unfair to monasticism. Any typology that lumps all forms of monasticism together and labels them as anticultural is simply inadequate.[24]

As with monasticism, so it is with Anabaptists. There are various types of Anabaptists, each of which have varying approaches to economics, education, missions, social service, and so on. The Mennonites are the best-known contemporary branch of Anabaptism, which originated in Europe in the sixteenth century as the Radical Reformation. Sometimes, when people speak of Mennonites, they have in mind a certain image of farmers who wear beards and suspenders and who drive horse-drawn buggies. In commenting on Niebuhr's reference

24. In an attempt to keep this account as simple and clear as possible, I focus on monasticism to the exclusion of convents. Female religious life exhibits a similar range of variation as male religious life does. I am merely attempting to stimulate reflection on the wide range of attitudes toward culture among those usually pigeonholed as anticultural.

to the Mennonites in *Christ and Culture*, Yoder says that Niebuhr appears to be thinking of the Old Order Amish.[25] But there are many different kinds of Mennonites and even more kinds of Anabaptists. All of them are committed to following Jesus in the way of peace, although they have evolved quite different ways of doing so

The main branches of the sixteenth-century, Continental Protestant Reformation were the Lutheran, the Reformed, and the Radical. A hodgepodge of various movements and figures are typically included under the label *Radical Reformation*, including pretty well everything that deviated from the Roman Catholic status quo but was not either Lutheran or Reformed.[26] Some basic distinctions, however, need to be drawn between Radical Reformers and heretical sects. *The Oxford Dictionary of the Christian Church* lists seven disparate movements as Anabaptist, including Swiss Brethren, South German Anabaptists, and Mennonites, all of which are basically orthodox, evangelistic, biblical churches whose theology differed from that of the Magisterial Reformers primarily in their rejection of the Christendom union of church and state.[27] But the list also includes the followers of Melchior Hoffmann, who taught a docetic Christology; Thomas Müntzer, a mystic who never actually practiced believers' baptism; the revolutionary movement at the city of Münster, where violence was used in an attempt to bring in the kingdom of God; and the Hutterite Brethren movement, which is distinct because of its Christian communism. In addition, Michael Servetus (1511–53) is mentioned, but since he denied the doctrine of the Trinity and never organized churches, he should not be classified as Anabaptist. (This is a bit like a Roman Catholic apologist referring to Arius in an article on Lutheranism, as if he were somehow relevant to the topic at hand.) Finally, the article also refers to Faustus Socinus (1539–1604), who denied the divinity of Christ and rejected infant baptism. (Again, one could mention that Arius affirmed infant baptism, but would that prove anything about those orthodox church fathers who affirm infant baptism?) Twentieth-century Mennonite historians, who have worked hard to distinguish between Anabaptism and various heretical and/or violent deviations, vigorously protest this kind of guilt-by-association historiography.[28] By mentioning various cultlike

25. John Howard Yoder, "How H. Richard Niebuhr Reasoned: A Critique of *Christ and Culture*," in *Authentic Transformation: A New Vision of Christ and Culture*, by Glen H. Stassen, D. M. Yeager, and John Howard Yoder (Nashville: Abingdon, 1996), 34.

26. For a good overview of the Radical Reformation, see C. Arnold Snyder, *Anabaptist History and Theology: An Introduction* (Kitchner, ON: Pandora, 1995).

27. F. L. Cross and E. A. Livingston, eds., *The Oxford Dictionary of the Christian Church* (3rd ed.; Oxford: Oxford University Press, 1997), 55–56 s.v. "Anabaptists."

28. See Harold S. Bender, *The Anabaptist Vision* (Scottdale, PA: Herald, 1944); William Estep, *The Anabaptist Story* (rev. ed.; Grand Rapids: Eerdmans, 1975); John Howard Yoder, *Christian Attitudes to War, Peace, and Revolution* (Elkhart, IN: Goshen Biblical Seminary, 1983); and Snyder, *Anabaptist History and Theology*; and their bibliographies of scholarly monographs, articles, and critical primary source editions.

Table 7. Types of Anabaptism

	Married Monasticism	The Quiet in the Land	Servants of the Poor and Peacemakers	Evangelical Congregations
Community	colonies of people who live in community with shared ownership of all goods based on Acts 2	family farms in rural areas with community life centered on local churches.	mission organization operated by Anabaptist churches working together	pietistic Mennonite branch with roots in renewal movements of nineteenth-century Russia
Emphasis	being self-supporting and not dependent on outside world; initiated some missionary work, but their history forced them to focus mainly on survival	separation from world and independence; very evangelistic in the sixteenth century, but centuries of fierce persecution led to reluctance to reach out	relief, education, agriculture, job creation, peace witness, and refugee ministry; works in 57 countries with many partners; focused on reaching out to hurting world	evangelism, outreach, and world missions; stresses need for personal conversion, ethical lifestyle, and meaningful worship
Focus	inward on community building	inward on family and church	outward on a hurting world in need of practical help	outward on a lost world in need of the gospel
Examples	Hutterian Brethren	Amish	Mennonite Central Committee	Mennonite Brethren Church

groups and heretics in the same breath as Anabaptists, Protestant churches have created an impression that all those who reject Christendom arrangements are outside the mainstream of orthodox Christianity—and this is factually incorrect. It is time that the superficial association of heresy and anti-Christendom views be put to rest. There is not space in this chapter to address this problem in detail, but in the examples that follow, I refer to groups that fit within the mainstream Christian faith, not to heretical groups that deny basic doctrines like the deity of Christ and the Trinity.

Four distinct approaches highlight the variety of ways in which modern descendents of the sixteenth-century Anabaptists relate to the wider culture around them (see table 7). These groups all have in common their Anabaptist heritage, commitment to following Jesus in discipleship, rejection of war and violence, and commitment to the major doctrines of historic, orthodox Christianity, such as the divinity of Christ, the Trinity, and the authority of the Holy Scriptures.

The Hutterian Brethren (or Hutterites) began in Moravia (in what is today part of the Czech Republic) in 1528–29 as groups of Anabaptist refugees from Switzerland, Germany, Austria, and northern Italy were forged together into a church under the leadership of Jacob Hütter, who was later burned at the stake for his faith.[29] By 1600 there were about 16,000 Hutterites in Moravia. They have had to migrate several times to escape persecution, living for a time in Slovakia, Romania, and the Ukraine before immigrating to the United States in 1874 and to Canada in 1918. About 40,000 Hutterites now live in various colonies in central and western United States and Canada. They support themselves through communal businesses and farming. All men vote and have a say in communal decision-making, but the leader of the colony is chosen by lot. The Hutterites have developed their own culture and seek to live according to their own ways in peace.

The Amish began in 1693 when a Swiss bishop, Jacob Ammann, and his followers broke away from the Mennonites.[30] They settled in Pennsylvania in the 1720s and 1730s as part of William Penn's holy experiment of religious tolerance and now live in twenty U.S. states and in Ontario. As of 1990, there were over 125,000 Amish in North America, and they are among the fastest growing population groups in the world. They earn their living by farming and live close enough to each other to be able to worship together in local churches. They are divided into many different groups, with most of the divisions caused not by theology but by disagreements over whether to adopt various innovations. Most Amish do not use electricity or own automobiles, but they do use gas and various machines operated by gas. A common misperception is that the Amish lifestyle never changes. Actually it does change, but much more slowly than it does for the rest of the world. They attempt to be discerning and refuse simply to assume that all change is for the better.

The Mennonite Central Committee is a relief, service, and peace agency of Mennonite and Brethren in Christ churches.[31] Founded in 1920, it has workers in fifty-seven countries working in projects as varied as health, education, agriculture, peace and justice, relief work, and job creation. Over their history, Mennonites often have been persecuted, often have been refugees, and often have been helped by others in time of need. Today, about fifteen denominations support the Mennonite Central Committee, which seeks to serve others in the name of Jesus. The Mennonite Central Committee usually works with partners and sees its role as being a facilitator, rather than seeking to control projects and institutions. Money is raised by means of sales of crafts, thrift shops, and individual donations. The Canadian Foodgrains Bank is a project founded by the Mennonite Central Committee, which enables Canadian farmers to donate grain and others to donate money to relief programs where there is hunger; the Canadian government matches its donations with four dollars for every one dollar donated. The Food Resources Bank is a similar program in the United States.

29. See John Hofer, Hans Meier, and John V. Hinde, "Hutterian Brethren (Hutterische Brüder)," Global Anabaptist Mennonite Encyclopedia Online website: http://www.gameo.org/encyclopedia/contents/H888ME.html (accessed May 5, 2005).

30. See Thomas J. Meyers, "Amish," Global Anabaptist Mennonite Encyclopedia Online website: http://www.gameo.org/encyclopedia/contents/A4574ME.html (accessed May 5, 2005).

31. See the Mennonite Central Committee website: http://www.mcc.org.

The Mennonite Brethren Church was founded in Russia during the nineteenth century. The Mennonites were named for Menno Simons, who was a priest until his conversion to the Anabaptist movement in 1537.[32] He played a large part in organizing Anabaptist churches, and the movement took his name after his death. For 250 years the Mennonites were known as "The Quiet in the Land" and lived peacefully in northern Europe. But the rise of Prussian militarism in the eighteenth century made it difficult for Mennonites living in that area, and they saw the announcement of land grants by Catherine the Great of Russia in 1763 as providential. By 1860 about 30,000 Mennonites were living in their own villages in Russia. As guests of the ruler, the Mennonites agreed to refrain from evangelization and were allowed a fair degree of self-governance. During this time, ironically, the Mennonites themselves took on many of the characteristics of the European state churches that they had opposed and that had persecuted the Mennonites.[33] For example, church growth was biological rather than by conversion, the church became identified with a certain ethnic group, and certain human traditions were elevated to the level of the gospel. Birth, rather than personal conversion, determined membership in the church, just as in Christendom. The Mennonite Brethren Church came into existence as a renewal movement in this context, emphasizing personal conversion, an ethical change of life after conversion, and biblical preaching. Today in Canada and the United States, Mennonite Brethren congregations tend to focus on evangelism, growth, Christian education, and worship. They have adapted to the North American environment by embracing the original evangelistic vision of the sixteenth-century Anabaptists and reaching out to non-Anabaptists. Rather than viewing the Mennonite movement as an ethnic religion, they stress cross-cultural outreach and have mission work in over twenty countries. As a result they worship each week in over twenty languages. The Mennonite Brethren conferences are not the only Mennonites that are evangelistic; they are just one specific example of how a church that had its missionary fervor nearly crushed out of it by persecution eventually found renewal.

We have only scratched the surface in this quick overview of various types of Anabaptist ways of living in the world. But hopefully the basic point is clear that it is unfair to accuse Anabaptists or Mennonites of being anticulture, just as it is unfair to paint all monasticism as anticulture. Hutterites and Amish work constantly at developing their own distinct culture. Although it is certainly different from the wider culture around them, it nevertheless is a viable alternative culture in its own right. Education, economics, agriculture, methods of self-governance, care of elderly and sick, recreation, marriage and courtship customs, and many other areas of culture have been developed in a distinct manner. To have a different culture is not to be against culture. Both monasticism and Anabaptism engage culture in

32. See Harold S. Bender and Myron S. Augsburger, "Evangelism," Global Anabaptist Mennonite Encyclopedia Online website: http://www.gameo.org/encyclopedia/contents/E9383ME.html (accessed May 5, 2005).

33. Yoder, *Christian Attitudes to War*, 198–99.

varying degrees and using various strategies, but neither can be said, as Niebuhr says, simply to be against culture. Every Christian is against culture to one degree or another, and this will be so until the world is fully redeemed. Niebuhr's Christ against culture type obscures the range of possible non-Christendom strategies for relating to culture. Hopefully, it is becoming clear that Christian ways of separating from aspects of the non-Christian culture around them need to be studied, reflected on, and mined for wisdom, rather than being summarily dismissed.

View of Christ Entailed by Type 6

The view of Jesus Christ presupposed by the Christ against culture type is the biblical portrait of Jesus Christ as the Lord of the church. Jesus is understood to be the incarnation of God who came into this world in order to seek and to save the lost. Jesus is the head of the church (Ephesians 4:1–16), which is his body (1 Corinthians 12:12–31). The church continues the incarnation in the sense that, as the Spirit of God fills the members of Jesus's body, the continuing ministry of Jesus takes place through those he has called to be his people (Acts 1:4–8). Jesus is the bridegroom (Revelation 19:1–10), and the church is his bride. Jesus is the Lord of the church because he is Lord of the whole cosmos, and the church is the new creation (Colossians 1:15–20). This is why Yoder entitled his 1980 Stone Lectures at Princeton Theological Seminary on the place of the church in social ethics "A New World on the Way."[34]

As history moves forward, the church carries the seed of the future kingdom of God, and therefore the church—not the nation-state or any human empire—is the meaning of history. The church will continue to exist after the judgment of this world; in fact, Paul tells the Corinthians that they will participate in judging the world (1 Corinthians 6:2), and he also tells them that they will one day judge angels (6:3). The church, therefore, is the presence of the kingdom here and now and the nucleus of the future kingdom in its fullness. The church appears to be only a small, weak minority of humanity, which is beset by sin and weak in and of itself. Yet the church is, in Yoder's pregnant phrase, the "new world on the way." As Lord of the church, Jesus is Lord of the whole cosmos, which is in the process of being renewed by God's work through the church. Jesus's lordship of the church is a means by which his lordship of the entire cosmos is being recognized.

Biblical Support for Type 6

The Christ against culture type appeals to the Bible in a very different way than the Christ legitimizing culture type does, in that type 6 reads the Bible

---

34. The first of these lectures was published in John Howard Yoder's *The Royal Priesthood: Essays Ecclesiological and Ecumenical* (ed. Michael Cartwright; Grand Rapids: Eerdmans, 1994), 102–26.

historically and views it as progressive revelation. Not every section of the Bible is read as equally applicable to us today. The Old Testament is valid revelation from God, but it is revelation that progresses in its unfolding and moves toward a point—that point being the incarnation of God in Jesus Christ. Since Jesus Christ fulfills the Old Testament law and sacrificial system, these aspects of the Old Testament revelation are viewed as pointing to him and are understood in light of him. Since Jesus Christ also fulfills and in the process transforms the Old Testament ideal of kingship, it is correct for the Gospels both to portray him as the promised messiah of Israel and to have him say to Pilate: "My kingdom is not of this world" (John 18:36). For type 6 human kingdoms that rely on violence are part of the past, not the future.

Type 6 appeals to several major themes of Scripture. It not only appeals to these themes in the sense that it chooses these particular themes out of the many other themes that it could just as easily have chosen; rather, the type 6 approach implicitly claims that these themes are central to a proper interpretation of the Scriptures and must be at the heart of any faithful reading of the Bible. To live a life of faithfulness to God in this world requires that we understand his will for our lives, and type 6 stresses that the grace of God is such that this will is made known to all those who earnestly seek it. In other words, God has not left his children in doubt about what it means to follow Jesus Christ as the people of God.

Creation

The first biblical theme stressed by type 6 is the original goodness but current fallenness of creation. The physical world is not evil in and of itself, but it is temporarily in the grip of evil in its current condition. The current state of creation is crying out for redemption (Romans 8:18–22) and waiting for God to act. Things are not normal as they are. This doctrine has two important implications. First, we must not attempt to read God's will from the way things are or from nature. It is not necessary to deny that the created order reflects the goodness of its creator in order to affirm that this reflection of God is marred by sin. We must also remember that human beings are affected by the fallenness of creation and therefore unable to interpret rightly what is right before their eyes. Natural theology should not, therefore, be used to overrule the plain teachings and example of Jesus Christ. Natural theology must be firmly subordinated to and controlled by revealed theology centered on Jesus Christ. A second implication is that the world is in need of redemption and that the current situation will not last forever. This is why separatists can give due weight both to the evil of the current world and the goodness of the original creation. The secret is eschatology. Any system of theology that does not have a lively futuristic eschatology will tend to oscillate back and forth between a gnostic tendency to view the physical world as completely evil and a naïve tendency to downplay the degree to which sin is actually manifest in the world. As we saw in chapter 3, Niebuhr's realized eschatology made it difficult for him to think of creation as both completely good and completely sinful at the same time.

People of God

The second biblical theme stressed by type 6 is the calling of God's people to come out from the nations and be separate. Yoder points out that ever since Abraham, God has been about the process of creating a people for himself.[35] The concept of the believers' church, the community based on the personal commitment of its members to God, is rooted in the Old Testament. After the confusing of the languages on the plain of Shinar and the scattering of the nations (Genesis 10–11), the biblical narrative focuses on God's call to Abraham and the covenant that God made with Abraham to bless all the nations of the earth through him. The making of Abraham's descendents into a holy nation through the events surrounding the exodus is part of the plan.

The prophets knew that election was not for privilege, but for service. Israel was supposed to be a light to the nations (Isaiah 60:1–3). Israel's failure was due to the desire of the people to be a nation "like all the other nations" (1 Samuel 8) instead of accepting God's call to be the means by which the grace of God comes to the whole world. Jeremiah's insight is that perhaps the exile is God's will for Israel—the means by which its mission might yet be fulfilled. They are to seek the peace and prosperity of the city of Babylon and accept the exile as God's will for now (Jeremiah 29:7).

Jesus founds a renewed people of God out a remnant of Israel (the twelve apostles), and from their witness comes the church. Paul's insight was that the "no" of Israel to Jesus as messiah is not a final answer but rather part of a mysterious opening for the Gentiles to come in (Romans 11). God has to allow the exile, has to allow his righteous servant to suffer and die, and has to allow Israel's eyes to be blinded so as to open a way for the Gentiles to come into the covenant. Christendom is a reversion to the old Israel of the monarchy, which had to be allowed to fall because it failed in its mission. The church is the suffering minority people of God that stands over against the world and by its distinctive witness makes it possible for people to convert by joining God's witnessing community of faith. Christendom makes conversion impossible by blurring the borders between church and culture; thus the church must take a stand against culture in order to make believing the gospel possible.

Discipleship

The third biblical theme stressed by type 6 is the call to discipleship, which involves a visible change of lifestyle. The discipleship stressed here is that of following Jesus in obedience to all that he taught. The overwhelming thrust of Jesus's

---

35. John Howard Yoder, *The Original Revolution: Essays on Christian Pacifism* (Scottdale, PA: Herald, 1971), 27–28.

ministry, as described in the Gospels, is a deemphasizing of religious rituals, customs, and rules and a corresponding emphasis on ethics, especially justice, mercy, forgiveness, and reconciliation. The lifestyle of discipleship leads to persecution by the world, which connects back to the previous theme because without a visibly separate church, the world has nothing to persecute. Discipleship and ecclesiology are thus visible.

The oft-repeated charge hurled at the separatists from the time of Augustine to the present is that this constitutes perfectionism and naïveté about the effects of sin. Often the charge is upgraded to Pelagianism and works righteousness. But to say that the church is visible is not to say that it is perfect. And to say that it is visible does not mean that one has to deny the reality of sin in the lives of Christians. In fact, a church made up of perfected saints would not be a community in which sinners would feel welcome. To say that the church is visible is merely to assert that there exists a community that confesses that it is sinful and that it has found forgiveness in the cross of Christ. The new lifestyle does not need to be one of sinless perfection, but need only be one of constant repentance and forgiveness. Interestingly the religious orders are not usually accused of this kind of pretension to perfectionism, even though the way in which they order their lives together is very similar to the way an Anabaptist congregation does.

Great Commission

The fourth biblical theme stressed by type 6 is the centrality of the Great Commission in the life and mission of the church. The great Roman Catholic missionary orders, such as the Jesuits, are examples of taking the Great Commission seriously. The church is to experience reconciliation, practice reconciliation, preach reconciliation, and hope for the day when reconciliation will be complete, rather than piecemeal and proleptic. Reconciliation is the heart of the gospel and the core of the identity of the church (Ephesians 2:11–22). The problem with Christendom is that the gospel becomes an internal matter of the individual, whereas salvation is a matter of the soul's destiny. Separatists oppose this individualism, even though they are often accused of fostering it. The nonseparatist demand is that our faith should be relevant to all of life—economics, politics, education, and so on—and the implication is that separatists narrow the focus to the soul and God. But actually, nonseparatists narrow the focus, with the result that the so-called relevance that the faith ends up having for the world is typically derived from natural theology rather than from the gospel. Separatists, on the other hand, come into such great conflict with the world precisely because they insist that the gospel is not irrelevant to issues of war and peace, marriage and divorce, capital and labor, and so on. The Hutterite insists on a particular kind of economic arrangement; the Benedictine insists on a particular political structure; the Mennonite insists on Christians talking to each other across national and ethnic boundaries even during a time of war. The problem is not that they make the gospel irrelevant; the real problem is that they make it too radical.

These biblical themes are often the implicit or explicit theological basis of type 6 movements. However, it is also common for many of those, especially in the monastic traditions, simply to base their lifestyle of chastity, poverty, and obedience directly on the commands of Jesus as found in the Gospels. A good example is Antony of Egypt. He heard the words of Jesus to the rich young ruler to sell everything, and he took them as applying to him and immediately obeyed. We can quibble about the soundness of his exegesis, but we must respect the absolute, literal obedience that many monks and nuns have given to what they considered the words of the Lord Jesus directly to them. Among many different Anabaptist and Brethren groups as well is found a similar direct obedience to the commands of Jesus.

Critique of Type 6

What can be said in critique of this type? The reader who has persevered to this point surely knows by now my conviction that Niebuhr's wholesale rejection of the radical Christ against culture type is the weakest part of his book. Furthermore, I also wish to counter the tendency of Niebuhr's work to convince his readers that the Christ against culture type must be rejected today in the name of responsibility and realism. I wish to rehabilitate the Christ against culture type and show that it does not necessarily lead to a failure to engage culture. Given these convictions, would it not be logical simply to affirm the Christ against culture type as correct and leave it at that? No, this course of action would be inadequate, for two very good reasons.

First, in the post-Christendom typology, the Christ against culture type is not the only alternative to Niebuhr's other four types. In the typology being proposed here, there are three non-Christendom types instead of only one, as in Niebuhr's typology. It would be wrong to leave the impression that it is all or nothing: support Christendom or separate from culture. Other possibilities will be explored in the next two chapters. Second, the Christ against culture type has been espoused at various points in history in ways that discredit the gospel and obscure the witness to the reconciling power of Jesus Christ. These failures must be acknowledged and not ignored if similar mistakes are to be avoided in the future.

One of Niebuhr's criticisms of the Christ against culture type, while it does not apply to all forms that this types takes, is on the mark with regard to some examples of the separatist approach. Niebuhr criticized the radicals for not understanding that the attempt to set up an alternative society is bound to crash into the reality of the universality of human sin. Niebuhr's observation is shrewd: "In his effort to be obedient to Christ, the radical Christian therefore reintroduces ideas and rules from non-Christian culture in two areas: in the government of the withdrawn Christian community, and in the regulation of Christian conduct toward the world outside" (71). What it comes down to is this: set up any kind of believers' church or separate community you like, and you will soon find that it is full of sinners, and you will inevitably find that the very sins you oppose in the world are also within your community of saints as well. There is considerable truth in this critique, and separatists would be foolish to ignore it. But is it grounds for abandoning the whole project of attempting to nurture a visible church? And have all separatists ignored this problem?

As a specific example, when the sixteenth-century Anabaptists suffered persecution at the hand of the Protestant and Roman Catholic churches and civil authorities, one of their responses was to move to areas where particular rulers were willing to offer them sanctuary. Quite often rulers like Catherine the Great of Russia wanted good farmers, who were known to lead quiet lives and not make trouble, to populate empty or underutilized lands. The tacit agreement between the Anabaptists and such rulers often involved freedom from military service and from persecution in exchange for paying taxes and refraining from evangelizing outside the community. The effect of this was to turn the Anabaptist colony into a ministate, led by religious officials, instead of being a church drawing members form the wider society around it. This change led directly to Mennonite colonies replicating some of the worst features of the Christendom they had originally attempted to challenge. Yoder puts it this way:

> The defensiveness and authoritarianism with which conservative mini-Constantinian establishments sometimes govern a rural colony or a church agency, the way in which immigrant farmers can without intending it be allied with authoritarian rulers against the interests of the previous, less technically advanced subjects of those same rulers, and the readiness to buy into some elements of the dominant culture while claiming to be clearly nonconformed on others, represent besetting temptations and at times direct moral failures in the Mennonite experience.[36]

Like the Puritans who fled religious persecution in England only to become persecutors themselves in New England, Mennonites who abandon evangelism and draw all new members from the children of members become a mini-Constantinian state. After a few generations have passed, the tendency is for most children of the colony to remain in the colony regardless of whether they possess a lively personal faith. This means, as Yoder puts it, that the world is now in the church.[37] The church is no longer separated from the world, and the line between the Mennonite colony and the outside world is now one of language, ethnicity, and culture rather than one of faith. Since the strategy of separation can fail, what is the solution?

We first must recognize that the criticism made by Niebuhr and the failures acknowledged by Yoder consist of the church becoming too much like the world;

36. John Howard Yoder, *The Priestly Kingdom: Social Ethics as Gospel* (Notre Dame: University of Notre Dame Press, 1984), 4. See also his discussion in *Christian Attitudes to War*, 198–99.

37. John Howard Yoder, *Nevertheless: The Varieties and Shortcomings of Religious Pacifism* (3rd ed.; Scottdale, PA: Herald, 1992), 104.

that is, the problem is that the believers' church becomes too much like the church of Christendom. The solution to this failing can hardly be Christendom! In other words, if the problem with the separated church is that it is too much like the nonseparated church, it can only exacerbate the problem by ceasing to be separate. What is needed is a better way to be separate, one that does not lead to replicating Christendom. How can this be achieved?

What Niebuhr is missing is a doctrine of the Holy Spirit and a conviction that the power of the Holy Spirit can make the separated church a community of equality rather than of authoritarianism. We also need to believe that the Spirit can make the Christian life a joyful expression of thanks to God, rather than a list of legalistic duties. In the end, apart from the work of the Holy Spirit, there is no hope for any church. Any church is going to degenerate into legalism, formalism, and authoritarianism over time unless there is continuing renewal and reform as the Holy Spirit repeatedly fills, empowers, and enlivens the community of faith.

When the separated church becomes so separate that it no longer functions as a witness to the surrounding culture, it is failing in its mission. It must be recognized that the call to come out and be separate is not a call to the church to become *absolutely* separate from the world. If God wanted to separate the church absolutely from the world, he could have accomplished that purpose by taking the church to heaven with Jesus in the ascension. But that would have defeated his real purpose. The church is to be distinct from the world in order to be a witness to the world. Separation must go hand in hand with witness, and so it can never be absolute separation.

The key here is for the church to retain its missional character—to keep at the center of its sense of identity its mission to witness to the gospel. The deal offered by rulers to end persecution if the church ends evangelism must be refused. In a strange way, this is the same deal offered by Constantine. If the church will become a department of the state and stop calling the state to follow Jesus, then the church will be favored rather than persecuted. Christendom can be any size. It can be a tiny Mennonite colony in Russia, a city like Geneva, a nation like the United States, or as large as the Roman Empire. The evangelization of the wider culture cannot be abandoned without the church losing its identity.

No bargain can be struck by the faithful church in which the central core of the church's mission is denied. Of course, this may mean no relief from persecution, and it may even mean the destruction of the church in some places at some times. But if God has told us to expect this outcome and if God is still sovereign, then we can focus on being faithful and leave the outcome in his hands. The church can always hope and pray for renewal. In the case of Russian Mennonites, this renewal happened in the rise of the Mennonite Brethren movement within the Mennonite colonies and later, in North America, in the twentieth-century recovery of the Anabaptist vision. There is no doubt that any faithful church (including ones that follow Niebuhr's prescription for attempting to facilitate the transformation of culture) can deteriorate and fall into sin. It happens throughout history to all kinds of churches. But there is also no doubt that the renewal and reform of the church can also happen and has been happening throughout church history.

What one must beware of is the temptation to identify the work of the Holy Spirit with only one tradition or one denomination and give in to the temptation to compromise in order that that tradition might be preserved. During the nineteenth century, a time of culture-Protestantism and reactionary Roman Catholicism, the future of the Anabaptist vision of the church looked bleak. But in 1900 who could have predicted the incredible explosion of Pentecostalism in the twentieth century? In 1900 who could have predicted the renewal of the Roman Catholic Church in Vatican II? Because of Pentecostalism, the believers' church has gone in one century from the smallest to the largest component of the worldwide church (other than the Roman Catholic Church). Who could have predicted that? At Vatican II, the Roman Catholic Church accepted the doctrine of religious freedom, for which thousands of sixteenth-century Anabaptists had died a martyr's death.[38] Who could have predicted that? It may well be that the vision of monks, Anabaptists, and other separated Christians—who have sought to make a visible community of Christians an alternative to the world—will live on in Protestant and Roman Catholic churches in the twenty-first century as Christendom ends and choices are made between renewal and death and between change and decline.

---

38. "Declaration on Religious Freedom," in *The Documents of Vatican II* (ed. Walter M. Abbott and Joseph Gallagher; Chicago: Follett, 1966), 675–700.

9

Christ Humanizing Culture
(Types 2 and 5)

In this chapter we examine types 2 and 5: Christ humanizing culture. Found second from the extreme right and second from the extreme left in table 8, they need to be examined together because they are very similar in many ways, although they also differ in important ways. The main difference, of course, is that they are on opposite sides of the central dividing line indicating acceptance or rejection by the church of coercive violence utilized by the state: type 2 is thus a Christendom type, and type 5 is a non-Christendom type. Those who embody type 2 regretfully accept the need for the employment of violent coercion in certain situations and therefore authorize Christian participation in most, if not all, forms of state-sponsored killing. Those who embody type 5, on the other hand, contend that Christians should not participate in violent coercion, whether state-sponsored or otherwise. Although both seek to humanize culture and although both recognize that violence is going to occur in a fallen world, exemplars of type 5 argue that Christians have their own, uniquely Christian calling and that they therefore should not allow themselves to be drawn into violence, whereas advocates of type 2 argue that Christians must participate in whatever violence is necessary for the defense of the innocent and the maintenance of peace and order in society.

Adherents of both types desire neither to be totally withdrawn from the world nor to be completely identified with the culture around them. They are, in this respect, like Niebuhr's mediating types. They both advocate the involvement of Christians outside the church in the wider world of culture, and they

Table 8. Post-Christendom Typology of Christ and Culture

	Christendom Types (accept violent coercion)			Non-Christendom Types (reject violent coercion)		
	Type 1: Christ legitimizing culture	Type 2: Christ humanizing culture	Type 3: Christ transforming culture	Type 4: Christ transforming culture	Type 5: Christ humanizing culture	Type 6: Christ separating from culture
Examples	• Theodosius I • Crusades • German Christians	• Luther • pietism • revivalism • Billy Graham	• Augustine • Columbus • Cromwell	• William Penn • Martin Luther King Jr. • Desmond Tutu	• Mother Teresa • Mennonite Central Committee • Brethren in Christ	• Antony of Egypt • Benedictines • Amish
View of Christ	symbol of ruling powers of society	unattainable yet relevant ideal	Lord of the cosmos	Lord of the cosmos	unattainable yet relevant ideal	Lord of the church
Biblical support	• conquest of Canaan under Joshua	• NT call to personal faith in Jesus (John 1:12; 3:16)	• Colossians 1:15–20 • OT Israel as theocracy	• Colossians 1:15–20 • Sermon on the Mount	• Jesus's parable of sheep and goats • early church in Acts	• OT exilic community • Revelation
Teaching of Jesus	denial of, even while using Christ as a cultic symbol to unify society	applicable only to private life (person/vocation dualism)	for all society and therefore should be imposed by force if necessary	for all society but should not be imposed by force, but preached by word and deed	for the church only, but motivates loving service to society	for the church only
Christology	docetic	partially docetic	inconsistently Nicene	Nicene	Nicene	Nicene

both believe that Christian involvement in culture will make society less violent and more just than it would be without the contribution of Christians to the culture. Both types believe that this improvement in society has its source in the personal morality of individual Christians, but type 5 sees that personal commitment being worked out in the context of community. For type 2, being a Christian makes one more honest, more dedicated to one's vocation, and more inclined to practice private charity, while for type 5 it makes you join a group working to serve the needy. It must be stressed, however, that although adherents of these two types may try to reform social structures, they would not try to Christianize them.

Neither of these two types believes that it is possible to have a Christian society or to convert whole nations, societies, and cultures to Christianity en masse, unlike those who exemplify type 3. But adherents of types 2 and 5 do believe that Christian involvement in secular society will make society better than it otherwise would be. This will occur through the conversion of individuals, who will then affect society by their personal morality (type 2) and also through their efforts in social service (type 5). Advocates of type 2 and type 5 want life to be more tolerable here and now, but they are realistic enough not to fall for the illusion of utopianism. Therefore, it is fitting that we call these two types "Christ humanizing culture." The meaning of this phrase is that Christ makes culture more humane, more civilized, and more reflective of that which is highest and best in human beings. It has nothing to do with secular humanism, which Christians reject as anti-Christian because it puts humanity in the place of God. The humanizing project envisioned here is one of making the world less violent and more just through Christians being salt and light in the world and influencing it for good.

Examples of Types 2 and 5

Martin Luther had no desire to end up like John Hus. Luther (1483–1546), the great sixteenth-century German founder of the Reformation in Germany, spoke out against false doctrine and church practices that obscured the gospel message. But, considering that Luther was attacking many of the same abuses and deformations of Christianity that Hus had attacked a century before, and considering that the Council of Constance had burned Hus at the stake, Luther had good cause for concern. Czech priest and reformer John Hus (1373–1415) was influenced by John Wycliffe and the English Lollards and shared many of their concerns about the corruptions of the medieval church, as well as their desire to reform it. He was lured to the Council of Constance by a promise of a safe conduct by the Holy Roman Emperor, but then was imprisoned anyway and burned at the stake on July 6, 1415. It was an example of the widely held philosophy that heresy has no rights. The medieval church could be cruel and unscrupulous toward anyone who challenged the status quo. When John Eck therefore labeled Luther "the Saxon Hus" after the Leipzig Disputation in 1519, the threat was unmistakable.[1]

Luther turned to the powerful princes of Germany in his attempt to escape the grim fate of the Czech reformer and to protect the Protestant Reformation from being crushed by forces loyal to Rome. So it was that the governance of the church was delivered into the hands of secular governments once again, this time even more completely than before. Like Hus and Wycliffe, Luther wanted to reform the church, not create a permanent division between Christians. And Luther certainly did not want to destroy the international character of the Christian church. But in turning to local governments for protection, Luther made these outcomes likely, if not inevitable. Luther's choice to make the Reformation a government program was to have long-term detrimental consequences for the gospel in the Western world.

1. Roland H. Bainton, *Here I Stand: A Life of Martin Luther* (New York: Mentor, 1950), 92.

Prior to the Reformation, the church was often controlled by various political powers, but there was, at least, a supranational entity, the papacy, to which appeal could be made. The papacy, at least in theory, symbolized the true character of the church as a body of believers drawn from many different linguistic, national, and ethnic groups. The Reformation changed all that in those areas of Europe that decided in favor of the Reformation. In Germany, England, and other Protestant countries, the church became a state church, and Christendom entered a new and even bloodier phase, as the devastation caused by the seventeenth-century wars of religion demonstrates. As the developing nation-states of early modern Europe gradually coalesced, each church became a national religion, controlled by the state and wedded to the interests of the state. This meant that nations fighting each other for power and influence now did so in the name of their own state religions, which became useful ideologies for motivating the population to fight against other states. It also meant that Christians now fought each other in the name of a nationalized faith. At the end of this road, four centuries later in Germany, lay the attempted fusion of *Volk* and church in the interests of German nationalism, which was to be one of the major causes of two horrific world wars in the twentieth century.

Evidence suggests, however, that the state-church approach was not Luther's first choice. In 1526 Luther published his version of the mass in the vernacular because he believed that ordinary people do not benefit from a service conducted in a language they do not understand. But what he thought would be ideal was what he called a "truly evangelical order."[2] This order of service was for a private service for those "who want to be Christians in earnest and who profess the gospel with hand and mouth."[3] Here is how he thought it would work:

> [They] should sign their names and meet alone in a house somewhere to pray, to read, to baptize, to receive the sacrament, and do other Christian works. According to this order, those who do not lead Christian lives could be known, reproved, corrected, cast out, or excommunicated, according to the rule of Christ, Matthew 18[:15–17]. Here one could also solicit benevolent gifts to be willingly given and distributed to the poor, according to St. Paul's example, II Corinthians 9. Here would be no need of much and elaborate singing. Here one could set out a brief and neat order for baptism and the sacrament and center everything on the Word, prayer, and love.[4]

Luther never established such a group of "earnest Christians." According to Donald Durnbaugh, "later he concluded that this was an impractical dream, and that to be

2. Martin Luther, *Liturgy and Hymns* (ed. U. S. Leupold in Vol. 53 of *Luther's Works*, ed. Helmut T. Lehman; Philadelphia: Fortress, 1965), 53ff. See also Donald F. Durnbaugh, *The Believers' Church: The History and Character of Radical Protestantism* (New York: Macmillan, 1965), 3.

3. Luther, *Liturgy and Hymns*, 53ff.

4. Ibid.

realistic, given the mixed multitude, he would have to turn to the prince in order to get on with the task of securing the Reformation."[5] But Luther's expression of the problem was backward. The mixed multitude and the political support for the Reformation were not a given; they were Luther's choices. *Given those choices*, this radical vision for a believers' church was not realistic.

As Roland Bainton notes, the growth of the Anabaptists, beginning in Switzerland in the 1520s, shows that it was possible to implement Luther's vision for a believers' church, even in sixteenth-century Europe. But it was possible only by breaking entirely with the territorial church concept; that is, with the concept of Christendom. Bainton says: "Luther's dilemma was that he wanted both a confessional church based on personal faith and experience, and a territorial church including all in a given locality. If he was forced to choose, he would take his stand with the masses, and this was the direction in which he moved."[6] Arguably, it is more accurate to say that Luther took his stand with the princes and nobles against the peasants, but Bainton's point—and he is exactly right—is that Luther chose the territorial church over the confessional church. Luther's choice was just that: a choice. Others chose differently. Whereas Luther chose the territorial church (or Christendom) model, the Anabaptists chose the confessional church (or non-Christendom) model. Granted, Luther died peacefully in his bed, and many of the Anabaptists suffered the same gruesome fate as Hus; nevertheless, the choice was there.

Luther chose the way of continuing Christendom even though it became fragmented into various geographical and political units. The church and state were to work together, and all the individuals within a given political unit were to be members of the state church. Everyone was to be baptized at birth, tithes were collected by force, heresy was illegal, and there was no tolerance of challenges to the religious status quo. The church, in such a system, inevitably becomes a mixed multitude of true Christians and unbelievers who outwardly conform because of fear of coercion. Christian morality can be expected only of the clergy; Christianity for the laity is a matter of ceremony and ritual, rather than ethics or discipleship.

The Lutheran concept of vocation was developed as a way of conceiving how a Christian could and should exercise his or her faith in the world. Niebuhr identifies Luther as the leading example of his Christ and culture in paradox type. This type, which Niebuhr calls the "dualist" position, is also known as the "two-kingdoms" position (170–71). The Christian is a citizen of the kingdom of God and also of the kingdom of the world. As a citizen of the kingdom of God, the Christian lives according to the gospel in his or her personal or individual life. But as a citizen of this world, he or she carries out his or her vocation in the world. One's vocation in the world is determined by the world—there is no such

5. Durnbaugh, *Believers' Church*, 4.
6. Bainton, *Here I Stand*, 243.

thing as a Christian cobbler, a Christian judge, or a Christian soldier. A Christian who is a cobbler, judge, or soldier simply attempts to be a good one. It is wrong to insert specifically Christian morality into one's worldly vocation; for example, a banker obviously must not give away the bank's holdings to the poor in obedience to Jesus's command to give to those who ask. A Christian soldier may personally love the enemy, but he or she shoots the enemy just the same in his or her capacity as a soldier. The hope for Christians influencing the world is that, if there are many Christians in society, their collective honesty, integrity, and dedication to doing a good job will make that society a better society than it otherwise would be. But Christianity does not really change the nature of society; it just changes the nature of some of the people in that society.

To a certain extent, however, the Christian prince is an exception to the rule that Christians do nothing different in their vocation from non-Christians, because it is the duty of the Christian ruler to enforce the Christian religion on society. This does not mean that everyone is expected to become a disciple of Jesus, but it means that the church has a privileged place in society and that some level of outward conformity to Christianity is required of all citizens. What is enforced is a religion that is neither a public discipleship nor a total life and world view. Religion is understood in the sense in which religion has been understood from the beginning of history—as the special sphere of life in which humanity relates to God or the gods. Religion is therefore not politics, education, economics, entertainment, or science. It is the relationship of the soul to God; that is, of one invisible thing to another invisible thing. The church's mission consists of its functioning as a department of the state looking after the religious needs of the population. The Christian prince ensures that this is done through the clergy of the church, who are employees of the state.

A second example of the type 2 approach grew up within the Lutheran territories once the revival that had accompanied the Reformation had cooled into a rigid, Scholastic orthodoxy. During the seventeenth and eighteenth centuries, a movement known as pietism arose within the Lutheran churches, which sought to promote personal religious experience and commitment.[7] This movement was a reaction against the formalism of the Protestant Scholasticism that dominated Lutheranism (and Calvinism) after the wars of religion. (Puritanism was, in some ways, a similar movement within Calvinism.) Pietism was a movement of clergy and laypeople that emphasized the need for a holy life in addition to doctrinal orthodoxy. A Lutheran minister, Philipp Jacob Spener (1635–1705), published his *Pia desideria* in 1675 with a list of six proposals for the restoration of true religion: (1) personal and devotional study of the Bible, (2) taking more seriously the priesthood of all believers, (3) emphasis on the practice rather than

7. F. L. Cross and E. A. Livingston, eds., *The Oxford Dictionary of the Christian Church* (3rd ed.; Oxford: Oxford University Press, 1997), 1286 s.v. "Pietism." For an excellent and concise introduction to pietism, see Dale W. Brown, *Understanding Pietism* (Grand Rapids: Eerdmans, 1978).

merely the knowledge of Christian faith, (4) winning the heart by love rather than coercion, (5) combining university studies in theology with heart religion, and (6) reforming preaching as a form of edification.[8] This program formed the basis of the pietist movement, which persists to the present day and which has been extremely influential in the development of modern Protestantism.

In defining pietism it is difficult to know whether a narrow definition or a broad one is most appropriate. Defined in its strictest and narrowest sense, pietism is that movement in Lutheran areas of Europe between 1675 and 1850 stemming from the work and writings of Spener and August Francke (1663–1727).[9] Respected church historian Kenneth Scott Latourette has a generally favorable treatment of pietism and tends to define it in this relatively narrow manner, although he acknowledges its wide influence.[10] Ernest Stoeffler, however, argues for a broader definition.[11] He says that we find running from the days of the apostles, through the history of the church, an experiential tradition. During the Middle Ages it expressed itself in a mystical approach to the Christian life, and during the Reformation neither Luther nor Calvin were free of its grip, while the Strassburg reformers, such as Martin Bucer, were strongly influenced by it. Anabaptists and other Radical Reformers were influenced by it as well, and during the seventeenth century it manifested itself in pietism. All streams of Protestantism have since been influenced by it. This kind of broad definition is too wide to be useful, so we will employ the narrower one.

At the same time, we must resist the temptation to explain pietism away as if it were nothing but something else in disguise. Some people view pietism as a mere extension of medieval mysticism and monastic piety, while others see it merely as a precursor of modern liberal Protestantism with its emphasis on experience. Yet, it must be regarded as more than merely a late blooming of medieval piety, because it has demonstrated remarkable adaptive powers in persisting over four centuries in diverse environments and in many forms. It must also be regarded as more than a precursor of liberal Protestantism, since it has persisted in a non-liberal form throughout the liberal period and may, in fact, outlive liberalism! Yet in saying that it is "more than" we should not deny that there are similarities. Instead of defining every kind of experiential religion as pietism, we should recognize the influence that German pietism has had on movements as diverse as Methodism, Pentecostalism, and North American evangelicalism. John R. W. Stott in England and Billy Graham in the United States, and those who rally around their respective ministries, could be called pietistic and may actually be modern examples of pietism.

8. Philipp Jacob Spener, *Pia desideria* (trans. and ed. T. G. Tappert; Philadelphia: Fortress, 1964), 87–122.

9. Brown, *Understanding Pietism*, 15.

10. Kenneth Scott Latourette, *A History of Christianity*, vol. 2: *Reformation to the Present* (rev. ed.; New York: Harper & Row, 1975), 894–97.

11. F. Ernest Stoeffler, *The Rise of Evangelical Pietism* (Leiden: Brill, 1971), 6–8.

The University of Halle was founded in order to promote pietism, and it was but one institutional expression of the movement's emphasis on mission.[12] Other expressions included an orphanage, a hospital, a widow's home, a teacher's training institute, a Bible school, a book depot, and a Bible house. Dale Brown is of the opinion that Calvinist influences on Spener led him to advocate a transformational ethic that was incompatible with the Lutheran two-kingdoms doctrine, which is more characteristic of German pietism.[13] A leading figure at Halle was Francke. Professor of theology, he also was very involved in promoting mission work. Count Nicholas von Zinzendorf (1700–60), who was raised by his pietist maternal grandmother and educated at Halle, created the Moravian church out of fragments of the Hussite movement at his family estate at Herrnhut. The Moravians are a pietist denomination and were the first Protestant group to engage in cross-cultural mission work, having sent out their first missionaries as early as 1732. Their influence on John Wesley was important in his spiritual development, and they have served as models for other denominations in the area of missions.

One could say that pietism stands halfway between Lutheranism and Anabaptism. Like Anabaptism, pietism stresses personal faith, Bible reading, prayer, evangelism, missions, conversion, fellowship, and discipleship. Historically, many have followed the lead of Albrecht Ritschl in regarding pietism as a revival of emphases of the Radical Reformation.[14] But not all pietists broke totally with the state-church model, as Anabaptism did. Pietists have often worked to create a church within a church; that is, a fellowship of believers that does not separate from the Sunday services of the state church but that supplements those services with prayer fellowships, mission groups, Bible studies, and so on. In many cases, pietist ministers occupy many of the pulpits of the state churches. A good example is the outstanding ministry of John R. W. Stott at All Souls Anglican Church in London in the second half of the twentieth century. Pietism is like Anabaptism in stressing personal faith and conversion, but it remains within the state-church structure like Lutheranism.

Unlike Anabaptism, in which conversion is a matter of becoming a part of a community of faith and ethical discipleship, conversion in pietism is primarily a matter of a change in the individual heart. What the doctrine of justification was to Luther, the doctrine of regeneration was to Spener.[15] The result of this is that the Lutheran two-kingdoms theology can be maintained and pietists can often function perfectly well within the constraints of Christendom. How-

12. For the information in this paragraph, see Robert G. Clouse, "Pietism"; idem, "August Hermann Francke"; and Richard V. Pierard, "Count Nikolaus Ludwig von Zinzendorf"—all in *The New International Dictionary of the Christian Church* (ed. J. D. Douglas; Grand Rapids: Zondervan, 1974), 780, 388, 1071; and F. L. Cross and E. A. Livingston, eds., *The Oxford Dictionary of the Christian Church* (3rd ed.; Oxford: Oxford University Press, 1997), 1112–13 s.v. "Moravian Brethren."

13. Brown, *Understanding Pietism*, 134.

14. Ibid., 19.

15. Ibid., 99.

ever, it should be mentioned that Spener and Francke both appealed for more religious liberty, especially in nonessentials of faith, than was common in their day. While believing that heresy should be fought vigorously, they argued that physical force should not be used, but only the weapons of prayer, love, argument, and persuasion.[16] This did not make them pacifist, but it did move them significantly in the direction of opposing violent coercion, which is a central mark of Christendom.

The strengths of pietism are the depth of its spirituality, the biblical and evangelical character of its faith, its missionary zeal, and its concern for the practical outworking of the Christian faith. But the reason why pietism is an example of type 2 instead of type 5 is that pietists do not usually challenge the existence or validity of Christendom. Although it is true that the emphasis on personal faith is in tension with the Christendom concept of coercion, it is nonetheless also true that pietism often works within a Christendom view of the church. Spener, for example, did not wish to eliminate the authority of the secular rulers over the church.[17] The concept of a pietistic chaplain in the army ministering to pietist soldiers is not contradictory to the spirit of pietism as such. Some pietist groups, as we shall see, do challenge the Christendom understanding of the church, but this does not always or necessarily happen in pietism.

If Billy Graham is a major modern example of the type 2 approach, Mother Teresa would be an outstanding example of the type 5 approach, a non-Christendom approach that rejects violent coercion as incompatible with the gospel. While the evangelical movement exemplified by Graham generally accepts Christian participation in state-sponsored violence, Mother Teresa and her Missionaries of Charity choose to witness to the gospel by serving the poor and needy in ways that preclude participation in violence. In fact, during the pontificate of John Paul II, the whole idea of Christian support for violence—whether the violence of war, capital punishment, euthanasia, or abortion—was subjected to increasing critique within the Roman Catholic Church. Graham's stand against the use of nuclear arms, despite his generally pietistic stance, represents a beginning of a potential trend toward convergence on this issue, although many disagreements still remain between evangelicals and Roman Catholics.

Another good example of the type 5 approach is the Mennonite Central Committee, discussed briefly in the last chapter. The work of the Mennonite Central Committee focuses on relief and development, refugee work, community development, and peacemaking. As an umbrella organization for about fifteen Mennonite and Brethren denominations, the Mennonite Central Committee provides opportunities for Christians to serve around the world in places where war, poverty, and natural disasters have created human tragedies. The work of the Mennonite Central Committee is similar to many other nongovernmental

16. Ibid., 43.
17. Ibid., 59.

organizations that do humanitarian work around the world, many of which are Christian, such as World Vision.

But one unique emphasis of the Mennonite Central Committee is its work in peacemaking, which arises out of its unique Anabaptist history and pacifist commitment. The multicultural makeup of the Anabaptist movement, which is due to its commitment to cross-cultural missionary work, and the minority status of the Anabaptist family of denominations allow Mennonite Central Committee workers to come into conflict situations, not as representatives of a certain nation-state or of Christendom, but simply as Christians. This means that the gospel becomes a radical, but hopeful, word to all concerned, rather than being a vehicle of cultural imperialism or a symbol of the West or the so-called British or American empire.

Another example of a type 5 approach is the Brethren in Christ Church, a movement that participates in both the Anabaptist and pietist streams of church history. The movement that became the Brethren in Christ Church began about 1870 in Lancaster County, Pennsylvania, when a group of Mennonites came under the influence of some German pietists who emphasized spiritual passion and a warm, personal relationship to Jesus Christ.[18] These pietist preachers also emphasized the necessity of a crisis-conversion experience. The Mennonites felt that these biblical emphases were missing from their churches, and they began a new fellowship that eventually became known as the Brethren in Christ. Later, around the beginning of the twentieth century, this group was influenced by the Wesleyan doctrine of holiness. The teaching of a second work of grace, which results in the believer receiving the ability to say no to sin, was accepted as official doctrine by this group. However, they continued to be Anabaptists, and so a life of discipleship (including pacifism) was a major emphasis.

Today, the group has its headquarters in Grantham, Pennsylvania, and includes about 270 local congregations in North America and 1,100 churches in twenty-three countries worldwide, with over eighty thousand members. The group operates Messiah College, a leading Christian liberal arts college in Grantham, and carries on cross-cultural mission work in twenty-three countries. The Brethren in Christ Church is one of the supporting partners of the Mennonite Central Committee. Radical discipleship, holy living, and evangelistic outreach characterize this denomination. Because the primary value of the typology is heuristic and because individuals and groups will not always fit perfectly into them, this pietist movement almost could have been classified as an example of type 2, but the influence of its Anabaptist heritage makes it an example of a non-Christendom type 5 movement.

One of the major questions facing the evangelical movement in North America is how it will adjust to the new situation that will arise as Christendom crumbles.

---

18. "About the Brethren in Christ: Our History," Brethren in Christ in North America website: http:// www.bic-church.org/about/history.asp (accessed May 16, 2005). See also E. Morris Sider, "Brethren in Christ Churches, General Conference of," Global Anabaptist Mennonite Encyclopedia Online website: http://www.gameo.org/encyclopedia/contents/B748ME.html (accessed May 16, 2005).

The pietistic heritage of evangelicalism does not offer a clear direction for a post-Christendom situation. In many ways, pietism is parasitic on Christendom; it presupposes the existence of Christendom and has adapted its emphasis on personal religion to the Christendom situation. What this means in practice is that pietism has attempted to avoid the stark choice between the territorial church and the believers' church, which divided the Magisterial Reformers from the Anabaptists in the sixteenth century. The Protestant Reformation represented a continuation of Christendom in a different form, and Anabaptism represented a rejection of the whole Christendom idea. Pietism, like the seventeenth-century Baptist movement, attempted to incorporate many Anabaptist ideals into a Christendom context. The Baptists moved further away from the Christendom model than the pietists in that they formed believers' churches, but they stopped short of the Anabaptist commitment to pacifism. As we move from the Christendom to the post-Christendom period, all the historical questions are back on the table once again.

Christian groups will gradually move in one of two directions: either toward becoming the culture-religion of the evolving post-Christian West or toward becoming a believers' church with a missional-church approach. (Even churches whose theology does not provide for a believers' church approach are increasingly finding themselves becoming believers' churches anyway, as more and more secularized people do not bother even to make use of the church for rites of passage.) The short- to medium-term future is likely to witness the realignment of historic denominations on a scale that makes the fundamentalist-modernist divisions of the early twentieth century look like a mere dress rehearsal. The liberal stream likely will emphasize sexual permissiveness and a vague emphasis on spirituality with a New Age or Hindu tinge and will retain churchly characteristics as it evolves and adapts its role as chaplain to postmodern, neopagan culture. The evangelical stream increasingly will become either the state church of a conservative political movement or a countercultural church of converts (a believers' church) and a witnessing minority in a pluralistic situation. The evangelical stream will maintain historic Christian orthodoxy as expressed in the canon of Scripture and the ancient, ecumenical creeds, and it will combine this orthodoxy with a missional emphasis that views the purpose of the church as bearing witness to the gospel in the world. This process will occur first in Europe and Canada, but the United States would be well advised to keep a sharp eye on these developments because the viability of American Christendom is increasingly questionable.

One of the concerns of this book is to point out the importance of the issue of pacifism for the future of the church. As we move beyond Christendom, any efforts perceived as attempts to resurrect Christendom or to impose Christianity on the population by coercive methods will increasingly be obstructions to the hearing of the gospel message. Therefore, we need to adopt and emphasize a pacifist stance for the sake of evangelism. The gospel of grace is fully compatible with evangelistic methods that respect the right of individuals to reject Christianity, but it is incompatible with violent coercion. As the privileged status of Christianity fades, more and more opposition will arise to any attempt to resurrect Christendom. Any such attempts will provoke a backlash, not only against Christendom, but also against the gospel. In such an environment, it is essential to the mission of the church that the church distance itself clearly from all forms of violence and coercion. The early church—rather than the church of Christendom—must be our model. The historic peace churches (Mennonites, Quakers, Brethren) have much to teach the rest of the church about living as a peaceful minority in a violent world.

View of Christ Entailed by Types 2 and 5

The view of Christ entailed by both type 2 and type 5 is that Christ represents an unattainable but relevant ideal. For both of these types, the incarnate Jesus Christ is authoritative for Christians in his humanity. This sets them apart from type 1, where the humanity of Jesus Christ is acknowledged theoretically but not allowed to become decisive for Christian discipleship. For type 2 and type 5 approaches, the humanity of Jesus Christ is seen as decisive for Christian discipleship insofar as the humanity of Jesus Christ is seen as the ideal. For both of these types, however, the ideal cannot be applied to human society in the fallen world successfully and so is, in a sense, unattainable.

What is meant by the word *unattainable*, however, is understood differently in these types. For type 2 approaches, the ideal human life of Jesus is unattainable because Christians are citizens of two kingdoms simultaneously and must live according to two different ethical systems at the same time. On the one hand the Christian must follow Jesus in his or her personal life, while on the other hand the Christian must carry out his or her vocation in society according to the rules and standards of the wider society. For type 2 the humanity of Jesus is thus an unattainable model for Christians in public life. But for type 5 approaches, the ideal human life of Jesus is unattainable in the sense that the church remains a minority and the non-Christian majority will never agree to follow Jesus in the way of discipleship. For type 5 the humanity of Jesus is thus an unattainable model for nondisciples. The final result is similar in a way: both approaches agree that we cannot have a Christian society if that means one in which the actual teachings of Jesus about money, sex, power, and violence are implemented in the institutions of society. For type 2 this cannot happen because Christians are not called to implement the actual teachings of Jesus in the wider society; these teachings are only for the individual and perhaps for the family and church. For type 5, on the other hand, it cannot happen because, as long as the church is a witnessing minority within a larger society, the teachings of Jesus can be normative only for the church and not for the society as a whole. In other words, the teachings of Jesus are for disciples, and there is no feasible way to impose them on nondisciples. In other words, for type 2 approaches, the teachings of Jesus are unattainable except for Christians functioning as individuals within the private sphere of home and church, while for type 5 approaches the teachings of Jesus are unattainable for those who do not confess Jesus to be Lord.

In both cases, however, the unattainable ideal of Jesus's teachings and example is relevant. But, again, they are relevant in different ways. For type 2 the humanity of Jesus is relevant as an ideal, which reveals what true human life is intended to be by the creator. The Sermon on the Mount radicalizes the Old Testament law in such a way as to emphasize the impossibility of keeping God's law or doing God's will in our fallen human condition. Thus, the sermon functions to drive us to our knees and to seek forgiveness for our sins. We cannot obey it literally in this fallen world; its strenuous demands must be mitigated by realism, common sense, and responsibility. But this is not to say that the sermon is irrelevant because it sets outs God's standards. Pietism is thus compatible with full participation in civil society, including violence. Even Christians who take very literally Jesus's teachings nevertheless feel that it is perfectly compatible with their personal discipleship to engage in worldly violence because not to do so would be irresponsible and unrealistic.

For type 5, however, the relevance of the Sermon on the Mount is more than merely negative; it has a positive relevance for the community of disciples who confess Jesus as Lord. That it cannot become the legislation for a society made up of disciples and nondisciples mixed together does not mean that it cannot function as the basis for the community of disciples. Type 5 stresses the relevance of the life and teachings of Jesus for the life of his disciples as they live together in Christian community. The sermon is not just a tool for inducing despair at our human inability to do God's will and keep the law of Christ. Of course, it does reveal to us the depth of our depravity and our need of divine grace, but it is also a positive program for kingdom living within the new polity created by the Holy Spirit. The humanity of Jesus Christ is attainable, but only by Spirit-filled disciples who have bowed the knee to Jesus Christ. It is unattainable by others and, thus, unattainable by society as a whole.

Biblical Support for Types 2 and 5

Type 2 appeals primarily to the biblical call to personal faith in Jesus Christ. The key text is John 3:16, which makes belief in Jesus Christ decisive for eternal life. John 1:12 emphasizes the need for each individual to receive Jesus Christ as Lord and Savior. Jesus's calling of the twelve disciples is understood to be proto-typical for the calling of all followers of Jesus. The disciples' mission of preaching the gospel and calling people to faith in Jesus—as, for example, Peter did on the day of Pentecost—shows that the same means is to be used to call people to faith in Jesus as Jesus himself used during his earthly ministry.

This biblical emphasis is often understood in terms of having a crisis conversion with a conviction of sin and an overwhelming sense of lostness and hopelessness, followed by a deep repentance of sin and trust in Christ alone for salvation. This type of experience is often seen as normative, even for the children of Christians who have been raised in Christian homes. However, this kind of conversion (usually recalled in detail, extending to the date and hour) is not always seen as normative for all Christians in the pietistic stream. Often there is openness to understanding the converting work of Holy Spirit as more gradual and less traumatic in certain cases. Not all Christians in type 2 can tell you the date and hour of their conversion; some believe they have been Christians for as long as they can remember. Nevertheless, they have no hesitation in preaching the need for others to have a crisis conversion if they are not already Christians.

While texts that emphasize the necessity of personal conversion may be important to some type 5 groups, type 5 inevitably appeals to texts that deal with the need for those who have experienced God's grace to serve the poor and needy in Jesus's name. The parable of the sheep and goats in Matthew 25:31–46 is a perfect example of this kind of text, although the Scriptures are full of texts embodying similar teachings. An excerpt from Mother Teresa's 1979 Nobel Peace Prize acceptance speech, given in Oslo, Norway, catches the spirit of what it means to practice Jesus's teachings in this parable:

> One evening we went out and we picked up four people from the street. And one of them was in a most terrible condition. And I told the sisters: "You take care of the other three; I will take care of this one that looks worse." So I did for her all that my love can do. I put her in bed, and there was such a beautiful smile on her face. She took hold of my hand, as she said one word only: "thank you"—and she died. And she died with a smile on her face—like that man who we picked up from the drain, half eaten with worms, and we brought him to the home—"I have lived like an animal in the street, but I am going to die like an angel, loved and cared for."
>
> And it was so wonderful to see the greatness of that man who could speak like that, who could die like that without blaming, without cursing anybody, without comparing anything. Like an angel—this is the greatness of our people.
>
> And this is why we believe what Jesus has said: "I was hungry; I was naked, I was homeless; I was unwanted, unloved, uncared for—and you did it to me." I believe that we are not really social workers. We may be doing social work in the eyes of people. But we are really contemplatives in the heart of the world. For we are touching the body of Christ twenty-four hours.[19]

The life and ministry of Mother Teresa and others like her exemplify the appeal to the parable of the sheep and goats, which is a key text for type 5.

Another key text for type 5 is the description of the early church in the book of Acts. This text pictures a community united by its faith in Jesus Christ prac-

19. Quoted from the Mother Teresa website: http://www.drini.com/motherteresa/own_words/ (accessed May 16, 2005).

ticing economic sharing and bearing witness to Jesus Christ even when bearing that witness results in martyrdom. Type 5 stresses not only the need to give the cup of cold water in Jesus's name, but also the need for communities of faith to embody this lifestyle in their communal lives: to care for widows and orphans in their affliction, as the book of James (1:27) puts it. To create communities that embody this ideal is a significant step beyond just pointing to this ideal as something that individuals should strive for on their own in private. To believe that the humanity of Jesus can be normative for the community of disciples requires one to take a further step in the direction of believing that the normative humanity embodied in Jesus of Nazareth is not only possible for humans to live, but also a feasible basis on which to construct a human community. If the kingdom of God is not pie in the sky, this latter claim must be substantiated in the daily life of the visible church.

Critique of Types 2 and 5

What can we say in critique of types 2 and 5? Despite their similarities, it will be necessary to consider each of them separately because different criticisms are warranted in each case.

The main criticism that must be faced by those who advocate type 2 approaches to the issue of how to relate Christ and culture is that a fundamental tension exists between its acceptance of Christendom and its attempt to let the humanity of Jesus Christ be normative for discipleship. Adherents of type 2 generally affirm a fully Nicene Christology in which both the divinity and the humanity of Jesus Christ are confessed to be true. When it comes to the personal sphere, the need for personal discipleship and holiness is affirmed quite readily. But in the public sphere, instead of advocating following Jesus in the way of the cross, there is acceptance of the necessity of compromise with the world when it comes to violent coercion. The Christian disciple is counseled to fight in war, support the state church and its coercive methods, and generally be a good citizen of the nation-state. This being the case, is the humanity of Jesus Christ, in which God's will for humanity is revealed, really authoritative for exemplars of type 2? This is a difficult question because it is not quite right to say that those who advocate type 2 have a docetic Christology or that they deny the authority of Jesus's life and teachings for the believer. But, on the other hand, there is no question that the authority of the life and teachings of Jesus are restricted to the personal sphere and not allowed to be normative for the public area.

In order for the life and teachings of Jesus to become normative for the public sphere, what would need to change for those who espouse type 2? What would need to happen for the adherents of type 2 to reject Christendom and to embrace a doctrine of the church as basic to discipleship? Discipleship cannot be a matter of individualistic efforts; it must be lived out in community. Once membership in the church becomes a higher priority and more central to one's identity than citizenship in a nation-state, then it becomes possible to view the radical teachings of Jesus as realistic. They are not realistic for individuals for whom the nation-state is their primary community, but they are realistic for members of close-knit communities of converted disciples living in covenant with one another. The rejection of violent coercion is the key to making one's membership in the church more fundamental to one's identity than one's citizenship in the nation-state. Once one rejects violence and begins to live out a life of discipleship within the church, one moves from the world into the kingdom of God. Once this happens, Jesus becomes Lord instead of Caesar. To make this move is to move from type 2 to type 5, and it is to move away from the idea of Christendom.

But is it enough to advocate moving from type 2 to type 5? Certainly, it is preferable that one make this move, but is it enough? Is type 5 an adequate form of Christian discipleship? Type 5 seeks to humanize society, and its typical form of outreach is social service. To heal the sick, visit the prisoner, feed the hungry, and comfort the afflicted is the agenda of those in this type, and there is no doubt that this agenda is biblical. But is it complete? Should Christians not also get involved in what could be called social action in addition to social service; that is, in politics in addition to social work? Should Christians not try to address the causes of the afflictions whose effects they seek to alleviate? If it is good to provide a home for a single mother while she is carrying a child instead of aborting it, would it not be better to try to influence public policy in order to reduce the number of abortions or even to eradicate abortion altogether? If it is good to send food to starving families in Africa, would it not be even better to provide those families with the training and the capital by which they could become self-sufficient? Or to change unjust international laws that prevent poor African farmers from selling their crops at a profit in the world market? If it is good to care for the dying, would it not be even better to build hospitals in an attempt to heal those who are sick? In other words, can those who advocate type 5 really avoid moving to a type 4 position and getting involved in attempting to transform society according to the concerns of Jesus? Is it enough to call for better treatment of slaves; is it not necessary to go further and call for the abolition of slavery itself?

A key issue here is the question of whether it is necessary to embrace violent coercion in order to move from social service to social action, from social work to politics. If one believes that in order to make this move, one must agree to support violent coercion, then it would seem that one could not move in this direction without embracing Christendom. Then it would come down to a choice between involvement in attempting to transform society and embracing violent coercion, on the one hand, or sitting on the sidelines and maintaining a pacifist stance, on the other. This is the choice that Niebuhr insists we must make: responsible involvement that accepts violence or irrelevant withdrawal that rejects violence. Either we can be good citizens and dedicate our lives to helping our fellow humans in the political sphere or we can follow Jesus's teachings literally and faithfully—but we cannot do both. Believing that this is our dilemma, Niebuhr therefore advocated the acceptance of Christendom and compromise with violence in the name of justice.

The burden of this book is to show that Niebuhr presents a false dilemma. Granted, many Christians have felt the force of this problem and sincerely believed that this dilemma is inescapable. From the time of Constantine to the present, many leaders of the church have chosen the path of responsible involvement over what they perceived to be irresponsible purity. But this is a false dilemma. First, it presupposes that kingdom ethics is irrelevant, when the reality is that nothing could be more relevant to the problems of this world. Second, it also presupposes that those who follow Jesus in the way of peace have nothing to say to the wider society that people outside the church want to hear. Third, it presupposes that the witness to the gospel is worthwhile only when it works; that is, when it is embraced by the world.

Actually, none of these presuppositions are true. First, nothing could be more relevant to a world perched precariously on the brink of nuclear annihilation than the message that reconciliation is possible and has already begun in the church. Surely it is not credible to call the work of the Mennonite Central Committee irrelevant. It most certainly is not irrelevant to the people from all around the world who directly and indirectly benefit from it, and someday we may wake up to find that we all have benefited from it because it has prevented nuclear holocaust. Second, many who do not confess faith in Jesus Christ nevertheless are ready to listen to what those who follow Jesus have to say about the crucial issues that all of us face. The awarding of the Nobel Peace Prize to Mother Teresa surely demonstrates the respect that people far beyond her religious order or the Roman Catholic Church have for her life's work. In light of her prolife, profamily, antipoverty message going so much against the grain of Western individualism and the culture of death, it is amazing that she has been able to win any kind of hearing at all. Third, it is not our responsibility to ensure that the world accepts the gospel; our mission is to be faithful heralds and to communicate the message. The Spirit of God is sovereign and can be trusted with looking after the results.

10

Christ Transforming Culture
(Types 3 and 4)

In this chapter we examine types 3 and 4: Christ transforming culture. Located in the middle of table 9, they are very similar, except that type 3 (a Christendom type) falls on the left side of the centerline, indicating that exemplars of this type accept the necessity of participating in violent coercion, while type 4 (a non-Christendom type) falls on the right side of the line, indicating that exemplars of this type reject violent coercion. Both of these types seek to transform society into a Christian society insofar as that may be possible. Both tend to be optimistic about the degree to which whole societies can be transformed, although more realistic representatives, who believe that society can be improved but never made perfect apart from a cataclysmic, end-time intervention of God, can be found in both types. Nevertheless, all representatives of both types believe that the attempt should be made. The only difference between them is that one type advocates Christian involvement in state-sponsored violent coercion, and the other believes that such involvement is an unjustifiable compromise with worldly methods.

Type 3 is certainly right to insist that someone must maintain law and order in this fallen world. Certainly, the Bible is not so idealistic and utopian as to suppose that, in this world of sin, there will ever cease to be a need for the sword. Most people on both sides of the centerline from all six types admit this fact, except for some representatives of type 3 (such as Marxists) and type 4 (such as liberal Protestants) who have allowed themselves to get caught up in the illusions

Table 9. Post-Christendom Typology of Christ and Culture

| | Christendom Types (accept violent coercion) | | | Non-Christendom Types (reject violent coercion) | | |
	Type 1: Christ legitimizing culture	Type 2: Christ humanizing culture	Type 3: Christ transforming culture	Type 4: Christ transforming culture	Type 5: Christ humanizing culture	Type 6: Christ separating from culture
Examples	• Theodosius I • Crusades • German Christians	• Luther • pietism • revivalism • Billy Graham	• Augustine • Columbus • Cromwell	• William Penn • Martin Luther King Jr. • Desmond Tutu	• Mother Teresa • Mennonite Central Committee • Brethren in Christ	• Antony of Egypt • Benedictines • Amish
View of Christ	symbol of ruling powers of society	unattainable yet relevant ideal	Lord of the cosmos	Lord of the cosmos	unattainable yet relevant ideal	Lord of the church
Biblical support	• conquest of Canaan under Joshua	• NT call to personal faith in Jesus (John 1:12; 3:16)	• Colossians 1:15–20 • OT Israel as theocracy	• Colossians 1:15–20 • Sermon on the Mount	• Jesus's parable of sheep and goats • early church in Acts	• OT exilic community • Revelation
Teaching of Jesus	denial of, even while using Christ as a cultic symbol to unify society	applicable only to private life (person/vocation dualism)	for all society and therefore should be imposed by force if necessary	for all society but should not be imposed by force, but preached by word and deed	for the church only, but motivates loving service to society	for the church only
Christology	docetic	partially docetic	inconsistently Nicene	Nicene	Nicene	Nicene

of human perfectibility through education and political/economic means. The debate between representatives of type 3 and type 4 is whether Christians are called to wield the sword. There is little doubt that someone is going to wield the sword in this fallen world; the doctrine of sin assures us of that fact. The question is whether Christians should be the ones to perpetrate the violent coercion necessary to prevent anarchy and injustice.

Sometimes that issue is cast as a matter of weak Christians who have no stomach for the brutal but necessary violence that is needed to maintain order and who prefer not to soil their hands with the dirty business of keeping the peace. If that were the whole story, then Christian pacifism would, of course, seem to be self-serving and even selfish. Indeed, many people argue that Christians should take part in violence in order to protect the innocent. However, a more important issue to consider is whether Christians have a mission given to them by the Lord Jesus Christ that is incompatible with the utilization of violence. If so, then the issue of faithfulness, not effectiveness, is the most important consideration. Yet, we should not underestimate the effectiveness of nonviolent Christian movements in sparking reform in society by creating dynamics of change from the bottom up, rather than from the top down.

Examples of Types 3 and 4

The Donatists were among the first Christians to be persecuted by other Christians in conjunction with the Roman Empire. In third-century North Africa, there was a major controversy over the issue of how severe the penance should be for those bishops and other clergy who had been guilty of *traditio*, the handing over of precious copies of the Holy Scriptures to government officials during the great persecution of 303–12. When Caecilian was elected bishop of Carthage in 311, it was alleged that one or more of those who ordained him had been a *traditor*.[1] For this reason, a large number of North Africans refused to recognize him. Majorinus was elected as a rival bishop and shortly thereafter succeeded by Donatus, for whom the schism was named.

After the Edict of Toleration in 313, the Roman government restored church property that had been confiscated during the recent persecution, and the Romans recognized Caecilian as the legitimate bishop of Carthage. Naturally, the dissenters appealed to the emperor to be recognized as the true church in North Africa, and Constantine arranged for a commission of inquiry, headed by the bishop of Rome, to look into the situation. On their recommendation, Constantine approved a policy of coercion to try to achieve a reunification of the church between 317 and 321. But this early attempt to enforce church unity by military means failed, and the Donatists became the largest party in the North African church. The identification of the catholic party with the Roman emperor inflamed local feeling against the Romans to the point where it became difficult to tell where the strictly theological dispute ended and the strictly political one began. (In some ways, the situation was similar to the Irish Catholic dispute with English Protestants and English government in modern Ireland.) In any case, this is one of the first-known examples of a Christendom approach to solving the problem of church unity by means of government power.

Augustine became bishop of Hippo in 395, and he became the main opponent of the Donatists. He eventually would call on imperial power to repress them,

---

1. This charge may well have been true because Augustine, a great foe of the Donatists, in one of his anti-Donatist writings, said that he did not know if the men who ordained Caecilianus were *traditors*. If he thought they were not, he surely would have said so because that would have taken a great deal of the wind out the sails of his opponents. Augustine, however, argued that it did not matter if the bishops who ordained him were sinners because the validity of sacraments does not depend on the worthiness of the minister. See Augustine, "A Treatise Concerning the Correction of the Donatists" (Nicene and Post-Nicene Fathers 1/4; repr. Peabody, MA: Hendrickson, 1994), 634.

appealing to Scripture texts that speak of "compelling them to come in" in Jesus's parable of the wedding feast. Augustine represented a confident, broad-minded church that expected to grow and take over the world for Christ, while the Donatists were obsessed with purity and with maintaining the distinct identity of the church over against all who would compromise that purity. The conflict was a complex mix of politics, ethnicity, regionalism, theology, ethics, and polity. Most of what we know of the Donatists comes from the pens of their enemies. We do know, however, that Donatism was deeply rooted in African Christianity and that it persisted for centuries despite persecution, until the conquest of North Africa by the Muslims in the seventh and eighth centuries and the resultant extinction of the Christian church in that region of the world.

The imperial persecution of the Donatists at the behest of the catholic church is an early example of a type 3 approach to the relating of Christ and culture. Perhaps it is at this point in history that we should begin to speak of the Roman Catholic Church as more Roman than Catholic and as one denomination among others, for the catholicity of the church is surely compromised whenever one section of it begins to utilize violence against another. When one branch of the church identifies itself so completely with the state that it collaborates with the state in perpetrating violence against other Christians, we have a failure of catholicity.

Although there was only one official church within the Roman Empire, there were other Christian churches outside the Roman Empire. As we saw in chapter 5, the alignment of the Nicene bishops with the Romans had disastrous consequences for the Christian church in Persia. By choosing to be Roman, Western Christians increasingly separated themselves from other branches of the worldwide church, which brought their claims of catholicity into question. Rather than viewing the Reformation as the beginning of the splintering of the church into factions, we should view the alignment of the church with the Roman Empire as the beginning of the splintering of the church into sects aligned with national or state entities. The Reformers merely accelerated this trend, which was begun by the fourth-century bishops who allowed themselves to be coopted by Constantine and which had come to full flower with Augustine's employment of state coercion against other Christians. The ecumenical implications of this argument are clear: identification with national or ethnic entities is a far greater barrier to true Christian unity than denominationalism. The practices that spawned modern divisions thus began even prior to Nicea!

By calling on Rome to utilize coercion against the Donatists, Augustine allowed the gospel to be confused with an ethnic conflict. The Donatists were not without blame either, because they seemed to be as ready to appeal to the ethnic and nationalistic sentiments of the rural, native, North African population as Augustine was to appeal to the Roman upper class of North Africa. This is not a happy story all the way around. Throughout church history we find the identification of Christianity, or a segment of Christianity, with preexisting class, ethnic, or nationalistic entities. In the late twentieth century in the Balkans, religion functioned as the ideology of Roman Catholic Croats, Orthodox Serbs, and Muslims, and it is very difficult to tell exactly where, for example, Serbian nationalism ends and Serbian Orthodoxy begins. We can also think of the identification of the Russian Orthodox Church with the nation of Russia and the identification of Christianity with the Spanish-speaking upper classes of South America up until the twentieth century. This pattern has been repeated over and over again in Christendom, and Niebuhr's sociological study *The Social Sources of Denominationalism* documents it in America as well.[2] The biblical gospel tends to be completely obscured in such situations as the warlike, hate-filled, and nationalistic aspects of religion are emphasized at the expense of themes like love, reconciliation, community, and peace.

A second example of the type 3 approach is one that we considered in chapter 4: Christopher Columbus. Columbus ventured to the New World as the representative of the king and queen of Spain, and he claimed all the territory he supposedly discovered for the Spanish monarchy. The invasion, conquest, and enslavement of the New World was deemed to be a just war because it was supposedly carried out for the purpose of spreading the Christian faith to the native peoples of the Americas. It was, of course, carried out mainly for gold, rather than for God, as the behavior of the invaders makes abundantly clear. Dead people cannot be converted, and genocidal policies cannot lead to the Christianization of the peoples of the New World. The Christianization of the territories of the New World involved the replacement of the native populations by colonialists, rather than the conversion of the native populations to Christianity.

A basic issue that underlies the whole invasion and conquest is that of the relationship between coercion and evangelism. Can valid Christian conversion be accomplished by force? If we say that it cannot, then the whole enterprise was a massive failure and even a farce. If we say that it can, then how do we square the idea of evangelism by force with the biblical teaching that God is love? How can forced conversion teach and communicate the true, biblical nature of God? It seems clear that forced conversion is inherently anti-Christian, and so the methods utilized by the Spaniards were not compatible with Christian evangelism. The cloak of religious legitimation thrown over the whole invasion and conquest needs to be torn off so that an honest appraisal of this period in history can be made.

As we look back on the Spanish conquest of much of South and North America, we must admit that it was detrimental to the whole cause of missions and evangelism in many ways. For one thing, the conquerors imposed their religion, and the official and public religion quickly became Christianity, yet the hearts of the people were not necessarily changed, nor were the majority of the people favorably disposed toward Christ. In fact, the opposite effect was undoubtedly widespread; many people became hardened toward the gospel and became enemies of Christianity, rather than simply neutral. Second, the threat of violence

2. H. Richard Niebuhr, *The Social Sources of Denominationalism* (New York: Meridan, 1962).

naturally led to a decision on the part of the native people to outwardly conform, all the while retaining their own pagan beliefs inwardly and often practicing these beliefs and rituals secretly. Thus, the stage was set for syncretism. A syncretistic religion became the main religion of society, and in such a Christendom situation Christianity was officially universal even though most of the population were not Christians. This led, third, to a lack of urgency in evangelism, since everyone was officially Christian. A good case can be made for viewing the use of coercion in religious matters during the invasion as hampering the cause of evangelism and missions insofar as the superficial conversion achieved by force preempted the slower, but more profound, conversion that could have been achieved if force had not been used.

The use of violence in promoting Christianity also discredited the Christian faith in the eyes of many of the native peoples, who came to regard it as the ethnic religious ideology of the Spanish. Some, no doubt, were driven to embrace their own gods all the more strongly because of the violence of the Christians. Others, who perhaps had a deeper knowledge of the Christian message, regarded the Spanish as hypocrites who preached love and practiced violence. Some, of course, became Christians and critiqued the Spanish twisting of Christianity from within Christianity. The net effect of Spanish violence, however, was to position Christianity as a nationalistic ideology of the Spanish invaders and to make it extremely difficult to see it as a multiethnic, international, universal message of peace, love, and hope.

A third example of the type 3 approach is that of the Puritan revolution in the English civil war led by Oliver Cromwell (1599–1658) and his New Model Army. The English civil war was one of many conflicts in history that appeared to those on both sides to be a religious war of good versus evil. Both Cromwell and King Charles I identified their own cause with that of God. Whereas Charles was convinced of the truth of the doctrine of the divine right of kings, Cromwell believed that reformation of church and nation justified the use of force. In fact, in the ferment of seventeenth-century English revolution, left-wing Puritanism "aimed at actualizing of the millennium for England and the world," which meant that the English civil war was "a holy crusade with just that goal."[3] Cromwell led the Puritans and independents to victory over the royalist forces, the Scots, and the Irish. Although he was instrumental in making the decision to execute the king, he refused to take the title of king himself. He ruled instead as Lord Protector from 1653 until his death.

Cromwell's ruthlessness in putting down revolt in Ireland cannot be understood apart from the contemporary fear that Ireland might be used as a base for foreign powers wishing to reinstall the Stuarts. However, the murder, rape, and pillage that characterized the repression of the Irish revolt had historical consequences

---

3. John Howard Yoder, *Christian Attitudes to War, Peace, and Revolution* (Elkhart, IN: Goshen Biblical Seminary, 1983), 286.

that extended far beyond the lifetime of Cromwell and his contemporaries and were out of proportion to his intentions. The subsequent history of the troubles in Ireland, which persist to this day, is proof that the cycle of violence is endless unless someone is willing to break it by absorbing hostility without retaliating.

When we employ this kind of extreme violence in pursuit of a political goal, what often happens is that the calculation of foreseeable effects is impossible. Violence has a way of spiraling out of control like a forest fire and destroying much more than we intended. A sixteenth-century problem was solved violently, and the problems caused by the so-called solution are still with us in the twenty-first century. To say that violence is effective in solving problems that peaceful methods cannot seem to solve is highly problematic at best.

When we turn to type 4 approaches, we often find that more positive social change is accomplished by those who renounce violent coercion than by those who employ it. This means that Niebuhr's argument that we must choose between irrelevant purity or effective compromise is not valid.

The first example of the type 4 approach is that of William Penn (1644–1718) and his so-called holy experiment in religious toleration in Pennsylvania. The usual reading of this experiment is that it was a failure because eventually the Quakers had to get out of government and let others govern who would prosecute war against the French and the Indians in 1756. John Howard Yoder, however, questions the usual interpretation of this experiment as a complete failure and as proof that pacifists must be irrelevant and detached from government.[4]

The underlying issue in this revisionist reading of pacifism in action is whether the state is inherently violent and thus fundamentally rooted in raw power rather than in justice. Is violence the central core of what the state is and therefore normal, or is violence on the extreme edge of what that state is and therefore abnormal? This debate goes back to Thomas Hobbes (1588–1679) and John Locke (1632–1704). Hobbes argued for the first position: that violence is at the core of the state and is normal. The essence of all government is tyranny, but tyranny is preferable to anarchy most of the time for most people because chaos and random violence make daily life so miserable. Locke argued for the second position: that a social contract is at the core of the liberal state and that violence is at the extreme edge of the state and thus abnormal. If Hobbes is right, then pacifism is completely irrelevant to politics, but if Locke is right, then pacifism is perhaps not entirely feasible, yet it is not entirely irrelevant either. If government is based on a social contract, then renegotiating that contract is always possible. If government is based on nothing but brute force, then negotiation is less likely to bear fruit.

The reading of the holy experiment in Pennsylvania as a failure is often taken to prove that pacifism does not work, that pacifism is possible only for a few people and is unrealistic when it comes to nations or large political units. Pacifism is thus viewed as irrelevant to politics, which opens politics to being done on the

4. Ibid., 269.

basis of theories that raise violence to the level of an ontological necessity; that is, something built into the nature of the universe. When violence is seen as an ontological necessity, then one can hardly be blamed for compromising with it in the same way as if violence were seen as a choice. From a theological perspective, we must say that violence is an *ontological reality* (against liberal utopians and in defense of the reality of the fall), but not an *ontological necessity* (against Christian realists and in defense of the doctrine that the creation was originally created good and remains fundamentally good). Christians must avoid the extremes of fatalism and naïveté if they wish to remain orthodox.

The question is whether it is feasible and desirable for a pacifist church, which rejects violence, to get involved in attempting to transform the society around it. Is pacifism relevant to politics? If pacifism is irrelevant, then those Christians who choose the type 4 approach are deluded and dangerous. They should be forbidden to try to transform society from a pacifist perspective because it leads to unrealistic utopian expectations that lead to disaster. On the other hand, if violence is a choice rather than an ontological necessity, and if violence is abnormal to the state rather than normal, then a pacifist church can challenge a state to be relatively less violent and relatively more just, and the state could be relatively transformed. All this is possible without succumbing to utopian fantasies.

The key to answering this question is to recognize that history moves, rather than standing still. What would have been seen as a utopian fantasy in the sixteenth century, such as religious liberty, for example, is now taken for granted as perfectly normal. The state did not collapse once infant baptism became optional, as many people in the sixteenth century thought it would. So we cannot predict in advance how much influence a pacifist church could potentially exert on the wider society. How far could it go? Also, would changing historical circumstances lead to rollbacks? History moves, but it does not progress continually in a straight line. Regression would seem to be just as much a possibility as progress. In the case of Pennsylvania, certainly, we see both enormous advance and also later regression, without all aspects of the advance being lost.

The Quaker movement began in the ferment of the English civil war.[5] Under Cromwell, the first Quakers had an ambiguous attitude toward war and aspired to political office. George Fox (1642–91), the founder of the Society of Friends, came to his decision that it is better to suffer violence than to inflict it as a result of a period of intense spiritual struggle in 1659. The backdrop to his struggle was the failure of Cromwell's rule to fulfill the theocratic dreams and the imminent restoration of the monarchy. Having hoped for the coming of the kingdom in society, Fox now turned to the coming of the living rule of Christ within the individual heart. Out of this apparent recipe for quietism, however, came an amazing tradition of social activism, including the Pennsylvania experiment, the movement for the abolition of slavery, and other

5. For the information in this paragraph, see ibid., 286.

constructive nonviolent movements for social change. In liberal Quakerism, the eschatological hope for the kingdom has been transposed into secular humanistic forms of social progress, just as in liberal Protestantism. More pietistic strands of Quakerism identified strongly with Anabaptist dualism as one of the historic peace churches.

William Penn was a second-generation Quaker from a noble family, which had been of major service to King Charles II.[6] Since the king did not have enough money to pay loans that they had made to him, he gave the family a hefty chunk of North America in the form of the colony of Pennsylvania. Penn found himself a landlord of a country that did not have a government, so he had to get involved, both in governing and in setting up the form of government as well. He had freedom in statecraft, but not complete freedom. For example, the death penalty for certain crimes could not be abolished because of the commitment to the crown. Penn and other Quakers governed Pennsylvania for about eighty years, from the 1680s to 1756. When the British decided to fight the French in western Pennsylvania, the government of Pennsylvania could not stay out of it. So the Quakers in government, who could not support war, withdrew from power and let others take over who could prosecute the war.

According to Yoder, we must note several relevant facts in evaluating the holy experiment in Pennsylvania. First, Penn used his relative freedom to "administer a system that was much less violent and much more humane than anywhere else."[7] For example, although the death penalty could not be abolished altogether, its scope was reduced and the number of executions was reduced greatly. Second, by the third generation, some Quakers did not equate the death penalty with war and began to see it as part of the legitimate police function of the state. This can be read either as a compromise or as the pioneering of a new approach to violence in which finer distinctions are made between some forms of violence and others. The possibility of abolishing at least some forms of violence was thus established. Third, the fourth-generation Quakers, who could not see how they could deal nonviolently with the French and Indian threat on the western border, had moved away from the strong commitment to nonviolence of Penn and Fox. This loss of commitment to nonviolence was coupled with an influx of non-Quakers into the western area of Pennsylvania and resulted in a political consensus that rejected total nonviolence. In this situation, Yoder argues, "it is a success of nonviolence, not a failure, to let yourself be voted out of government."[8] Overall, Yoder argues, "it is not a fair test of any position to ask whether it will work when most people don't believe in it." While pacifism cannot work in a society in which the majority does not embrace it, the same could be said of constitutional democracy, religious liberty, and freedom of the press as well. A social consensus needs to be

6. For the information in this paragraph, see ibid., 270.
7. Ibid.
8. Ibid., 271.

established that views pacifism as something basic to that society; without such a consensus, pacifism is not viable.

In arguing that a pacifist minority being voted out of office by a nonpacifist majority does not prove that pacifism does not work, Yoder is undoubtedly correct. But it would be even more precise to say that pacifism can work for a voluntary community only if people choose to embrace pacifism. It certainly can work for a church, and it could theoretically work for a country, but only where the country is made up of pacifists or at least an overwhelming majority of committed pacifists. It is questionable whether such a country could exist for many generations, if at all, given that not all children of Christian parents will embrace the faith. Nevertheless, the possibility of such a situation arising in the future cannot be ruled out completely.

Yoder insists, however, that we recognize that the Quaker government did work for eighty years, which is not an insignificant length of time. People who raised families during that time reaped the benefit of Quaker policies, and many things tried during that time could, on later reflection, be considered desirable. Maybe it is not feasible to impose the entire Quaker experiment on a later historical situation, but that does not mean that prison reform or democracy or open immigration or some other particular policy could not be beneficially implemented elsewhere. The holy experiment had value as a laboratory for future social experiments.

The example of Pennsylvania can be read in two ways. It can be read pessimistically as a story that shows how impossible it is for consistent, nonviolent Christians to be involved in government just because it did not last forever. It can also be read as a story of a relatively successful participation of pacifists in the civil community for a considerable length of time. The first reading is dependent on Hobbesean presuppositions brought to one's interpretation of the historical facts, while more Lockean presuppositions would lead one to gravitate toward some version of the more optimistic second reading. Which set of presuppositions is most consistent with Christian doctrines of creation and eschatology?

Perhaps it would be fair to conclude that this experiment reveals both the limits and the possibilities of Christian involvement in politics and social change. The limits have to do with the fallenness of creation and the kingdom of God not yet having come in its fullness. We cannot expect a utopia in the present historical situation. The possibilities, however, are much greater than those who dismiss pacifism as irrelevant often are willing to admit. Specific changes in specific places and at specific times, for example, the abolition of capital punishment in modern Canada, are possible, and the degree to which society can be changed for the better is not predictable in advance. As history moves along, it is impossible to say whether a given reform or improvement will be possible. This is why the church has to keep on bearing its witness to the cosmic lordship of Jesus Christ and keep on trying to call for greater justice, a more stable peace, and less violence. That is why a type 4 approach is not unrealistic at all times, but rather necessary at all times in order to establish the limits of progress in each generation and each situation.

A second example of the type 4 approach is that of Martin Luther King Jr. and the American civil-rights movement of the 1950s and 1960s. This nonviolent church-based movement confronted the larger society with a specific set of injustices and called for legal, economic, educational, and attitudinal change. The basic outline of this story is well known, so I will focus on one specific leader (King), one specific ideological component of the struggle (the philosophical commitment to nonviolence), and one specific example of the implementation of that ideology (the Montgomery bus boycott).

King (1929–68) was a black Baptist preacher and the son of a Baptist preacher. He cannot be understood properly apart from his biblical and Christian distinctiveness. He championed civil rights for African Americans, but his ultimate purpose was much broader than simply obtaining more power for one group at the expense of another. He wanted the reconciliation of the black and white races in America and believed in the need for forgiveness and reconciliation, not just for a redistribution of power alone. King's dream was for the change of hearts and minds, not just of laws and institutions.

King preached and practiced nonviolent methods of working for social change. Marches, boycotts, speeches, symbolic acts, voter registration, the creative use of the courts to mount legal challenges to unjust laws, and other nonviolent tactics were used to confront, unmask, and disarm the powers. The appeal was to the conscience of the nation, particularly the white majority, rather than to the power of laws alone. Between the historic Brown v. Board of Education of Topeka decision in 1954, by which the U.S. Supreme Court ruled that segregation in public education was unconstitutional, and the Civil Rights Act of 1964, which prohibited racial discrimination in public institutions, the civil-rights movement pushed forward with many outstanding successes.

In 1955, a black woman named Rosa Parks did a radical thing. She refused to give up her seat near the front of a bus to a white passenger and move to the back when told to do so by the bus driver. She was arrested and jailed, but the incident sparked a boycott of the Montgomery, Alabama, bus system by blacks and their white sympathizers, which garnered national media attention and proved to be a catalyst to a decade of nonviolent social action. King, a local Baptist minister, was asked to speak at a meeting of the Montgomery Improvement Association, and he gave a great oration that launched his career as a civil-rights leader. With King leading the boycott, the protest went on for a full year and ultimately led to a Supreme Court decision that invalidated Montgomery's segregationist laws.

King, who had a PhD from Boston University, turned out to be both a master strategist in the social struggle and an orator of uncommon gifts. He advocated a philosophy of nonviolence and, as long as he lived, was able to make progress toward justice through the use of nonviolent means. He wrote: "The beauty of nonviolence is that in its own way and in its own time it seeks to break the chain reaction of evil. With a majestic sense of spiritual power, it seeks to elevate truth, beauty and goodness to the throne. Therefore I will continue to follow this method because I think it is the most practically sound and morally excellent way for the Negro to achieve freedom."[9]

In the midsixties, King was challenged by younger, proviolence leaders such as Stokely Carmichael for leadership of the movement, and he argued against their growing impatience with the pace of change. Responding to the new slogan "Black Power," he wrote: "One of the greatest paradoxes of the Black Power movement is that it talks unceasingly about not imitating the values of white society, but in advocating violence it is imitating the worst, the most brutal and the most uncivilized value of American life."[10] King's murder was a major blow, not only to African Americans and to the civil-rights movement, but also to America as a whole and to world Christianity. The nonviolent vision of King resonated in the hearts of oppressed people around the world, however, and his dreams for racial reconciliation have never died.

A third example of the type 4 approach is that of Desmond Tutu and the Truth and Reconciliation Commission in South Africa. The struggle against apartheid was long and hard in South Africa, and many times it appeared that the outcome was going to be civil war, a convulsion of violence, and perhaps genocide. Yet, to the astonishment of the entire world, on behalf of the entrenched white minority, on February 2, 1990, President F. W. de Klerk announced the lifting of bans against the political parties opposed to the white apartheid regime, including the African National Congress and even the South African Communist Party. Nine days later, Nelson Mandela was set free, after twenty-seven years of imprisonment, and the stage was set for a peaceful transition from white minority rule to majority rule. On April 27, 1994, the new, democratically elected government of South Africa was sworn in, and apartheid had been overcome without the bloodbath that most observers had thought inevitable.

The question then arose of what to do about those who had committed crimes during the years of oppression. What about the Soweto uprising of June 16, 1976, when unarmed school children were shot for demonstrating against the use of Afrikaans as the language of instruction? What about the Magoo's Bar bombing of June 1986 when three people were killed and sixty-nine injured by a car bomb planted by Umkhonto we Sizwe, the armed wing of the African National Congress? As in many historical situations, there were atrocities on both sides of the conflict. And there is no doubt that the apartheid regime was unjust and that the arrival of democracy in South Africa was a good thing. If the new regime had decided to take vengeance on its enemies, it would have been no great surprise—just a continuation of the seemingly endless cycle of violence and retribution. The

9. Martin Luther King, *Where Do We Go from Here? Chaos or Community?* (New York: Bantam, 1967), 73.

10. Ibid., 74

Nuremberg Trials after World War II are an example of victor's justice, where war criminals from the conquered nation were tried and punished. Would the new South Africa be able to extract itself from the cycle of violence even after the end of the apartheid regime?

An amazing thing happened after the government of Nelson Mandela took power. South Africa established a Truth and Reconciliation Commission, and all those who had committed crimes during the apartheid years could apply to it for a pardon in exchange for full disclosure of the truth and remorse. Desmond Tutu points out that this decision was key to the achievement of a negotiated settlement because the security forces would have been much less likely to cooperate with a peaceful transition of power if they had thought that the new government was going to bring the force of the law against them for their actions committed during the apartheid years.[11] The terrible human-rights violations that took place under apartheid could not be ignored. Yet, retribution would only perpetrate further (endless) cycles of violence. National healing and peace were achieved through a process of confession and forgiveness.

This whole historical story is complex and rich in lessons for the future of the world, but I wish to stress just one point. Sometimes, the renunciation of deserved violent retribution can be the thing that sets in motion a process of reconciliation and ends the cycle of violence. In fact, it is difficult to see what else can ever do this. The cross is just such a point where an innocent victim absorbed violence and evil without retaliating. Now forgiveness is on offer to whoever is willing to confess his or her complicity in the violence that came to a climax in the crucifixion of the Son of God. Christians believe that it is through this process and no other that the redemption of the world is occurring. How can anyone make the astonishing claim that nonviolent action is irrelevant to the public engagement of culture? How can anyone think that violence is the only way to end violence and yet also profess to believe with the apostle Paul that in Christ God was reconciling the world to himself?

View of Christ Entailed by Types 3 and 4

Both type 3 and type 4 view Jesus Christ as the Lord of the cosmos. Both of them view Jesus as Lord of the whole creation, not just of the church. For both types, the reason why Christians legitimately can ask the wider society to adopt Christian morality is that Jesus is Lord. He rules now at the right hand of the Father, and someday he will return to earth to set up the kingdom in its fullness. At that time, every knee will bow and every tongue will confess that Jesus Christ is Lord to the glory of God the Father (Philippians 2:10–11).

11. Desmond Tutu, *No Future without Forgiveness* (New York: Doubleday, 1999), 20.

For both types, there is thus a tension between Christ and the powers of this world at the present time. He claims to be Lord, but they do not recognize his claim. The biggest difference between the two types is that type 3 holds that, since Jesus is the rightful Lord of this earth, it is therefore legitimate to implement that lordship by violent coercion if necessary. The reasoning is that, since this is what is going to happen in the second coming, we should do it if we gain enough temporal power to do so. Type 4, however, while agreeing that Jesus will use coercion to establish his lordship in the second coming, disagrees with the further step of saying that we should do this in anticipation of the apocalyptic intervention in history by God. Type 4 says that we are not God and that we should not trust ourselves to use violence. It is not our calling; our calling is to witness to the gospel of Jesus Christ. His calling is to be the Lord of the cosmos, and when he returns he will do what only he can do with perfect justice.

Biblical Support for Types 3 and 4

Both type 3 and type 4 appeal to Paul's great description of Christ's cosmic lordship in Colossians 1:15–20. Both types see in this passage the proclamation of Jesus as Lord of the church and also Lord of the whole cosmos. But type 4 views Jesus's current reign in the church as being a nonviolent one, while type 3 advocates the use of violence by the church in the assertion of the lordship of Christ here and now.

Type 3 appeals to the Old Testament example of Israel as a theocracy and sees Israel as a model for nations today that want to be ruled directly by God. Its reading of the Old Testament is that this model can be applied validly to our situation today. Type 4, however, disagrees with this interpretation and argues that no contemporary nation (including modern Israel) is equivalent to Old Testament Israel and that the church is the focus of God's working in the world today. The church is to be a contrast society—an alternative to the nation-state.

Type 4 appeals to the Sermon on the Mount as the basic constitution of the church. By living according to values that appear to be absurd to the world, the church exemplifies a new kind of existence in the world and is a foretaste of the kingdom of God. The basic mission of the church is not to bring in the kingdom, as in type 3, but rather to bear a faithful witness to the kingdom. The category of witness is very important. The church, as a witness, points away from itself to that greater thing, which is still future and yet has been partially revealed in the life, death, and resurrection of Jesus Christ. To the extent that the church participates in the reality of Jesus's resurrection, the church participates in the fullness of the kingdom and by participating in it is able to embody it in a very weak and fragmentary way. Nevertheless, the participation of the church in the kingdom makes possible a witness to the kingdom that, while always remaining imperfect, consists of more than mere words.

Critique of Types 3 and 4

What are the strengths and weaknesses of these two types? We can speak of their main strength jointly because both of them bear witness to the cosmic lordship of Jesus Christ. Both of them attempt to embody the reality that Jesus, not Caesar, is really Lord. They both witness to the lordship of Jesus Christ not over just the individual soul or the private space of men and women and, perhaps, families and churches, but to the lordship of Jesus Christ over politics, education, economics, science, and entertainment—over all of human life and nature as well.

However, the problem with type 3 is that it believes that it is right to impose the lordship of Jesus Christ upon all of society, regardless of whether the members of that society confess Jesus to be Lord. The teachings of Jesus are for all of society, and so they should be imposed by force if necessary. Those who advocate type 3 often argue that, if this is not done, then Christians leave themselves open to the charge that they do not really believe in the cosmic lordship of Christ.

Type 4, on the other hand, contends that it is not our place to impose the teachings of Jesus by force, but that we are limited to the means of preaching, teaching, persuading, and witnessing. Those who advocate type 4 approaches to social action are free to use any and all methods to get people to acknowledge the lordship of Jesus Christ up to but not including physical coercion or violence.

Both type 3 and type 4 can be said to be Nicene in their view of Jesus Christ in that they both take seriously both the humanity and the divinity of Jesus Christ. However, type 3 is inconsistent in that it attempts to acknowledge the authority of the humanity of Jesus Christ for us but makes an exception in the matter of violent retaliation against evil. We follow Jesus on many points, but when it comes to suffering injustice without retaliating as he did on the cross, we think we must make an exception and not follow him at that point. But if we take following Jesus seriously and if we listen to his explicit command to "take up your cross," then we must be honest enough to admit that not to follow him at the point of the cross is to not really follow him at all in the New Testament sense. If a person says, "Yes, I want to follow Jesus by healing and serving others and by giving my life in humanitarian work, but I am no masochist and I will compromise with violence and killing just enough to preserve my life and allow me to get on with my medical work," then that person is not really following Jesus. To do good deeds, to help others, and to be altruistic are all very good ideals. But they are not the equivalent of taking up our crosses and following Jesus to the point of being willing to be killed for our refusal to participate in the warped and sinful violence that the world considers to be normal. Yes, a life of nonviolent service and love sometimes does lead to suffering and death—that is precisely what the life of Jesus teaches us. Yet beyond death there is resurrection, and that is also what the life of Jesus teaches us. Jesus was fully human, but we learn from his humanity that to be in this world and totally surrendered to the Father's will places us in tremendous tension with the world as it is currently structured.

Only type 4 approaches are consistent in allowing the humanity of Jesus to become fully authoritative for us by following Jesus in the way of peace. The humanity of Jesus is understood to include his entire life, ministry, teachings, death, and resurrection, not just his ministry and teachings. Nineteenth-century liberal Christianity sought to make Jesus an exemplar of all things good and beautiful and said that we should follow his teachings, such as the Golden Rule, because he taught good things. But New Testament Christianity says that we should follow him because he taught a doctrine that is absolutely unique because it is centered on his person. We do not follow him in order to add anything to his atoning sacrifice or in order to actualize in the world his lofty ideals. We follow him for one reason only: so that we can witness to him by reminding the world that *this man* once walked the earth and that his life, death, and resurrection have changed the world forever.

Type 4 is susceptible to the temptation to romanticize the world and to expect a too easy victory over evil. The example of William Penn and his holy experiment should serve as a constant reminder that the coming of the kingdom is not a straight-line march of constant progress. There are bound to be setbacks as well as victories, and sometimes ground gained at great cost will later be lost again. The task of witnessing to the coming kingdom must never be allowed to degenerate into the assumption that the kingdom has already come. We can rejoice whenever we find a new instance of Christ's lordship being acknowledged in this world, but we should not be so naïve as to think that we can bring in the kingdom in our own strength.

Nothing is so romantic and unrealistic, however, as the concept of war as a noble enterprise carried out with dignity, restraint, and morality. The reality of war is dirty, degrading, and disgusting and will never be anything but. Karl Barth knew the horror of modern war and wrote movingly of how it does not ennoble us, but rather degrades our humanity:

> Today, however, the increasing scientific objectivity of military killing, the development, appalling effectiveness and dreadful nature of the methods, instruments and machines employed, and the extension of the conflict to the civilian population, have made it quite clear that war does in fact mean no more and no less than killing, with neither glory, dignity nor chivalry, with neither restraint nor consideration in any respect. The glory of the so-called military profession, which incidentally has become the profession of everybody either directly or indirectly, can now feed only on the relics of ancient illusions long since stripped of their substance. . . .
>
> Does not war demand that almost everything that God has forbidden be done on a broad front? To kill effectively, and in connexion therewith, must not those who wage war steal, rob, commit arson, lie, deceive, slander, and unfortunately to a large extent fornicate, not to speak of the almost inevitable repression of all of the finer and weightier forms of obedience? And how can they believe and pray when at the climax of this whole world of dubious action it is a brutal matter of killing? It may be true that even in war many a man may save many things, and indeed that

an inner strength may become for him a more strong and genuine because a more tested possession. But it is certainly not true that most people become better in war. The fact is that war is for most people a trial for which they are no match, and from the consequences of which they can never recover.[12]

To idealize modern war as if it were a matter of romance, chivalry, and heroism is to exhibit an attitude that is far more out of touch with reality than is pacifism, far more trusting of fallen human nature than is pacifism, and far less rooted in the brutal experience of humanity in the twentieth century. The demonic face of war has been unmasked, and there can be no going back to the past. Modern war is not something that Christians should be prepared to engage in at all. It should be renounced, rejected, and distrusted by those who take up their cross and follow Jesus.

12. Karl Barth, *Church Dogmatics* III/4 (trans. Geoffrey W. Bromiley et al.; ed. Geoffrey W. Bromiley and Thomas F. Torrance; Edinburgh: T & T Clark, 1957–77), 453–54.

Conclusion

Jesus Christ, as he is testified to us in the Holy Scripture, is the one Word of God, whom we are to hear, whom we are to trust and obey in life and in death. We repudiate the false teaching that the church can and must recognize yet other happenings and powers, images and truths as divine revelation alongside this one Word of God, as a source of her preaching.

Barmen Declaration, article 1

The New Testament sets aside any nationalistic understanding of God's reign and with it the instruments of power requisite to national survival. Israelite nationalism has more in common with Augustine's post-Constantinian vision of an imperially sanctioned Christianity than it does with Jesus' preaching that "to repent and believe in the gospel" is the proper way to recognize that "the kingdom of God has come near."

Sally Cahill, *Love Your Enemies*

Uninterruptedly absorbed in progress toward its own deification, the state feels less and less the need that God should be spoken about.

Karl Barth, *Church Dogmatics*

Indeed in every strand of the New Testament evidence it is made clear that to follow Jesus means to accept the way of the cross—that most potent symbol of absolute rejection by the world. . . . What I have been saying—and I have been trying faithfully to represent the teaching of the New Testament—suggests a total discontinuity between the gospel and the life of people apart from the gospel, a total discontinuity between the gospel and culture.

Lesslie Newbigin, *Signs amid the Rubble*

11

Jesus or Constantine?

In this final chapter, I need to sum up the argument of this book. There can be no doubt that if we reject the Christendom model of mission and embrace a post-Christendom approach, there will be far-ranging consequences for the life and ministry of the church. In this chapter, I want to spell out more clearly what the choices that we face actually involve.

I began, in chapters 2 and 3, by taking dead aim at a famous classic that almost everybody likes and arguing that it led us astray because it presupposes the old Christendom paradigm. I argued that the Christendom presupposed by Niebuhr is now in the process of passing from the scene—and that this is a good thing. Obviously, the decline of Christendom is more advanced in Europe and Canada than in the United States, but this does not mean that Christendom is likely to recover in the West. We need to adjust to living in the post-Christendom situation because we are going to be living in it for a long time, so far as anyone can see right now.

The problem with Christendom is that it requires the church to merge with the church's host culture to the point of denying the lordship of Jesus Christ. Being in the world is fine; the church must be in the world in order to carry out its mission. But becoming a worldly church is not fine because a worldly church is nothing more than an echo of the world's own wisdom. It is important to grasp the point that the reason we want to avoid worldliness is not because we do not care about the world and have no compassion for people. In fact, the exact opposite is true. A worldly church has no good news to proclaim that the world would not know in any other way. A worldly church simply says "me too" to the culture's highest and best wisdom and becomes a culture-religion. The world needs the church to be the church so that the world can know that God loves the world and that redemption is therefore possible. The church is a sign of hope in the world, but if it does not remain distinct from the world it loses its ability to point to the transcendent God.

The church can make common cause with non-Christians on an issue-by-issue basis and does not have to oppose everything in secular culture. The church should be involved in all aspects of culture and should be culturally creative and always appreciative of beauty, goodness, and life whenever and wherever it finds these good things. So how do we define worldliness? A key issue is the point where the church accepts the state's authority to tell Christians when and who to kill. Once we go past this point, we have functionally negated the lordship of Christ. Niebuhr understood this better than did many of his readers. He was concerned to provide a justification for Christians' participating in war and other forms of state-sponsored violence, even though it goes against the commonsense interpretation of what Jesus taught in the New Testament. He needed to provide a rational framework for making compromises in the name of realism and responsibility. His book is a masterpiece of rhetorical effectiveness, clarity, and civility. He succeeded in his purpose admirably and has amassed a huge following.

Since I am an evangelical, I am particularly concerned that my fellow evangelical Christians have been persuaded by Niebuhr (and others) that they need to compromise with violent coercion as a means to the end of gaining cultural influence. The kind of arguments made in *Christ and Culture* have been accepted by evangelicals. In an odd sort of way, Niebuhr's arguments are responsible for the rise of the religious right (which must make him roll over in his grave!). But think about it. All you have to do is accept the whole argument of his book and just substitute some adherent of Adam Smith for F. D. Maurice in the last couple of pages and there you have it. Let us not forget that capitalism and socialism are both secular ideologies born in the Enlightenment. Both subscribe to the ideas of the authority of autonomous human reason, and both look to science as the source of human progress. Both are worldly systems of salvation with which the church is tempted to compromise and say: What we mean by the gospel is pretty much summed up in socialism; or, What we mean by gospel is pretty much summed up by liberal, democratic capitalism. When you say it like that, it sounds so ridiculous that one is tempted to think that no one would believe that. But millions do.

The rise of the religious right in the United States poses a tremendous problem for those of us who think that the gospel is about Jesus and his teaching, his death, his resurrection, and his lordship. By aligning itself with the Republican Party, the religious right aligns itself with capitalism, militarism, and extreme nationalism. For the sake of a few moral issues (e.g., abortion and homosexuality), the religious right mutes the Christian witness on behalf of the poor, the environment, and peace. The religious right has recently become just as big a problem as the religious left has been for the past century. Liberal Christians have been saying for a long time that the kingdom of God is a human sociopolitical project in which all we have to do is implement socialism and we are home free. This makes Jesus completely unnecessary except as a cheerleader and brand spokesperson for our ideology. The religious right blanks out Jesus's teachings in much the same way as the religious left blanks out Jesus's death and resurrection as decisive for the salvation of the world. One ends up with a human Jesus who seconds our motions, and the other ends up with a divine Jesus who seems to have no concern for the poor and the oppressed. The most charitable way to look at this is to see each as right in what it affirms and wrong in what it ignores. But that is not really an adequate way to conceptualize the problem. The deeper problem is that both the right and the left have a false Jesus, a Jesus created in their own image and not the Jesus of the New Testament. How can we preach the true gospel when these two deformations of the gospel are so dominant in the culture? How do we break through the incredible power of these human-centered gospels and speak clearly about the Jesus-centered one? The answer is not for conservatives to become more left wing, any more than it is for liberals to become more right wing. The answer is for everyone to cease being either left or right, either liberal or conservative, and to embrace the radical Jesus of the Bible.

I do not see any hope for getting beyond this impasse until we as Christians repent of the whole Christendom project (as I advocated in chapters 4 and 5). In our situation today, the way to affirm the lordship of Jesus Christ is to disavow Christendom. This is the contemporary equivalent of declining to burn the pinch of incense to Caesar in the early church. Only when we do this will it become clear that we really have something new and different to say that the world does not already know. We need to serve notice that Jesus is no longer available as a prop to the cultural projects that various people are promoting. Jesus is not backing any candidates this year, and he is dead serious about already having replaced the rulers of this world as king of the world. This is our message.

Once we let go of our capitalist and socialist projects and our science and technology projects and our world peace through values clarification projects and all the other great ideas that people have had for fixing the world, then and only then are we ready to let the cross and resurrection of Jesus stimulate our imaginations as to how Christians can engage the world redemptively. The purpose of chapters 6–10 was to give our imaginations a workout, to stimulate new ways of thinking within the new paradigm of post-Christendom. Good questions to ask are these: What could a peaceful minority people do that a culture-religion could not do? What do we as followers of Jesus have to say that the world does not already know? If God took the church out of the world tomorrow, what could not be replaced out of the resources of the many fine social service organizations and other world religions? How do the cross and resurrection inform our approach to social justice issues?

Once we start asking questions like these, we are on the verge of being able to imagine what it would be like to bear a faithful witness to Jesus Christ in a fallen world, which is desperately in need of grace. Somebody else can run the government, fight the wars, and struggle for power, money, and fame. Christians have better things to do. We need to imitate our Lord and strive to live lives of forgiveness, reconciliation, and service to the poor. We need to live together in community and put the needs of each other ahead of our own selfish desires. We need to worship joyfully and give sustained, humble, careful attention to the word of God. We need to obey Jesus's teachings and prove to the world that they make sense and lead to fulfilled lives. And we need to call others to join us in the life of discipleship.

The exact shape of the missional congregation in the post-Christendom Western world of the twenty-first century will vary from place to place. We can draw inspiration from the monastic movement, and probably the best possible response to the current politicization of Christianity embodied in the religious right would be to form monastic communities that renounce violence, power, and wealth. These could be communities in which people take vows of celibacy, or they could also be forms of so-called married monasticism, which draw inspiration from Mennonite and Hutterite groups. Other Christians will respond to the post-Christendom challenge in different ways. Many churches will continue to function in the same ways, except that the members will become more intentional about resisting the powers and opposing injustice. We need to do little things as well as big things. Plant a garden. Decline a promotion that requires you to travel too much to be a good parent. Visit a senior's home once a month with your youth group. Join an environmental organization. Give money to an organization that works against hunger. Volunteer at a pregnancy care center. Learn to distrust those who tell you that if you just support their cause the world can be reformed in one big blow. Laugh at advertising and laugh at the devil (you can usually do both at the same time).

The purpose of this book is not to provide a how-to manual for those who wish to start another movement or church trend with a packaged, seven-step program to making your church a growing and successful post-Christendom church. If pastors take the ideas in this book too seriously, they may well get fired. If churches take them too seriously, they may lose members or budget and have a hard time making mortgage payments. So if these are your top preoccupations, I suggest that you ignore what this book is saying. We have had the church-growth movement, the seeker-sensitive movement, the ancient-future-church movement, the emerging-church movement, and the missional-church movement, and the last thing we need is another movement. The problem is that the level of our knowledge already far exceeds the level of our obedience. We just need to take Jesus's words seriously and see where it goes.

The point is to stimulate imaginations so that various groups of people all over the Western world can learn how to follow the leading of the Holy Spirit in their own particular situations. If you reject Christendom, you will sometimes appear left wing to your right-wing friends (or enemies) and you will often appear right wing to you left-wing friends (or enemies). When everyone has a problem with you, then you will know that you are doing something right: "If you belonged to the world, it would love you as its own" (John 15:19). All that I have done in this book is to identify the key point of spiritual resistance to the powers: the repudiation of coercive violence. If we get this one right, then the odds are dramatically increased that we will avoid become worldly on a wide range of issues and that we will retain our ability to witness faithfully to the lordship of Jesus Christ. It is not that this one issue is the only important one; it is rather that it functions as a dividing line between those who can be absorbed into the unredeemed world system and those who cannot. Our goal is to be indigestible to the world.

The Temptation of Jesus

In his great novel *The Brothers Karamazov*, Fyodor Dostoevsky has one of the characters, Ivan Karamazov, present a poem called *The Grand Inquisitor*, which portrays Jesus returning to earth during the height of the Spanish Inquisition.[1] Jesus appears in Seville on the day after a hundred heretics have been burned. He raises a little girl from the dead, and the crowds shout for joy and acclaim him. But then the Grand Inquisitor appears: a ninety-year-old cardinal, whose face is drawn, his eyes sunken, and yet stands tall and erect. He arrests Jesus and later that night visits his cell to talk with him.

In the conversation, which is really a monologue because Jesus never speaks, the Grand Inquisitor justifies what the church has done since Jesus founded the church. The Grand Inquisitor implies that Jesus has no right to say anything, since Jesus has handed over his authority to the pope, who now wields it. He claims credit for having done away with human freedom and for giving happiness (defined as the reliable satisfaction of material needs) to humanity. The Grand Inquisitor's view of humanity is that humans just want to be ruled and to have their needs provided for and that they will gladly give up their freedom in exchange for these things. He tells Jesus frankly that when "the wise and dreaded spirit of self-destruction and non-existence" spoke to him in the desert (a reference to Matthew 4:1–11 = Mark 1:12–13 and Luke 4:1–13), Jesus was wrong to refuse to accept his advice. The advice was basically to take human freedom away from humans by overpowering them with miracle, mystery, and authority, so that it would be possible to make them happy by providing for their needs. Instead, Jesus gave them more freedom. He accuses Jesus as follows:

> Instead of seizing man's freedom, You gave them even more of it! Have you forgotten that peace, and even death, is more attractive to man than the freedom of choice

1. Fyodor Dostoevsky, *The Brothers Karamazov* (trans. A. R. MacAndrew; New York: Bantam, 1970), 297–318.

that derives from the knowledge of good and evil? . . . You wanted to gain man's love so that he would follow You of his own free will, fascinated and captivated by You. . . . You made man decide about good and evil for himself, with no other guidance than Your example. But did it never occur to You that man would disregard Your example . . . as well as Your truth, when he was subjected to so fearful a burden of choice? In the end they will shout that You did not bring them the truth. . . . You Yourself sowed the seeds of destruction for Your own kingdom, and no one else is to blame.[2]

The Grand Inquisitor believes that people need to be ruled by a paternalistic leader who does what is best for the masses because the masses would never be strong enough to act in their own best interests. They must be coerced into belief. Jesus is dismissed as an unrealistic idealist, whose way is well intentioned but finally ineffective because he did not have the stomach for coercion.

The Grand Inquisitor's interpretation of the temptations in the wilderness is interesting because it is presented as the devil's interpretation; yet it is an interpretation that must be defended by those who believe in Christendom. Jesus rejected Christendom in the desert, but in the fourth century his church accepted what Jesus had rejected. At the very outset of his ministry, after his sense of calling as messiah had crystallized, Jesus was confronted with the issue of what kind of messiah he was going to be. The devil did not try to dissuade him from putting himself forward as messiah; the devil merely tried to tempt him to be a certain kind of messiah. The devil has never been against religion; he just would like to be the object of worship. And if he cannot arrange that, then at least he can try his best to ensure that the worship of the true God will be corrupted, twisted, and turned back on itself so that humans end up worshiping either themselves or an idol. The Grand Inquisitor's view is that in the advice the devil gave Jesus there was no temptation at all, but wise advice, which was spurned by Jesus. The Grand Inquisitor claimed credit for taking the devil's advice and correcting Jesus's mistake.

The temptation that Jesus faced in the desert was the temptation to found Christendom; that is, an integrated economic, political, and religious system that assumes sovereignty over the complete life of society. This is not a common interpretation of the temptations, but I think it is the correct one. John Howard Yoder interprets the first temptation as an economic one.[3] The devil advised Jesus to make bread out of the stones, presumably to feed the multitudes and thereby to win the favor of the people. He interprets the second temptation as sociopolitical in nature. Certainly it is wrong to gain power by worshiping Satan, but is Satan's being worshiped the only thing wrong with this offer? Yoder comments, "Are we to imagine some sort of Satan cult? Or does it not yield a much more concrete

2. Ibid., 307.
3. John Howard Yoder, *The Politics of Jesus: Vicit Agnus Noster* (2nd ed.; Grand Rapids: Eerdmans, 1994), 25.

meaning if we conceive Jesus as discerning in such terms the idolatrous character of political power hunger and nationalism?"[4] If we interpret the temptations not as three totally separate temptations, but as three aspects of one central temptation, then it is easy to see how economic and political approaches to rule relate to each other. Yoder interprets the third temptation as being for Jesus to put himself forward as a heavenly messenger from on high in an overpowering manner that could not be withstood by the people. It would also be the signal for the messianic revolution against the power of Rome to begin—the kind of sign the many pseudomessiahs would have loved to be able to provide. The temptations were for Jesus to set himself up as the economic, political, and religious Lord and to centralize all power and authority in one entity. Is this not exactly what happens in Christendom? The message of the Gospels is that Jesus was the messiah, but not the kind of messiah that many people expected.

The Davidic/Maccabean messiah who would lead a war against Rome and set up a renewed throne of David to exalt Israel over all the other nations was the kind of messiah that many of Jesus's contemporaries, apparently including some of his disciples, expected. Yet Jesus said no to that program and chose a nonviolent confrontation with the powers, which resulted in his death on the cross. Jesus, as he is presented to us in the Gospels, apparently trusted that somehow God would use this innocent suffering to redeem the world and that the resurrection was the triumphant vindication of this faith. Jesus explicitly calls his disciples to take up their crosses and to follow him (Matthew 16:21–28; Mark 8:31–38; Luke 9:21–27). In all three Synoptic Gospels, this teaching immediately follows the confession by Peter that Jesus is indeed the messiah (Matthew 16:13–20; Mark 8:27–30; Luke 9:18–20). Once the disciples recognize his messiahship, it is important to define messiahship. Jesus explicitly calls his disciples to take up their crosses, which means following him in the new way of being messiah that he has chosen, the way of suffering at the hands of evil without retaliating in order to expose the ultimate powerlessness of evil. When Jesus tells Pilate in John 18:36 that his kingdom is not *ek tou kosmou toutou*—that is, "not of/from/out of this world"—what is he saying? He is saying that his kingdom is not limited to the weapons of this world and therefore does not employ them. This conversation takes place a few hours after Jesus told Peter to put up his sword in the Garden of Gethsemane (John 18:11). Jesus's kingdom is not defended by the sword. It can neither be established nor defended by the sword. It is not Christendom.

The Temptation of the Church

The church of the fourth century was tempted to embrace Constantine's offer of respectability, wealth, freedom from persecution, wielding the imperial sword

4. Ibid., 26.

against heretics and unbelievers, and high social status—all this in exchange for becoming the religious arm of the empire, the Roman state church, the official religion of the empire. The Davidic/Maccabean vision of a powerful sword raised against the enemies of God seemed to be on the verge of fulfillment. The kind of messiah longed for by so many for so long appeared to be at hand. R. A. Markus writes these astonishing words about that historical moment:

> The conversion of an emperor, followed by the large-scale christianisation of their society within a few generations, seemed to transform the conditions of Christian existence dramatically, and certainly more visibly than the great divide of the Incarnation. The miracle which turned a persecuting empire into the political embodiment of their religion, into its protector, promoter and enforcer, almost succeeded in seducing Christians from their sense of the homogeneity of these "last times." They were almost lured into believing that a new messianic age had dawned with Constantine's conversion. . . . How could such a miraculous triumph of their only recently oppressed religion be anything other than God's mighty work?[5]

Was the conversion of Constantine actually of greater world historical significance than the incarnation? Did it really change the world more visibly than the incarnation did? Were the fourth-century Christians *almost* seduced and *almost* lured into believing in a new messianic age? Or were they *actually* seduced into it? This was the temptation of Christendom.

The church in the fourth century was tempted to accept the advice of the "the wise and dreaded spirit of self-destruction and non-existence" that Jesus had rejected. Constantine offered bread for the bishops to distribute to the masses, thus enhancing their image and role as providers. Constantine offered to unify the church with the state so that reverence for one would rub off on the other. Constantine offered the so-called miracle of the conversion of an emperor (surely an event as dramatic as the messiah throwing himself off the top of the temple and surviving), with the power to compel an empire to follow. The church of the fourth century accepted the deal, not realizing, perhaps, that it was a deal with the devil. The bishops of the church saw the conversion of Constantine in providential terms and developed a theology of empire early on. This was done primarily by Eusebius of Caesarea, of whom Jaroslav Pelikan says: "At the hands of Eusebius, this historical and theological interpretation of Constantine's victory and kingship as an achievement of Christ the Victor and King through the sign of his cross became a full-blown theology of history and an apologia for the idea of a Christian Roman Empire."[6] Can a Roman Empire be Christian, or is this a contradiction in terms? This

---

5. R. A. Markus, *The End of Ancient Christianity* (Cambridge: Cambridge University Press, 1990), 89.

6. Jaroslav Pelikan, *Jesus through the Centuries: His Place in the History of Culture* (New Haven: Yale University Press, 1985), 51.

is why an *apologia* was needed, for the pre-Constantinian church would have assumed it to be a contradiction.

The bitter fruits of Christendom were not accidental; they were not just collateral damage. They were an inevitable outcome of doing it the devil's way. In chapter 4 I labeled the Christian persecution of the people of God, the Jews, and the Christian persecution of the people who were most like Jesus, the Anabaptists, as mysteries. Only when the true nature of Christendom is revealed as surrender to the temptations of the devil that Jesus had rejected can the mystery be understood. How could Christians be so un-Christ-like, even anti-Christ? It was possible only when the way of Jesus has been abandoned for the way of Constantine.

Jesus or Constantine?

We have a choice today between Jesus or Constantine. Who will we follow? Let us try to be as honest as we can about the contrast between the two.

Two Kinds of Messiah

First, we have two kinds of messiahs. The concept of a messiah developed during the years of exile for the people of Israel. The Jews have lived in exile for most of the period from the destruction of Jerusalem in 586 BC to the present. The message of Jeremiah to the exiles (Jeremiah 29) that they should marry, plant gardens, and settle down in Babylon was the beginning of a gradual dawning on the Jewish people that perhaps God's will for them, and the mission to which the Jews were called by God, could be fulfilled in exile. Perhaps they could be a light to the nations as a witnessing minority among the nations. Yet they always hoped for a return to the land and for the rebuilding of Jerusalem, the temple, and the nation. Gradually, however, the realization grew that only a decisive intervention of God through a special figure—the messiah—would be sufficient to accomplish this miracle in such a way that Israel would not simply fall back into its old ways of disobedience to Torah. A complex of ideas—keeping Torah perfectly, a miraculous divine intervention, and the coming of messiah—gradually coalesced.

Jesus took these ideas and mixed them with the mysterious Suffering Servant of Isaiah and the Son of Man of Daniel and came up with a concept of a messiah that had not been imagined before. He knew that a mere return to the kingdom of David and Solomon was not enough to accomplish the redemption of the world. The problem of evil lay deeper, and so there was a need to expose and defeat the principalities and powers that rule this world. But they could not be defeated by picking up their own weapons to use against them. Rather, they must be defeated by divine intervention. Jesus kept Torah perfectly, allowed himself to be called messiah, and went to Jerusalem to confront the powers nonviolently, knowing that he must suffer but trusting in God to use this innocent suffering somehow to redeem the world and to intervene, which God did in the resurrection. And according to Peter preaching on the day of Pentecost, this is what happened: "But God raised him from the dead" (Acts 2:24).

When Constantine is viewed in messianic terms, the definition of messiah in play is far closer to the Davidic/Maccabean ideal than to the concept that Jesus embraced. The kind of messiah that Constantine represented was not only a different kind of messiah from the concept that Jesus embraced, but it was also one of the concepts of messiahship that was available to Jesus and that sorely tempted Jesus. It is not that Jesus never considered the idea of being a political messiah; Jesus was tempted in precisely that direction but rejected the temptation. Constantine's messiahship was not new—it was a reversion to the Old Testament as an alternative to Jesus.

Two Views of Power

These two types of messiahship involved two contrasting views of power and violence. Jesus was born into a violent world. Herod massacred the infants in an effort to assassinate Jesus, which forced Jesus and his parents to become refugees. The Romans ruled the Holy Land ruthlessly by the sword. Zealous Jewish bandits, a combination of brigand and guerilla fighter, harassed the Romans. Jesus was surrounded by people who believed that power comes from the sword. But Jesus confronted the violent sociopolitical system of his day by rejecting both quietism and violence, and the logical outcome of his stance was the cross. Those who claim that Jesus was apolitical and interested in only what goes on in individuals' hearts have a difficult time explaining how he could have ended up antagonizing the political powers enough to get himself crucified. Those who portray him as a prototypical freedom fighter have a difficult time explaining why he taught his disciples to love their enemies and not to resist an evil person. Jesus does not fit any of the usual categories.

Jesus calls us to follow him in renouncing the world's reliance on power that originates in violent coercion and to rely instead on a witness that consists of proclaiming and living out the good news of the gospel. Like Jesus, we are called to live lives that make no sense if there is no such thing as the resurrection of the dead. Like Jesus, we are called to live lives that make no sense if God does not exist. We look to God to use his power to overcome evil; our role is to witness to what God has already done in Jesus Christ to defeat the powers. Ultimately, our faith is in the power of love to overcome evil, but apart from the hope of resurrection this would be foolish idealism.

The Constantinian view of power assumes that violence in defense of justice is necessary in this world of sin. So did the Davidic/Maccabean view of power that Jesus rejected. Constantinianism distinguishes between violence used for good purposes and violence used for evil purposes. But Jesus and the New Testament (especially the book of Revelation) assume that violence can be utilized legitimately only by God himself. For us humans, it always rebounds on us and perpetrates an endless cycle of retribution. This cycle is broken in the cross, and the function of the church is to bear witness to this truth.

Two Views of the Cross

The cross is the most widespread and common symbol of Christianity. But what does it symbolize? In the use made of it by Jesus and Constantine, we see two very different views of the meaning of the cross. Constantine put the cross on the shields of his army and used it as a symbol by which to conquer the world. He made it a symbol of the kind of power that flows from violence—the power of the sword. Certainly, many people have experienced the cross as a symbol of an oppressive, violent, imperial power coming to dispossess, conquer, kill, and loot. That was certainly the experience of the Native American cultures at the time of the European invasions of North and South America. It was also the experience of Jewish people thorough the long history of Christendom. Recall the words of Ernie to Golda quoted in chapter 4: "The Christians say they love him, but I think they hate him without knowing it. So they take the cross by the other end and make a sword out of it and strike us with it!"[7] The concept of the cross being turned into a sword is very perceptive; this is exactly what has been done in Christendom.

To Constantine, the cross means embracing the sword and trusting in military power, but to Jesus it means rejecting the sword and trusting in divine power. We as a church today have to choose Jesus's way or Constantine's way; we cannot have both. We can take up our crosses in one of two senses: to carry our cross up our Calvary to identify with Jesus in suffering at the hands of the world, while trusting in God for vindication, or to take up our crosses and turn them into swords to use in coercing others to profess the Christian faith.

Two Kinds of Church

Depending on which view of messiahship, power, and the cross we adopt, we will adopt one of two very different concepts of the church. If we follow Constantine, we will adopt a view of the church as the institution that serves the religious needs of society. The church will have a defined and limited role, which is to be a part of the one whole entity called Christendom. The state will have responsibility for much of life, including a good part of the responsibility for extending the faith to conquered peoples, a process in which the church, of course, cooperates. The Constantinian church is focused on ritual, rather than on ethics. No moral change of life and minimal participation in the actual worship of the church are required of members. Since the membership of the church automatically contains all citizens of the state through infant baptism, there is little emphasis on evangelism and outreach.

7. Andre Schwarz-Bart, *The Last of the Just* (trans. Stephen Becker; New York: Atheneum, 1960), 324–25.

If we follow Jesus, on the other hand, we will have a very different view of the church. The church will be a counterculture in tension with the rest of society. There will be a clear line of distinction between the church and the world, and conversion will consist of crossing that line. Niebuhr stressed the responsibility that the church has to the world and defined it as the responsibility to compromise with the world in order to have influence on the world. But the most important thing the world needs from the church is for the church to be separate from it. Only then can the world know itself to be the world. Only then can the world realize its unredeemed character and its need of God's grace.

An ecclesiology developed from a commitment to follow Jesus will be a missional ecclesiology. A missional ecclesiology is one in which the priority for the church is its mission to bear witness to the gospel of Jesus Christ. By living out of a different narrative than the world does, the church confronts the world with the choice of following Jesus. A missional church consists of those who have made the commitment to follow Jesus in the way of discipleship and who are witnessing to the lordship of Jesus Christ as they follow him. To follow Jesus is to take up one's cross and to reject violent coercion. The gospel does not need to be backed by the threat of the sword, because it is good news. It is the best news in the history of the world—that God has not abandoned his fallen creation, but rather has acted to redeem it through Jesus Christ. To force the confession of Christ upon people is to betray a lack of belief in the reality of the message being proclaimed, for if this news is true, then no coercion is necessary. If the gospel is rejected, there is no point trying to force acceptance, because outward conformity to the religion of the conquerors is not faith in Jesus, is not love of God, and is not the result of the working of the Holy Spirit.

Two Kinds of Eschatology

The two ways of Jesus and Constantine are rooted in two different eschatologies. The Jesus of the New Testament went to the cross, not in despair, but in faith in the intervention of God. Apart from the hope of God acting in history in a similar way to how the Old Testament portrays God as having acted in the history of Israel, Jesus's whole concept of messiahship makes no sense whatsoever. Only a believing Jew could have come to a view of messiahship like his. It is a forward-looking eschatology. It looks forward to God's providential guidance of history to its consummation, which will involve a decisive divine intervention in history.

On the other hand, the eschatology of Constantinianism is backward looking. The view of history developed by apologists for Christendom is one in which the decisive interventions of God have already happened. The future is projected to be more of the same as we are experiencing now. And the dualism of the temporal versus the eternal becomes more important than the already-but-not-yet tension inherent in New Testament eschatology. Eschatology is more of a matter of "down here" versus "up there," and salvation is defined in terms of what happens when we die.

The kingdom of God has already come in that it appeared when Jesus appeared. The decisive victory over the powers achieved in the cross and vindicated by God in the resurrection is expressed in the New Testament in the ascension of Jesus to the right hand of God—the place of authority and rule. Jesus is now Lord, even though not every eye yet sees and not every knee has yet bowed. Nevertheless, Jesus reigns, and the kingdom is present wherever his reign is confessed. Yet it is not present in its fullness and will not be until the unveiling (apocalypse) and appearing (parousia) of Jesus Christ at the end of this age.

Two Kinds of Discipleship

Finally, we need to consider that there are two different kinds of discipleship, depending on whether one follows Jesus or Constantine. To follow Constantine, the primary issue relates to being a good and loyal citizen of the state. To be a good Roman *is* to be a good Christian. One simply lives up to one's birth.

But in order to be a good follower of Jesus Christ, one has to make a deliberate choice to acknowledge Jesus as Lord. To be a good Christian is to be something less than totally devoted to serving the state and obeying the political authorities, for one's obedience to the state must always take second place to one's obedience of Jesus Christ. One first requests and then needs to live up to one's baptism, something that is possible only in the power of the Holy Spirit.

The kind of church we need is one that facilitates such discipleship and takes it up into its very heart, rather than rejecting it or marginalizing it, as the Constantinian church does. In the Constantinian church, a devotion to Jesus Christ that leads to literal and serious discipleship is possible, but it is channeled in the so-called religious life, where it does not threaten the so-called secular life lived by most people. The life of discipleship is seen as heroic, worthy of admiration by all, but not possible for all. Those who call the entire church to the path of discipleship are rejected as fanatics and persecuted in Christendom.

The Choice We Face Today

The church today faces the same choice—or, perhaps we should say, the same temptation—as did the church of the fourth century. From the fourth to the twentieth centuries, Christendom existed in its various forms. Now, Christendom is dying in some places and dead in many others. The church in the fourth century had not yet embraced the sword and had not yet accepted the way that Jesus had rejected. But it faced the choice. Today, we have another opportunity, for as Christendom dies we have the chance to renounce it once and for all. We need to renounce Christendom and reaffirm our faith in Jesus Christ and his church. We need to make the opposite choice to the one made by the church in the fourth century.

If we do not, there are at least three foreseeable negative outcomes. The first possibility is that the church will cling to political power as long as possible and in its determination to maintain the church of Western culture stance, even at the expense of historical and biblical orthodoxy, will end up becoming a pagan-state church of a pagan state. Regrettably, this appears to be an inevitable outcome for much of liberal Protestantism unless there is revival and reform. The second possibility is that the church will become the ideological cover for a reactionary, fascist takeover of one or more nations as the disintegrating effects of individualism and the sexual revolution weaken the state to the point where external threats (Islam? China?) become too dangerous. This is a very possible scenario for conservative Protestants. The third possibility is that by trying to cling to political power as long as possible the church will provoke a strong enough reaction by the pagan forces that increasingly control Western civilization with the result that the church will be persecuted and hounded underground.

The first possibility would result in the loss of the gospel witness in the West. The true church of Jesus Christ would simply disappear. The second would disgrace the gospel by identification of it with an inhuman and evil regime. The equivalent of the German Christians would win out. The long-term outcome of the third possibility is impossible to predict. But in the worst-case scenario, it is possible that the church could be eradicated in at least some parts of the West as thoroughly as it was in North Africa and Asia Minor. If that happens, we trust that the Holy Spirit will continue to work in the southern churches, just as the Holy Spirit worked in Europe and North America after the decline of the church in North Africa in the seventh and eighth centuries and in Asia Minor after the fall of Constantinople in 1453.

Whether the culture will move toward Christ or farther from Christ is not within our control. We do not control history. We need to focus on the choices that actually are up to us. Basically, the church today faces a choice between following Jesus or following Constantine. We need to choose the way of Jesus if we wish to be faithful witnesses to the gospel in the world. But there must be no illusions about choosing Jesus and also, at the same time, clinging to whatever vestiges of Christendom may remain to us in our particular part of the Western world. The two are not compatible. The burden of this book has been to argue that a choice is necessary, that a future other than Christendom can be imagined, and that the church of Jesus Christ need not fear the end of Christendom. Christendom is dead, but Jesus is eternally Lord!

Subject Index

Author Index

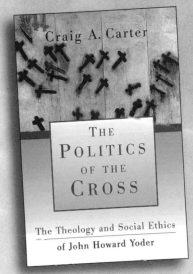